THE

Common Weal

Oxford University Press

London   Edinburgh   Glasgow   Copenhagen
New York   Toronto   Melbourne   Cape Town
Bombay   Calcutta   Madras   Shanghai
Humphrey Milford Publisher to the UNIVERSITY

THE
Common Weal

WRITTEN

By the Right Hon. HERBERT FISHER, M.P.

F.B.A., F.R.S., LL.D.

'Our duty is—our aim ought to be—to employ the true means of liberty and virtue for the ends of liberty and virtue.'—Wordsworth.

OXFORD
AT THE CLARENDON PRESS
1924

Printed in England

PREFACE

WHEN last spring I was invited under the terms of the Stevenson Trust to deliver a course of lectures upon Citizenship to the University and City of Glasgow, I realized that I could not hope, within the limited time available, to make a systematic contribution to Political Philosophy. My best chance of interesting my hearers would be, I felt, to allow my thoughts to play freely and discursively round some of the topics which have at different times, either in the course of my reading, or my travels, or my parliamentary and official experience, impressed themselves upon me as being of special interest and importance. Thus, many subjects which would properly fall within the scope of a well-planned volume on Citizenship have been omitted, while others which to the philosophic mind may seem to be too closely ' immersed in matter ' are lightly touched upon.

I have felt the more emboldened to take this course

by the reflection that my friend, Sir Henry Hadow, who delivered the Stevenson Lectures last year, has spoken upon the whole subject with the elegance, the precision, and the philosophic completeness to be expected of so great a master.

Sept. 30, 1923.

CONTENTS

I

THE CALL OF THE STATE

Malgré tous les efforts d'un siècle philosophique les empires es plus civilisés seront toujours aussi près de la barbarie que le fer le plus poli l'est de la rouille.—RIVAROL.

In spite of all the efforts of a philosophic age, the most civilized empires will always be as near to barbarism as the most polished steel is to rust.

NOBODY has any wide experience of life without being conscious of the generally low standard of human behaviour. Great crimes are happily rare ; indeed in every well-organized state the number of persons who undergo imprisonment or are made the subject of criminal prosecutions constitutes a comparatively small fraction of the population. But open any daily newspaper, and how uncomfortable and unquiet a spectacle it appears to disclose ! Foreign countries are behaving badly. Some of our own statesmen are held up to opprobrium. The reports from the law courts evidence a good deal of dishonesty and immorality. The columns devoted to public meetings indicate that in spite of all the efforts which have been made to reform the world a great deal still remains to be done. The Churches complain of religious apathy ; and the critic says that if the world does not act on Christian principles, the Churches are to blame.

To those who have been concerned with the task of government, this impression comes home with peculiar force. Every morning the foreign telegrams bring news of troubles and difficulties from every quarter of the globe. There is a plot in Kabul, a nest of cosmopolitan anarchists in Chicago, a plan for stirring up hatred against all the white races in Ethiopia and

Baluchistan, a bitter feud between peasants and industrials in Southern France, an outbreak of one of the moral, religious, or political epidemics habitual to Russia, an Anti-Semite passion leading to outrage in a district in Hungary. The Poles and Lithuanians snarl at one another across the frontier like angry dogs. India violently complains that her nationals are ill-treated by the Union Government of South Africa. A story of a negro-lynching comes in from Texas. Extracts from the cosmopolitan press reveal a wide dissemination of sensational and inaccurate news. An hour with the daily batch of foreign telegrams is not calculated to foster an encouraging view of the wisdom with which the human race accommodates itself to the governing conditions of life.

The world, of course, cannot be fairly judged from the statesman's morning budget of intelligence. His business is to know of troubles and to deal with troubles. The foreign observer does not report fair weather but only the premonitory symptoms of storm, so that the great spaces of quiet are left out of the picture, which by these omissions assumes an aspect a good deal more formidable than the reality.

Nevertheless, a massive impression remains that human beings, by reason of manifest defects in behaviour, are making of the world a much more unpleasant and uncomfortable place than it ought to be.

The statesman comes to a conclusion the reverse of rosy on a bird's-eye view ; but is he not confirmed by a narrower inspection ? Let us assume, as without undue modesty we are entitled to do, that the standard of public conduct is higher in Great Britain than in many other countries, is it adequate or nearly adequate ? Is it not notorious that the subscription lists to public objects almost always exhibit the fact how very small is the circle of those who give anything to hospitals or universities or public playgrounds, and how comparatively large is the number of well-to-do persons who do not regard it as any part of their duty to make such contributions ? Is it not equally notorious how small a fraction of society takes any interest in the conduct of public affairs ? [1] how important Trades Union issues, such as a strike, are left to be determined by a handful of the men who are vitally concerned ? how great a part is played by catch-phrases and relatively unimportant local issues in our political elections ? how large a proportion of the electors in a democracy vote for the party out of whose policy they expect to derive a personal advantage ? and with what indulgent laxity persons concerned with the charging of expenses against public funds interpret their responsibility ?

Another reflection, equally commonplace, strikes every observer of contemporary life. The system which governs industrial life in our modern communities has at any rate one thing in its favour. It works. Unlike some Utopian schemes for the formation of human societies, it is founded upon certain natural and moral truths which mankind in all ages has recognized. It assumes that man is entitled to the proceeds of his labour, however roughly and imperfectly it gives effect to that principle. And it assumes that labour should be adjusted to human wants. But with what waste, with what friction, with what abounding signs of incompetence does the system work ! How much still remains to be done to relieve mankind of the heavier types of labour, to diminish drudgery and to cheapen the cost of necessaries to the consumer ! How much of the business ability of the world is squandered in making money profits when it should have been solely directed to the manufacture of commodities of the type,

---

[1] 'In no county in England, as far as I am aware, does the number of persons really active in politics amount to 10 per cent. of the electorate.'— GRAHAM WALLAS, *Human Nature in Politics*, p. 233.

scale, and price most adapted to serve a wholesome public need!
How costly and imperfect is our machinery for eliminating the
industrially unfit! How defective, in spite of great recent
improvements, is our machinery for insurance against the
wastage of human capital due to unemployment! What
a burden upon the springs of industry is over-capitalization!
What huge economic losses to the community result from the
chronic misunderstandings which divide labour and capital!
The indictment, which is levelled against all classes, could be
greatly prolonged.

A third reflection, not less discouraging, arises from a con-
templation of international relations. Every Government
is naturally served by naval and military advisers, and naval
and military advisers are professional alarmists. ' If you believe
the doctor ', wrote a great Prime Minister, ' nothing is wholesome, if you believe the theologian nothing is innocent, if
you believe the soldier nothing is safe.' [1]

And the more brilliant the soldier, the more insecure is
the world in which he dwells. As the Irishman views his
national history as a series of revolutions against Britain, so
to the soldier the past and future take shape as a procession
of wars. Every power, however friendly, is a potential enemy
against whose possible attack adequate security must be taken.
It is not the soldier's business to take into account diplomatic
alliances; he must advise for every contingency, and it is the
province of the politicians to discount his dangers, to pare down
his plans, and to correct his perspective. There is then all
over the world a great body of professional military opinion,
nourished upon the study of war, interested in war, saturated
with the conception of war as an enduring and recurrent
factor in human affairs. And such a body of opinion sometimes
exerts a decisive influence upon the public mind and upon the

[1] *Life of Robert, Marquis of Salisbury*, vol. ii, p. 153.

course of Government policy. After a great war, the number of individuals professionally interested in the science and art of war is immensely increased. A vested intellectual interest in war is created, which only long years of peace can effectually weaken.

It was one of the many cheerful views entertained by Herbert Spencer that the world was passing from a military into an industrial age. Commerce and industry were to kill war. Free trade was to knit nation to nation in bonds of common interest ; as education increased, the fundamental unreason of war would be progressively realized, and quarrels, formerly settled by the sword, would be referred to arbitration. It is clear now that Spencer was too optimistic. There is no cause of war more potent than the competition for markets and the desire to secure what is sometimes vaguely called ' a trade ascendency '. It is indeed by no means fanciful to assign, as one of the many causes which led to the late World-war, the opening out of Africa and the disappointment of Germany at the relatively small share which by reason of the weakness of her navy she was able to obtain of the African spoils. The philosophic historian of the war would open with Dr. Livingstone, that pious Scottish missionary from whose self-denying and evangelic labour there have sprung storms of strong and tempestuous passion which have shaken the world.

The economic panic-monger is as formidable as the military. He sees everywhere the spectre of shortage. It may be coal, or oil, or wheat, or vanadium. His company, his trust, his nation must seize what they can while the opportunity offers. The backward or ill-organized portions of the world offer themselves to this form of commercial exploitation. A great Trust, like the American Oil Trust, pushes its conquests into every continent, subsidizing newspapers, influencing Senates and Parliaments, acquiring concessions, brow-beating diplomats.

China, Mexico, the small Central American States, the weak and distracted monarchy of Persia, the continent of Africa offer tempting fields to the hunter for concessions. There is much talk of developing the backward parts of the world. It is too often forgotten that the only sound way of developing a country is to develop its inhabitants. The competition of the advanced countries for the control of the industrial resources of the backward and semi-barbarous, without reference to the well-being of the inhabitants, has been in the past and threatens still to be in the future, despite the excellent provisions of the Covenant of the League of Nations, a source of international disturbance.

In other words, we are met everywhere with evidence of misconduct, waste, unnecessary drudgery, unnecessary dearness, unnecessary quarrels, and by the spectre of possible wars. The art of living comfortably and harmoniously upon the planet has not yet been achieved. Science has proved to be a double-edged weapon, as formidable in the destructive processes of war as it is beneficent in the development of the arts of peace. We create wealth ; but we also accumulate instruments for its wanton destruction. It is even contemplated as a tenable political thesis that sixty million white men in the centre of Europe can be and should be kept in a permanent state of economic weakness because experience has shown that they cannot be trusted to keep the peace.

Is it not then worth considering whether the conduct of human affairs cannot and should not be improved ? whether apart from probable advances in scientific invention, or in the machinery for organizing the more efficient production and distribution of wealth, there may not be in the moral and political sphere special considerations to which weight should be attached ? Is the cure for our ills necessarily so recondite ? May it not be found in a mode of thinking and a direction to conduct ? In a word, in a livelier and more general sense of civic duty ?

This is no academic question, but for Europeans of to-day most practical and urgent. Europe is the trustee for civilization. The art, the literature, the philosophy which move the world are largely European. The principal hope and promise for humanity lie in the preservation and improvement of that high standard of life and achievement which has been reached after long centuries of evolution by the more gifted peoples of Europe. What does not the world owe to the imaginative genius of the Greek, to the sense of law and organizing power of the Romans, to the measured taste of France, to the music and profound scholarship of Germany, to the great creative artistic impulses of Italy and Russia, to the combined aptitude for poetry and politics evinced at every stage of their history by the Anglo-Saxon race ? In the generation which immediately preceded the war, fresh prospects of beauty and knowledge seemed to be opening out in every direction. Russia, whose voice had for many centuries been mute or muffled, began to speak in tones which spread a thrill throughout the world. Her music, her imaginative literature, her science, seemed to promise an almost measureless enrichment of the spiritual resources of man. And the lesser Slavonic nations were experiencing something of the same intellectual fermentation. Civilization seemed to be spreading with effortless rapidity. The high general level of education in the Scandinavian countries, the diffusion of schools and colleges in the Balkans, the serious contribution made by small countries like Finland to the progress of scientific and historical research, the almost universal prevalence of a high level of technical proficiency in lyrical poetry, the rapid multiplication of mechanical improvements, were symptoms of a degree and intensity of intellectual activity and interest such as the world had not previously experienced.

There was much collective thinking, much organized intellectual activity, but there were giants also. There were Pasteur and Tolstoy, Kelvin and George Meredith, Wagner and Brahms, Taine and Renan, Mendeléeff and Ibsen, Mommsen and Maitland.

It would never have occurred to any one before the war to doubt that this civilization possessed the stability of one of the great inscrutable ordinances of nature. We believed that it could be improved, for we believed in progress. We believed that it could and should be extended, for we were much concerned with our duties to the depressed members of our own community and with our obligations to the backward races of the world. But that the fabric of European civilization should be itself insecure, that it should be capable of destruction from within, that was a fear which had not occurred to any one of substantial judgement. Wars were, of course, expensive ; revolutions were destructive ; but neither war nor revolution was likely to affect to any permanent degree the solid and brilliant fabric which had gradually been built up by the efforts and sacrifices of generation upon generation of the most gifted and vigorous members of the human race acting under the most favourable natural circumstances of climate and position.

There is not quite the same confidence now. The world has been in eruption, the burning lava has not yet cooled, and the survivors of the volcanic fires ask themselves whether they are in truth on solid ground. The civilization of Europe is no longer founded upon the secure and unshakeable basis of agriculture. A few European countries such as Bulgaria are still purely agricultural, but they are not in the van of progress. The brilliant and originating part of European civilization rests not upon agriculture but upon something far more delicate, far more easily disturbed, far more liable to grave and even fatal dislocation. It reposes upon the basis of modern industrialism, with its interlocked system of world transportation, its minute subdivision of labour, its intricate mechanism of credit and speculation, of paper currency and bills of exchange, of banks and accounting houses. A severe shock administered to the nerve centre may paralyse the whole organism. We have seen how a highly civilized state may by successive inflations of its note-issue impose a capital levy upon the middle class of its population so severe as to incapacitate it from carrying on the intellectual work of a nation. We have seen how countries dependent in part upon imported foodstuffs may be driven to the brink of ruin by a long continued spell of adverse exchanges. We have seen how the paralysis of a great industrial area like the Ruhr may inure to the injury of the whole world. We have witnessed the widespread desolation of Russia through the destruction of economic confidence, St. Petersburg reduced from a position of great wealth and luxury to the squalor and poverty of an overgrown Asiatic village, its population decimated, its culture extinguished, its *litterati* dead or scattered, and famine, the creature of drought and misgovernment, striking down millions of peasants in one of the great granaries of the world. We have witnessed Vienna, long famous as the gayest and most brilliant of European capitals, driven almost desperate for lack of food ; and we are now menaced by the prospect of scenes in Germany recalling that grim period of moral and economic prostration which succeeded the Thirty Years' War. How narrow is the margin which divides European civilization from chaos is made alarmingly clear by this experience.

The disease, of course, is not to be wholly attributed to the economic structure to which we are now fatally and, I think, rightly committed. That structure exposes civilization to risks, but these risks proceed not from the nature of the credit instruments by which economic exchanges are effected, but from something more fundamental, from the fears and passions and appetites of man. The real malady of Europe is not economic, but moral and political. It consists in the conflicting ambitions and inveterate feuds of the European races which keep the world in a perpetual fret and fever of uneasiness, but for which, as yet, no anodyne has been found or seriously sought. So long as these hatreds persist and are not overborne by countervailing motives and sentiments, European civilization is exposed to danger, and the more highly organized the economic structure of society the greater the danger will be.

To the Titanic struggle there has succeeded a period of comparative peace. The strain of the war has produced a natural exhaustion. For the most part men are desirous of living quietly and reaping a little material prosperity after all the efforts and sacrifices which have been endured. But though the map of Europe has been arranged upon a plan more closely adjusted to the desires of its populations than ever before, seeing that our present state-system is now based upon the two principles of nationality and democracy, the violence and suddenness with which these great changes have been carried through has produced an accumulation of freshly smarting wrongs and grievances. Old sources of irritation have been removed, new poisons have been introduced, less formidable, let it be hoped, than those which produced the disruption of the three great military Empires of the Continent, but still sufficiently active to call for care and vigilance. On all sides goes up the bitter cry of the proscribed and beaten victims of the world revolution, from the Russian exiles in many lands, from the ruined Loyalists of Southern Ireland, from the defrauded Magyars of Transylvania and Serbia, from the Germans submitted to the ungrateful yoke of the Poles and Czechs. The problem of political persecution which confronted our ancestors during and after the wars of the French Revolution and Empire has returned upon us in a form infinitely more intractable and more complex, and in a world each part of which has grown, through the development of science and industry, increasingly sensitive to the disorders of every other section of the whole. We cannot, therefore, afford to be indifferent to the conduct of affairs upon which so much depends. The great cause of world peace and world prosperity affects each one of us. Islanders as we are, we cannot regard it as irrelevant to our interests if, in any part of Europe or indeed of the world, cruelty and injustice and oppression continue to flourish. The questions whether clemency and justice are to prevail over the spirit of revenge, whether the new régime is to be made as tolerable as may be to those who are in any case bound to suffer under it, or whether the rôles of persecutor and persecuted are merely to be reversed, affect the whole prospect of European peace. In the preservation of that peace we are all interested. To the removal of the causes which are likely to endanger it we may all contribute. But let there be no illusion as to the difficulties which lie before us or as to the gravity of the election with which Europe is confronted. If one road be taken, all the ample and brilliant promise of civilization may be realized. The other way leads straight to the cataract and the rapids.

It is no part of my present plan to discuss the philosophical basis of political obligation, to ask the question why, if at all, we should obey the State, and within what limits that obedience should be rendered. I shall ask you to assume with Aristotle that man is a political animal, endowed with physical and mental gifts which clearly point to a life in the society of his fellows, and that it is only through a life passed in the Commonwealth, and for the common weal, that he can deploy to the best advantage the gifts with which he has been endowed and realize perfection. I shall ask you to assume that there is such a thing as morality and that morality consists in ' the disinterested performance of self-imposed duties '. And I shall ask you further to assume (with Green) that the real function of government is to maintain conditions of life in which morality should be possible. It is not my present purpose to argue these theses, to discuss with you whether there is such a thing as duty, or what duty is or what metaphysical postulates the conception of duty may involve. All these inquiries are important, but we have no space for them here. Let us for the present assume that man is a social animal, that it is his duty to perfect his being, that this he can only do as a member of a commonwealth so instituted and organized as to maintain conditions under which it is possible to lead a moral life.

Neither shall I delay you with an analysis of the various human motives which in fact determine mankind to obey the laws which are enacted for their governance. What part of political obedience is founded on imitation, what part on rational self-interest, what part on inertia, what part on sympathy or the psychology of the crowd, and how far the relative importance of these motives may be altered by place or time—these speculations, so interesting to the political psychologist, must be left on one side. It is sufficient here to indicate that in this direction lies a rich field for exploration.

My purpose is humbler and more practical. I propose to invite you to consider the duties of the citizen in the light of the experience which we have now gained from several thousand years of recorded history. My belief is that the conditions of modern civilization make it of increasing importance that an intelligent appreciation of civic and political issues should be spread through the community, and that unless the standard in this respect be kept high, the facility with which short-tempered and ill-grounded opinions are diffused by the press constitutes a new and formidable obstacle to the sound conduct of public affairs.

This proposition does not involve the thesis that we should all be politicians. There may come an age—it seems far distant now—when the public will repose as much confidence in a British Cabinet as it now has in His Majesty's judges, and may be content to leave the transaction of political business to a professional and highly-trained class in the assurance that it will be well and efficiently conducted. Indeed, a great part of the business of government, and that the most important, is under existing conditions transacted by the permanent Civil Service, in whose ability and integrity there is a widespread and well-founded trust. But, however much confidence may be placed in politicians, public opinion in a democratic civilization is the ultimate arbiter of affairs, and public opinion is made up of the particular opinions of individual persons. Nor is it unimportant what these opinions may be, or how seriously they are treated. The chance remark of an average man in a third-class carriage or on the top of an omnibus has its weight, and may be taken by the listening pressman as an indication of the way in which the wind is blowing. The customer who buys a newspaper chiefly for its sporting news may be abetting the spread of political or social doctrines abhorrent to his better judgement. It may be taken as an axiom that the greater the number of people in a State who take trouble to form opinions of their own on public affairs or upon the characters of the men and women who are chosen to conduct them, the more wholesome the complexion of public opinion will be. It is, then, a matter of importance that the citizen should think about the commonwealth and think help-fully, that he should be active not passive, that the circle of his interests and his sympathies should not be bounded by self.

Heaven forbid that we should all set up to be saviours of

society. 'I am not', says Mr. Henry Ford, 'a reformer.
I think there is entirely too much attempt at reforming in
the world and that we pay too much attention to reformers.' [1]
Mr. Ford was thinking not of the good man's efforts to improve
his surroundings and help his neighbours, but of the ambitious
man's appetite for grandiose schemes of social reconstruction
either by revolution or legislative enactment. He was con-
trasting his own methods of helping mankind, which consisted
in putting on the market a cheap and serviceable motor-car,
and in giving employment to several thousand operatives at
a high wage and short hours, with the ambitious scheme of the
Russian Bolshevists, who in their defiance of nature and morality
have plunged the Russian people into economic misery. The
cosmic reformer is in fact a very costly article. Unless he
strikes a pact with Nature he is beaten. The world must rely
for its stability and progress not upon these great and ambitious
schemes, though they may have ideas of value in them, but
upon the acts and thoughts of innumerable men and women
of goodwill, most of them entirely unknown, like Johnson's
friend, Dr. Levett, who spent his life tending the poor :

> His virtues walked their narrow round
> Nor made a pause nor left a void ;
> And, sure, the eternal Master found
> The single talent well employed.

But if we cannot all be politicians or reformers or professional
philanthropists or experts in social and economic problems, we
can all be good citizens. We can all regard our task, however
humble it may be, not merely as a bread-winning operation,
but as a contribution to the well-being of the community of
which we are members. If we can feel with the great causes
which move the world, so much the more gracious is our state.

[1] *My Life and Work*, by H. Ford.

The larger a man's view of life, the keener will be his zest in living it, the more exciting the call to the full employment of his powers. But, to those to whom it has not been vouchsafed to have political ambition or the impetus to social improvements, there remains a great fund of civic direction and support in the jealous observance of the codes of honour and etiquette which have been evolved by the principal callings and professions of mankind. Some of these codes are higher than others. Some are very old. The principle that a medical man should never conceal a scientific discovery from the brethren of his craft, and never divulge confidences obtained from his privileged position in the sick room, comes down from the body of writings attributed to Hippocrates, the great Greek physician of the fifth century B. C. But whether old or new, austere or indulgent, these codes generally combine, with some elements that are narrow and sectarian, a conception of duty to the Commonwealth.

To obey them is to obey something higher than appetite and larger than self. The good and honourable physician who has never voted at an election, never spoken on the platform, never worn a party colour and never read a book on political economy or attended a lecture on citizenship, may, nevertheless, be a better citizen than many a notorious scene-painter of political grievances. Nay, if he gives his best to the community, what more can the community demand ?

II

SOCIAL DEBT AND SOCIAL CREDIT

' Really we have no fixed classes. We have men who will work and men who will not.'—HENRY FORD.

' If a single postcard is to reach its destination, all the railways of the world must tremble beneath the thunder of the locomotives.'—WALTHER RATHENAU.

IN the present state of the world there are no words more unhappily familiar than debt and indebtedness. We can hardly open a newspaper without coming across some reference to our war debts and the best means of reducing them. Now we read of Germany having cancelled the greater part of her internal debt by the simple process of inflation, and are given to understand that the German middle class have been ruined by the process ; or conversely we are reminded of the heroic methods by which the currency in this country has been deflated to the advantage of the debt-receiving and to the disadvantage of the debt-paying class. These transactions clearly raise large financial issues, but they also raise large moral and political issues as well. How far is a Government justified in writing down its debt and ruining its middle classes ? In what circumstances may a Government justifiably say to itself : ' We are so placed that we must sacrifice everything to industrial production. We must say to our doctors and lawyers and authors and civil servants, " You have rendered great service to society and in recent years have advanced considerable sums to the State. This, however, cannot save you from present ruin. We do not propose to repay you : we propose to write off the greater part of your claims against us. Art and science and learning must suffer. The primary object of the state must be the revival of industry, and in the interests of industrialism we tax the people lightly and meet our obligations by paper issues. In other words, we impose a high capital levy upon the fund-holding class." '

The converse procedure of deflation opens up similar streams of moral and political speculation. The State which after a war endeavours to balance its budget and to restore credit by imposing heavy taxation saves its middle class but creates a severe, though passing, depression in trade, since no one is prepared to make purchases if he has reason to think that prices are going to fall further. The advantage of a policy of deflation is considerable. Credit is improved ; imports are purchased more cheaply. The cost of living falls. On the other hand, the burden of the debt is appreciated instead of reduced, and the debt-holding class enriched at the expense of the debt-payers ; and since the fall in prices is in some cases more than counterbalanced by a fall in wages, and the burden of taxation presses heavily on the springs of industry, the poor may be temporarily injured rather than benefited by the process.

These two alternative methods of handling a national debt have been much canvassed by publicists. Which is preferable, it is asked ? But this question clearly stands in need of further definition. What do we mean by preferable ? Do we mean materially advantageous to the whole State at the moment ? Or do we mean materially advantageous in the long run ? Or is the advantage to be considered not merely material ? Should the statesman take into account ethical or aesthetic advantages as well, for instance the advantage of preserving a class of artists and men of letters, quite apart from material considerations, or the importance of helping the poorest members of the community quite apart from the profit and loss account ?

These questions arise when we are considering the duty of the statesman in respect to one only of his many civic functions. But there is a larger and a prior question with regard to civic obligations which affects not statesmen only but the whole community. It is this : what is our civic obligation and how is it to be discharged ?

We are familiar with the distinction between social creditors and social debtors. There are some persons plainly who are burdens on the community. The habitual drunkard is such a burden. He is a misery to himself and to his family. The young spendthrift who runs through a fortune at the gaming tables and lives ever after on the benevolence of his friends and relations without doing a stroke to earn an honest livelihood is again a clear instance of a social debtor, of a man who has received everything from society, the advantage of settled laws, of an established régime of private property, of a laboriously constructed system for the distribution of goods, but has given nothing in return. In sharp contrast is the hard-working doctor whose working days are divided between the accumulation of medical knowledge and the practice of his art, the philanthropist who spends his life in the advocacy of great causes, the inventor by whose scientific ingenuity the control of man over nature is immeasurably increased, the musician whose skill gives delight to millions of his fellow beings. We cannot indeed strike an exact balance between the credit and debit side of the account. We cannot say with confidence of any of our friends : A. has given back to society 10 per cent. more than he received, or A.'s credit and debit account exactly balance ; but, broadly speaking, we have a fairly confident impression in many instances that A. is a social creditor and B. a social debtor, that A. has done some good with his life, and that B. has wasted his opportunities and might as well not have existed. In many other instances we are less certain, and in some instances we feel that we have too few data upon which to form a judgement.

In general, however, we should say that a man who during his working years has earned his living honestly, brought up his children decently, paid his taxes, and made some provision for his old age, is to be classed rather among the creditors than among the debtors of society. His life may have been on a commonplace material plane. He may have been an uninteresting type of bourgeois, with no elevation or breadth of outlook, with no schemes for the improvement of his fellows, with no aim higher than the attainment and preservation of a decent standard of family comfort according to the canons and conventions of his class. In society rather a bore, in local affairs a nullity, yet a man who by his exertions made his way and brought up his family to take their part as breadwinners in society. Such a man we should, I think, be justified in classing among the creditors of society. The balance of credit to his account would be slight, but it would be a balance. He had paid his way and something over.

How far, however, would such a verdict hold, if the occupation out of which the livelihood had been made had been of no social value or even anti-social in its character and effects? A man who is actually producing fresh wealth for the community is clearly performing a distinct service to society. He is adding to the national dividend; but what of a livelihood formed by betting on the turf or by speculating on the Stock Exchange or by gambling at cards? Do such pursuits as these, however honestly conducted, disqualify those who follow them from admission to the class of social creditors? Can an honest bookmaker say after his retirement, ' I have repaid all and more than all that I owe to the society in which I was born. It is true that I have not added to the wealth of my country. I have not caused two blades of grass to grow where one grew before ; but racing and betting are permitted by the laws of my land. They are pleasures which claim many devotees : they are pursuits indeed which attract many rogues ; all the more important is it that there should, in the betting community, be a nucleus of honest men. Further, I am one of the conduits by which the wealth of the spendthrift is guided into the channels of prudent and profitable investment.'

Our judgement upon the case will be affected by the view which we take of racing. If in our view the innocent pleasures resulting from the breeding, training, and racing of thorough-breds outweigh the undoubted evil associated with the race-course, then we should think no worse of the man who earns his living in the racing stable than we do of the professional on the cricket field or the golf course. If, on the other hand, we hold that racing is anti-social, that it is a bane to society, that it ought to be prohibited by law, then we are compelled to conclude that all economic services rendered in connexion with racing are wasted. The jockey, the trainer, the stable boy, no less than the bookmaker, the starter, and the judge, are economic debtors. They may earn their living ; they may never run into debt ; but so far as they are engaged in these occupations connected with racing they are running up an account against society. That account may be offset by services of a real and substantial character. The jockey or the stable boy may serve in a national war or use such leisure as they possess in helping their friends and relations, or make admirable fathers of a family, but when their civic accounts are compared with those of men who earn their livelihood in banks or on farms, they stand at a disadvantage by reason of their occupation.

A livelihood earned by keeping a disorderly house or an opium den is clearly a livelihood earned by anti-social practices. It would be difficult to imagine how any services rendered by persons habitually engaged in such pursuits could lift them out of the category of the heavily and profligately indebted. What, however, of the honest man or woman whose life is spent in dispensing alcoholic liquor to the thirsty across the bar of a public house? Here again the judgement will be determined by the views which we may happen to hold as to the morality of the trade in strong drinks. The prohibitionist would doubtless contend that the evils of intemperance were so great that any livelihood derived from the sale of strong drink to the community was a livelihood ill-earned and deleterious to the public welfare, while others would draw no distinction in point of social utility between the distribution of drink, food, and clothing, arguing that in each case the evil does not consist in the thing supplied but in the excessive or abusive use of it.

From these illustrations it will be seen that we open up a wide field of casuistry as soon as we attempt to determine who are or who are not social creditors, and to estimate the infinitely varying shades and degrees of credit to which their activities are entitled. Looked at from the purely economic point of view, the welfare of any community as of any household depends upon the workers being in sufficient numbers and putting forth sufficient output of productive energy to support not only themselves but the drones. No society can thrive which does not produce a sufficient stock of wealth to feed the children and the sick and the old as well as to support the labouring population and to supply a stock which will enable fresh productive work to be undertaken. A society composed of drones or social debtors would perish of its own inaction. It is not, however, sufficient that a man should live : it is to be desired that he should live well, that he should be able to develop his capacities, whatever they may be, to the best advantage, that his desires should be refined rather than gross, and that his whole course in life should be directed by reason and forethought rather than by blind appetite or the urgent impulsion of elementary material needs. What is true of man is true of society. It is not sufficient that a society should be able to command a supply of goods and services adequate to the maintenance of its existence. Something more is needed. We do not measure nations only by the volume of trade, by the amount of their exports and imports. We judge them by the quality of their civilization, by the taste which they show in the beautiful, by their achievements in the sphere of knowledge, and by the success with which they plan the national life so as to yield a maximum of rational happiness and diffused interest. It follows that if a society is to be regarded as adequately embodying the ends for which man may be assumed to exist—and these may be summarized in the term ' the good life '—something more is needed than economic labour devoted to the supply of economic needs. A society composed of a number of people merely actuated by the motive of hustling one another and trampling upon one another in their pursuit of economic gain, and holding before their eyes as the one aim and object of human existence the getting of material wealth, would probably fail in the long run, even as a money-getting machine, either through the necessary wastefulness of competition or through lack of disinterested science, or through the exploitation and over-driving of the immature, or through the want of that larger imagination which gives inspiration to human character, and it would certainly fail from the first and all the time to give satisfaction to the higher needs of man. The members of such a society would be paying their way : in the vulgar term they would be ' earning their keep '. A society of ' purely economic men ' could not in the strict sense of the term be accused of being a society of social debtors. And yet such a society, attending exclusively to present values, might to the eye of the best contemporary wisdom appear to be deficient in moral, intellectual, and aesthetic virtue; and to posterity, to have been guilty of ruinous imprudence in its use of material wealth.

The moral is that a life based on a motive of mere egotism, however laborious, is not strictly a civic life. It may be valuable to society, but if all lives were lived on the same low, though energetic, plane, it would be found that its constitution would be insufficient even to secure a permanence of material welfare. Without some civic spirit the State must perish. There must be some planning for the whole as well as some apprehension of the part, some vision of the future as well as some grasp of the present, some feeling for the needs of others as well as some appetite for the advancement of self. In the industrial sphere it has already been found by experience that the more the worker is enabled to appreciate and understand the whole mechanism, character, and purpose of the business upon which he is engaged, the more zeal and intelligence will he display in his manipulation of the highly specialized process upon which he is engaged. This is very natural. The human mind requires something intelligible to feed on, and a single process is not intelligible until it is viewed in connexion with all the other processes and with the end to which it and they jointly contribute.

It has thus been a common feature of Christian education to give to children a certain philosophy of history. The history of that philosophy is in itself a curious study. It originates with the Book of Daniel, which describes the succession of the empires and the destiny of man. And the philosophy of history contained in the Book of Daniel has been handed down and accepted by generation after generation of ecclesiastical historians. It is, for instance, the philosophy expounded by Bossuet, and is still the recognized academic tradition in

Catholic Europe. It is not my purpose to consider how far this conception of the historical development of the world is to be regarded as complete or adequate in the light of present knowledge. The prophet Daniel took no cognizance of India or China or Japan. Nevertheless, the conception of a Providence guiding the course of human history according to a pre-ordained and divine plan has formed so large a part of the moral and civic education of the civilized nations of the world, and has been so generally regarded as a valuable prophylactic against cynicism, inertia, and despair, and as an encouragement to the exercise of the active virtues, that it is a matter for consideration whether human nature can give of its best to society without the aid of some such teleology. Let us for a moment assume the converse. Let us imagine that the belief is universally held and inculcated in our schools that the world is a vast comedy, half divine, half infernal, but wholly irrational, capricious, and mysterious, that we are the playthings of ironic chance, and that when the time comes for the terrestrial globe to explode or to freeze, mankind will not even survive as a memory, so that in the sum of things it is indifferent what we do, and how we do it : would it not be reasonable to infer that the sense of civic obligation would be sensibly weakened? It is true that we might find shelter from the harsh caprices of cosmic weather by the reflection that experience has shown us that honesty is the best policy, that we are more comfortable under a well-ordered than a disordered State, and that whatever may happen to the cosmos, we at least have acquired a certain technique for deriving a modest revenue of content from the circumstances of destiny. But what argument would we cogently address to those who would maintain that there was no such thing as social duty? If the sum of things is irrational, no argument founded on reason.

Even if it be not given to him to philosophize about the cosmos, the member of a State in which civic spirit has attained any development, will generally have a working belief that man exists for some good end, and that things are worth while. He will proceed on the assumption that he is sent into the world for some purpose other than mere enjoyment, that he has a part to play, and that it matters to himself and to others how he plays it. This sense of purpose sometimes receives additional power from a belief which may be and generally is founded on the flimsiest rainbow of speculation, that a nation has a particular mission to accomplish in the world. Such a conviction of a divine and providential destiny has clearly been a powerful spring to action among the Jews throughout their history. Similarly the belief in a grandiose but undefined mission for the Prussian State, fostered by the learning of a great school of Prussian historians writing between 1870 and 1914, had obtained an almost Messianic intensity before the war, and was, whatever may be thought of its quality, a most powerful incentive to social service and to patriotic abnegation.[1] Writers in Austria are now complaining of the great evil resulting from a lack of this sense of State mission. They tell us that the public mind of Austria is paralysed by uncertainty as to the destiny of the State, as to the political end to which public action should be addressed. Ought Austria to aim at a junction with the German Republic? Ought she to lay out her life as a second Switzerland? Ought she to work for a Federal Union with the Succession States? In the lack of any clear and imperious direction, the civic conscience of the country is fatally embarrassed.

[1] It is interesting to observe that tha experienced Russian statesman Count Witte held that the 'historic and sacred mission of Russia' to protect the Balkan Slavs was 'a romantic and obsolete chimera', M. Paléologue, *La Russie des Tsars*, vol. i .p. 119.

If the absence of a clear political purpose is a hindrance to the development of a State sense in the new Republic of Austria, the gift of political enfranchisement has an opposite effect in countries like Poland and Czecho-Slovakia. There men and women who had never thought about civic obligations before have become ardent patriots. The State is an object of general interest, of universal pride. It is a new thing : it is on trial : great achievements are predicted of it. There is a widespread desire to show the world that the liberated peoples can govern themselves wisely and well, and that in painting and music, in literature and science, as well as in war and commerce and government, the new European States can vie with the old. It is probable that the advantages derived from this exaltation of civic feeling and interest largely counterbalance the loss naturally due to the transference of power and authority from experienced to inexperienced hands.

In all these cases it seems to be undoubtedly true that the sense of civic indebtedness is exalted by the presence and depressed or diminished by the absence of a conception of or a faith in national destiny. It is, indeed, not the most difficult thing in the world to play upon what has been called the ' psychology of the crowd ', and to stimulate the strong gregarious instincts of man even to the point of the extreme of self-abnegation by the picture of a clear national purpose, such as success in war, to be achieved by a defined and intelligible course of action. It is also not difficult to stimulate class-consciousness by an appeal to class appetites, and class has its martyrs as well as creed. It is, however, a question whether a citizen ought to be ' class conscious '. Ought he to regard himself as owing a debt to his class which it is his duty to pay by a life spent wholly or partly in its service ? According to a fashionable school of Labour opinion, the primary civic allegiance of man seems to be to his class, and to his class independent of national boundaries.

Let us pause for a moment to examine this contention. What is a class? We speak of the aristocracy, and of the middle class, and of the working class, and in speaking of these classes we assume that they have opposed interests. Or again we may prefer to divide society into two classes, capitalists and wage-earners, and again assume an opposition of interests. But however we may subdivide society, whether it be by the criterion of birth, or wealth, or economic status, two things are clear : first, that under a democratic constitution, persons are always passing from one category to another, rising here, sinking there ; and second, that the points of economic antagonism within a class are quite as numerous, if not more numerous, than the points of economic antagonism between one class and another. Has the wage-earner whose livelihood depends on the price of cereals the same interest as the wage-earner whose livelihood depends on the market for coal? Has the buyer the same interest as the seller while they wrangle in the market? Have the operatives engaged in two industries hotly competing against one another for the same market an identical interest? If there is a job of work which can either employ 100 men at £4 a week or 200 at £2 a week, and 200 men seek employment, and those who are trade unionists claim that no wage lower than £4 should be taken, is there not a fierce opposition of interest between the 100 who are taken in and the 100 who are left out? Is it not then clear that even if a class may be defined as a body of men with identical economic interests at some point, it is necessarily composed of men whose economic interests differ at other points? And if this be so, is it not also clear that to base allegiance to class on grounds of economic self-interest is to build the house of social obligation on the sand ?

C 2

It may further be asked what a man owes to his class that he should be inspired to dedicate his life to its service? No one doubts that a child has obligations to his parents. No one doubts that in normal cases these obligations are considerable. Nobody again doubts that a citizen has obligations to the State whose laws protect his life and property. But what are the obligations which the aristocrat owes to the nobility, the bourgeois to the *bourgeoisie*, the poor manual toiler to the proletariat? The supreme gifts of life are not owing to any one class. Consider the gift of language. To whom should the Briton render thanks for the great inheritance of speech which distinguishes him from the brutes and makes him free of the kingdom of reason? Certainly not to any class in society, but to generations after generations of men and women who have used and developed the language, and more particularly to those among them who have through their writings stamped upon the national speech an enduring impression of their genius and power. What is true of language is also true of all the great branches of the human inheritance. It is true of knowledge, of art, of religion. No one of these is the gift of a social class.

To what then are we to attribute the very wide diffusion of a belief that duties are owing to one's own class? Is it not due to the fact that, according to the old proverb, birds of a feather flock together, or, as Aristotle put it, that friendship is among equals? Men of similar fortune are apt to have similar experiences, similar pleasures, and a similar outlook. It is easier to form friendships within your own class than outside it; and man is naturally inclined to pursue the line of least resistance. A very slight tincture of social envy for those above or of social contempt for those below is sufficient to develop these tendencies, to consolidate them into a hardened body of class feeling. There still, however, remains no basis

for the assumption that a man has received the great boons of
life from his class or that he is bound to consider the claims
of class as paramount or indeed as important in the hierarchy
of social obligations.

Indeed, a moment's reflection shows that the privileges
obtained by the efforts of one class may become the rights
and the liberties of a nation. Magna Carta was wrested from
King John not by the people but by the barons ; the revolution which established constitutional government in this
country was the work of a Whig oligarchy ; the Reform Act
of 1832 of a Parliament of propertied men ; that of 1867 of
a Tory Government. The right of every child to an education in a State school in Great Britain was not won by the
artisans and peasants of the country, but by the bourgeois
members of a bourgeois Parliament. The Labour parties all
the world over enter into a political heritage which has been
created by the struggles and efforts of middle-class men. If
the rich owe much to the complaisance of the poor, the poor
have also a debt to the public spirit of the rich.

The truth is that as soon as we begin to examine the problem
of social indebtedness, the more difficult is it to confine it
within a narrow circle. Our debt is, in reality, to the whole
society and to nothing short of it. We may feel allegiance to
school and college, to locality and to class, to the organized
body representing our trade or profession, to our church, our
club, our particular friends ; from all these we may have
received benefits, which we can define to ourselves, do
not propose to repudiate, and are anxious to repay. Yet it
is clear that all these institutions and pleasant facilities imply
an established social order and would be incompatible with
political chaos. They imply a government, a police, a judiciary,
a system of taxation ; they imply protection for life and
property ; they imply such a distribution of goods and services

that a surplus available for the support and education of the young is available ; they imply in other words the whole network of modern civilized life, and bespeak a debt of which, if the truth be told, humanity past and present is the one and only condition.

One contention of recent origin has now assumed so much importance with certain honest minds that it deserves some special consideration. This is the view that the world can only be regenerated by a class-conscious proletariat. Now this doctrine is held in two forms. There are some who maintain that the class struggle is an end in itself, that honest open class violence is a great deal better than corrupt compromise and intrigue, and that the moral life of the State is enriched by the sustained clash of embattled material interests. Such is the gospel of Georges Sorel, the philosophic prophet of syndicalism and the author of a well-known book entitled *Réflexions sur la violence*. M. Sorel has no patience with adjustments and accommodations. He thinks social peace a fraud and a delusion. For him passion is the lever which moves the world, the action of hot blood on hot blood, and of hot thought on hot thought. There must be an end of palliatives and anaesthetics. The workers must be nerved to fight by the vision of a general strike, which will bring about the downfall of capitalism.

What then? M. Sorel is not concerned with the sequel : but it is clear that if violence is the condition of moral health, a general strike which inaugurated an era of social peace would be an ethical catastrophe of the most complete description. We are not therefore presented with any positive picture of the consequences of the world victory of the proletariat. The general strike is rather, in M. Sorel's view, to be regarded as a moral ideal than as an economic contingency. It is a battle cry, an inspiration, one of those ' noble lies ' assumed but never realized which philosophers have often told us are necessary to the well-being of the Commonwealth. In reality, M. Sorel would be unhappy in a classless world, because for him class contest is the salt of life.

Other professors of class-consciousness regard it not as a joy for ever but as a transitional historical necessity which will pass away when the victory of the proletariat is achieved. Their ideal is a classless world only to be attained by a spell of intense class-consciousness exploding in a general engagement with the enemy. They argue that as no army wins a victory without concentrated discipline, the workers must submit to a military exclusiveness if they are to attain their objective. They must think and act together, for if there be any flaw in the cohesion of the class, the keen spear of the capitalist foe will pierce through the armour to the flesh.

In their zeal for the intensification of class-consciousness, the more revolutionary thinkers go so far as to advocate a complete severance of intellectual ties between the manual workers and the residue of society. As one of the more ardent spirits has put it, ' Not general culture, professedly unbiassed, but a fighting culture, admittedly tendencious, is the avowed aim of the revolutionary proletariat.' Not only must economic science be recast from the workers' point of view—' untendencious economics are as absurd as untendencious football '—but there must be a proletarian poetry, a proletarian art, a proletarian science, and proletarian schools in which this new, comprehensive, and liberating theory of life is expounded to the young. The revolutionaries are nothing if not thorough-going. As one of the proletarian poets has himself sung :

> The warfare of the classes isn't honey and molasses,
> And you'll need a sharper weapon than a kiss.

And, indeed, if this school of highly sectarian thought

should prevail there will be little prospect of more honey from Hymettus.[1]

Now it is easy to point out the absurdities of this extreme doctrine of proletarian culture. A fighting culture is, of course, no culture at all. It is destructive of all the things that lie at the root of culture, love of truth, love of beauty, love of justice, sense of evidence. Moreover, it is essentially material. A musician does not ask what Beethoven's income was before he accords his admiration to the Violin Concerto in D major. The class origin of Van Eyk or Raphael or Sargeant has as little relevance to the excellence of their painting as the price of meat in Leadenhall Market. Let wages be what they will, the law of gravitation is serenely impartial in its operation, so that whether a man be employer or employed, should his foot slip on the edge of the precipice, he tumbles in the same direction. You cannot alter the laws of number on the plea that poverty exempts you from the income tax, or escape the physical consequences of debauchery because the rules of hygiene have been drawn up by a bourgeois profession.

It may indeed be true that a class bias enters into our treatises on political economy. If so let the bias be corrected, but do not substitute one bias for another. No subject of serious study, affecting the welfare of men, deserves to be treated with such disrespect. What would be thought of a class-conscious viscount who set out to rewrite the text-books on medicine, on the ground that they were deficient in aristocratic flavour? The whole conception of learning and culture would be degraded by such snobbery.

Moreover, consider for a moment the enormous spiritual impoverishment which the acceptance of such a doctrine

[1] For a picture of the length to which this extravagance can go, see E. C. Paul, *Proletcult*.

involves. It is hardly excessive to say that all that is best in the common heritage of men is rejected by these extreme sectaries. If the extravagant and patently false notion is accepted that the intellectual work of man must always bear the imprint of his material circumstances and social outlook, then the democracy is warned off nine-tenths of the poetry and music, the history and the science, the philosophy and the art, which constitute the chief glory of the human race. From the purely sectarian view of the fighting socialist no means could be more aptly devised to cripple the intellect, confine the imagination, and lessen the general power and influence of his supporters, than this attempt in advance to prejudice the free contact of the mind with the great body of profound thought and exquisite feeling which is enshrined in the art and literature of the world.

Fortunately this extreme sectarian doctrine finds few supporters among the level-headed industrial workers of Great Britain. What, however, does receive a very wide measure of acceptance among decent, honest, tolerably sensible working men and women is the doctrine of class-consciousness and class-war. Great things have been hoped of the class-conscious working man. An admirable social observer even gave it as his opinion in 1908 that the class-conscious working man was the chief safeguard against the horrors of a general European war.[1] And though this hope has been signally frustrated in the event, the fact that it should have been entertained at all by a competent thinker points to the need of stating the case for class-consciousness with full allowance for its possible merits.

What is it then that these workers feel? They feel in the first place that the present social system is unjust; that there are great inequalities of wealth, that the large fortunes are

[1] Graham Wallas, *Human Nature in Politics*, p. 238.

not in most cases earned by commensurate service to the community, but are the result of good luck, or dishonesty, or an oppressive use of an initial economic advantage, and that these inequalities tend to depress the status of the worker and to promote luxurious expenditure in a way which is bad for stable employment. And they feel, in the second place, that wars are always ruinous to the class to which they belong, and that if the industrial workers all over the world could unite, they could put a stop to war once and for all. They say that these two grand aims, greater economic equality and universal peace, cannot be obtained without the formation of a disciplined international labour army, strong in class-consciousness and prepared in the last resort to use the instrument of the general strike.

Now let us assume that these critics of the existing universe are right in their diagnosis. Let us assume that the two principal evils which affect mankind are, as they say, the uneven distribution of material wealth and the liability to war, and let us further assume, what requires, of course, a great deal of investigation, that a real improvement in the lot of man could be effected, if not by the abolition, at any rate by a considerable modification of the capitalistic system in the direction which they suggest. Do these assumptions sanctify the doctrine of class-consciousness and class-war? A cause is either right or wrong, just or unjust, reasonable or unreasonable, congruous with the nature of things or dissonant from it. If a cause be right, just, and reasonable, then it should be commended not to a class but to mankind. It should owe its triumph not to force but to persuasion. The establishment of a party, bound together by an intellectual principle, to advance a particular cause is an entirely legitimate operation : but it is belief in the cause which should determine the frontiers of the party, not the accident of material position. A man who claims that social justice is the exclusive concern of his own class, and that all other classes in society are moral pariahs, does not know what social justice is. He sins against the very doctrine of human solidarity which he is confessedly desirous of promoting.

There is, however, a sound as well as an unsound form of class-consciousness. The unsound form is exclusive, warlike, narrowly sectarian, bitterly doctrinaire. The sound form is based on honest self-respect, legitimate pride in good work achieved, humane desire to help those members of society upon whom the pressure of our economic system most cruelly descends, coupled with a readiness to appreciate the argument of the other side. The workers of Great Britain have no small reason to be proud, as they look upon the great industrial fabric which owes so much to their labour and mechanical skill, or as they reflect upon what has been done by their own efforts through trade unions and provident societies, and the principle and practice of co-operation to benefit members of their own class. What neither they nor their employers are entitled to do is to forget that they are members of a society so closely bound together by debts and credits of every kind, each member so dependent on every other, and all so much the creatures of a common history (seeing that even the most gifted of mortals brings less into the world than he receives), that to prefer strife to conciliation, and class war to mutual help, is nothing less than the abdication of rational morality itself.

III

THE CLAIMS OF BODY AND MIND

' Of all things a man has next to the Gods his soul is most divine and most truly his own.'—PLATO.

SOME years ago I was standing with a friend on a railway platform in Central India waiting for the Bombay Express, when a slow train, composed almost entirely of third-class carriages, drew up, and discharged part of its crowded burden. From one of the carriage windows there was protruded the head and shoulders of a middle-aged man, the singularity of whose appearance at once attracted my attention. His beard and hair were coloured a bright vermilion, and his eyes shone with a strange glow of abstracted excitement. By a curious chance my friend, who some years before had been Principal of an important college in India, recognized the man as an old acquaintance and engaged him in conversation. The man of the vermilion beard had, as it appeared, been the college photographer, but had suddenly discovered religious scruples which had led him to give up his art and his means of livelihood. He was now in the prime of life, a saint and a pilgrim dependent on the charity of others for sustenance and wholly absorbed in the welfare of his own soul and in his relation to the Supreme Being. He seemed radiantly happy and had nothing, he said, to regret. The train was bearing him to a famous shrine with a crowd of fellow pilgrims.

Such abrupt conversions are by no means uncommon in the religious atmosphere of India. In a lonely spot in the Vindhya hills I once came across a young hermit of twenty-one who, after a brief course at the Calcutta University, had tired of the common way of active life and decided that only in solitude, meditation, and idleness could he achieve perfection. In such cases the sense of allegiance to the community is reduced to a vanishing point. The Indian saint owns no debt to his fellows. If he were reproached for his lack of civic spirit he would not understand the force of the grievance. Were he pressed for an apology he might reply, that to solicit alms is to give occasion for the exercise of virtue in others, that to practise sainthood is to furnish a shining example to the world. But he would not consider it necessary to provide an apology grounded on social service. He would say that the duty to the individual soul transcended all other duties.

Consider, by way of contrast to this Indian otherworldliness, the case of Jeremy Bentham. At the age of twenty-one Bentham made a will directing that his body should be dissected for the benefit of Science. ' This ', he wrote in 1769, ' is my will and special request I make not out of affectation of singularity, but to the intent and with the desire that mankind may reap some small benefit by my decease, having hitherto had small opportunities to contribute thereto while living.' Now Bentham was not one of the great altruists of the world. He was not, nor did he ever claim to be, a heroic or a saintly character. Nobody could class him with Father Damien or with St. Francis or with William Tyndale. He belongs rather to the prosaic but eminently useful class of benefactor, among whom Franklin is also to be numbered, who are driven by an irresistible impulse to improve the society in which they are found. Bentham himself never laid claim to superlative moral merit. He was, he said, as selfish as a man could be, but somehow his selfishness had taken the form of benevolence. At the age of twelve he was inspired, by the reading of a book in which the delays and complexities and injustices of the law were portrayed, to find in Chicane his great enemy; and the appetite for legal improvements which he first conceived as a boy grew upon him with advancing years, and was the source of a huge mass of social activity, all relevant, and almost all useful.

Another prophet of social reform who has left a deep mark upon our modern way of thinking about the State has equally with Bentham disclaimed any special gift of unselfishness. In the first number of *Fors Clavigera* Ruskin writes as follows:

' I will put up with this state of things passively not an hour longer. I am not an unselfish person nor an Evangelical one; I have no particular pleasure in doing good; neither do I dislike doing it so much as to expect to be rewarded for it in another world. But I simply cannot paint, nor read, nor work at minerals, nor do anything else that I like, and the very light of the morning sky has become hateful to me, because of the misery that I know of, and see signs of when I know it not, which no imagination can interpret too bitterly.'

Ruskin could not be at ease in a world defaced by so much ugliness and misery, just as Bentham could not be at ease in a world full of so many absurd and oppressive institutions, the accumulated legacy of years of prejudice and sinister interests. In both men the civic impulse was stirred by the spectacle of abuses which it was an imperious need in them to denounce and to remove.

It was no false modesty in Bentham and Ruskin to disclaim unselfishness. Each in his life-work obeyed the law of his own nature; and each would have been wretched had he pursued any course other than that which he in fact adopted. The foundation of altruism is a good healthy stock of egotism. Nobody can do his duty to the city unless he first does his duty to himself. Herbert Spencer has sometimes been derided for laying stress in his *Data of Ethics* upon the moral importance of attending to personal health. His ideal of the rosy, healthy man, who always takes the right amount of exercise and the right amount of sleep, who never overworks his brain or over-taxes his digestion, but comes bounding down to breakfast every morning in exuberant spirits, has seemed to many superfine critics to embody a somewhat commonplace ideal of human conduct. But surely there is a large element of good sense in this teaching. In order to live well, it is first necessary to live ; and in order to live it is necessary to observe certain elementary rules for the conduct of our physical existence. Properly understood, it is everybody's duty to make himself as healthy as he can be. What, however, it may be asked, is physical health? Is it something which we can define by reference to fixed standards? Clearly not. It would be a waste of time for a lawyer or a doctor to submit himself to the laborious training required of a professional athlete. The kind of health required for the efficiency of the pugilist is not the kind of health required for the proficiency of the parlia-mentarian. Indeed, the one kind of health is incompatible with the other. It would appear then that when we speak of the pursuit of physical health as being not only desirable in itself but essential to the effective discharge of civic duties, we are using the term 'health' not as denoting a fixed bodily condition which every one, whatever his vocation, should endeavour to attain, but a condition of the body which is found by experience to be conducive to the most effective development of the particular functions which any individual may be called upon to discharge.

With this qualification, the care of physical health is clearly one of the primary civic duties. Lord Cromer used to contend that accessories of physical health had a greater importance in affecting the course of events than historians are willing to allow, and has cited the instance of his unfortunate sore throat on the occasion of General Gordon's stay in Cairo on his way to the Soudan as having not impossibly been the source of that very train of circumstances which led to the death of Gordon and to the Khartoum expedition. Certainly nobody who has seen politics at close quarters can fail to be impressed by the immense part which physical health plays in the direction of affairs. At a great crisis the strain of work exhausts and discomforts all but the very strongest. The statesman who rises to the front rank must be able day after day, week after week, and month after month, to bear a burden of work and responsibility which would break down any but an exceptional physique. He is always doing important things : he is almost always doing difficult things ; and he is exposed throughout to vigilant and continuous criticism.

Robust health, then, is certainly of all the gifts that which is most indispensable to the man who seeks to shine in the public life of his country. Intelligence is of little avail without it. A certain degree of physical power is necessary to obtain an audience for your views and to pull them through against opposition in Council or Parliament.

The duty to self involves, of course, a great deal more than attention to physical health. It implies self-improvement in all its ranges and degrees. John Stuart Mill once laid down as among the conditions of a happy life these :

' That there should be a decided predominance of the active over the passive and that more should not be expected of life than it is capable of bestowing.' [1] There is little doubt that both these counsels are wise, the first as preserving in healthy exercise and repair the social faculties, the second as a prophylactic against bitterness and disappointment. Mill is probably right in thinking that a life exclusively dedicated to meditation or to self-culture or to scientific speculation is not,

[1] Bain, *John Stuart Mill*, p. 114.

however valuable and ennobling these activities may be, so conducive to happiness as a life in which the practical part of man receives adequate scope and employment. This, however, does not imply that such lives may not be necessary to the higher progress of the race. It may be part of the price of progress that many lives should be lived upon a plan which excludes much of the ordinary kind of happiness, though yielding moments of exquisite satisfaction far beyond the reach of average mortals. Science has been built up by such voluntary self-mutilation, and as Goethe has observed, Art too requires, as its primal law, renunciation. The question may also be raised, whether literary, artistic, and scientific work, when carried out with a serious sense of responsibility, is not to be regarded as practical activity in Mill's sense of the term. No professional philanthropist could have had a higher reward in the consciousness of services rendered to mankind than Pasteur; but even when scientific investigations have a less direct and obvious bearing on the practical needs of mankind, even when they seem to be utterly remote from any possible social relevance, the interconnexion of the various parts of knowledge is such that nobody can be certain that the very purest parts of pure science may not some day or other minister to the practical needs of man.

The scientific worker may, then, be regarded among society's creditors even if he has never voted at an election or shown any active interest in social affairs. His work, if it is to be effectively carried on, requires a high degree of specialization; and we may forgive him much negligence of our common civic interests, provided that in his own peculiar province he makes real contributions to knowledge.

The same proposition applies to the specialist in art or letters, if he gives to the public nothing less than his best and that best is better than any service he could render in any other sphere of activity. The dilettante stands in a different category. His tastes may be innocent and pleasant ; but a life exclusively spent in their indulgence cannot be described as the life of a citizen.

The principal argument for self-development on wide lines is the truism that that which a man can give is dependent on what he has. A rich nature is prodigal of gifts ; the stream overflows its banks and fertilizes the fields on either side. If the sense of enjoyment is atrophied by disuse, a great part of a man's social utility vanishes. To be too highly specialized leads to blindness even within the limits of our speciality. There is nothing more valuable than the cross-fertilization of ideas : physics aiding geography, crystallography aiding medical research, bacteriology leading to the conquest of malaria, the science of acoustics harnessed to the campaign against the submarines. In general, the wider a man's education, the richer and more varied his equipment of ideas, the greater the span of his interests, the more valuable will he be to his fellows.

But whether the range of a man's intellectual interests be wide or narrow, there is one central overshadowing duty imposed upon him as a thinking being which he cannot neglect without a lowering of his whole nature and usefulness to his fellows. It may be described as the formation of a habit of intellectual thoroughness. By this is meant not that everybody should set out to make himself a solemn prig, or to pronounce *ex cathedrâ* upon subjects which he ill understands, or to play the missionary among people better informed but more reticent than himself ; but that there should be in the mind and throughout the conduct of life a continuous recognition of the fact that truth is one thing and falsehood another, that opinion may be either correct or incorrect, wise or unwise, wholesome or pernicious, and that it is a matter of transcendent importance to each individual whether his life is to be lived on makeshifts and make-believes or on painfully tested reality. The duty of thoroughness means, therefore, that the good man should acknowledge some intellectual responsibility, that he should take some trouble to form serious opinions upon the great issues of life and mind, and that if he has arrived at conclusions which are real to himself he should not surrender them out of cowardice or for material reward. ' Truth ', says Plato, ' is the beginning of every good thing both to gods and men.' And perhaps in the last analysis the idea of truth as an end so precious that it should be followed at all costs and hazards is the one certain mark of a divine quality in the human soul.

The presence in any society of a body of men devoted to the disinterested pursuit of truth is a great moral antiseptic, quite apart from the value which may attach to the results of their unfettered speculation. The mere fact that here and there within the community there are thinkers to whom the ordinary rewards of life are as dross in comparison with the claims of speculative truth is a standing reminder of the high levels at which human existence at its best may be led. Nor is the value of such an intellectual priesthood diminished by the fact that ultimate principles both in science and religion are never likely to be enthroned beyond the region of controversy. For each individual intellectual peace may be the achieved result as it is the desired goal ; but such a result is no proof or measure of moral excellence. The beauty of the life consists not in the end, but in the dedication.

Is it necessary to labour the consequences to society of keeping high the standard of intellectual thoroughness ? A moment's reflection will show that the great changes which have come over the world have been mainly due either to passionate religious insight or to the disinterested movement of intellectual curiosity, and only in a very small measure to the clash of political forces. When we consider the present state of human society and compare it with that which prevailed at the dawn of history, how small a fragment of the enormous difference which presents itself can be attributed to the action of statesmen or to the texture of political controversy! Take the longest, the most fundamental, the most animated of political debates—the secular controversy between the Empire and the Papacy—how meagre are its results compared with those of the wheel, the compass, the printing-press, the steam-engine! Behind all the fuss and clamour of competing parties in Church or State, quiet thinkers are patiently listening for the secrets of nature and steadily harnessing her powers, one after the other, to the use and the profit of man.

All this may be admitted, and yet the critic may urge that the number of persons qualified either to advance scientific knowledge or to discuss with any profit to themselves or the community the first principles of religion and science constitutes so small a minority of the human race, that the best working rule for the ordinary citizen is to accept what is given him in the prevailing creeds of his age without challenge or criticism. Now we are far from wishing to deny that there are a vast number of human beings who are not intellectual, for whom it is a pain to exercise even such slender intellectual faculties as they may possess, and to whom accordingly no better advice can be given than that they should be loyal members of such bodies, ecclesiastical or temporal, as those in which they happen to find themselves, and that when in doubt they should follow the lead of men whose characters and motives they trust. But it does not follow that because a man is devoid of the power of abstract reasoning, he is incapable of reaching sound conclusions on practical affairs. A certain moral instinct coupled with good sense and native tact often keeps a stupid man right where the quicker brain falters. Mere cleverness, then, is no passport to the formation of that habit of intellectual thoroughness which lies at the base of good citizenship. What is essential to any useful contribution to social welfare is that important issues should be treated as serious and that a man charged with the decision of grave matters should bring all the resources of his nature and experience to bear upon them.

It is, then, no valid justification for intellectual indifferentism to urge that big questions are difficult. Nobody is called upon to pronounce on problems altogether outside the scope of his knowledge or powers of apprehension. But there is a wide range of questions, moral and political, not so complicated but that they can be grasped by the resolute application of any sound intelligence, and entering as fashioning principles and guiding motives into the public life of the country. With many of these, at least, the good citizen may be expected to make himself familiar. Indeed, if his outward acts are to exhibit any inward coherency of character, he cannot escape the labour of framing opinions and conclusions as to the principles which should dictate his public conduct. There are some topics with respect to which a mind that is open is a mind that is empty. If a man says that he has an open mind as between the Tories and the Labour Party, or as between a policy of Free Trade and Protection, we know at once that he is ignorant of the alphabet of politics. His mind is open, not because his judgement is suspended after an exhaustive examination of the issues, but because he has never seriously applied himself to the issues at all.

The temptations to a superficial indifferentism are so great in an age of cheap printing, easy locomotion, and diversified amusements that the austere calls of the practical intellect may easily pass unheeded. It is a comparatively simple course to accept the current dogmas of a political or religious party without examination and to defend them in a spirit of party

zeal ; but no good comes of it. For another kind of temperament it is equally attractive to drift into an elegant Pyrrhonism,
finding flaws in every doctrine, limitations in every truth, and
nowhere in the whole ocean of speculation an anchor for settled
belief. The hard road lies between these two extremes, in
the intellectual process, at once sanguine and sceptical, which
discovers, with a full sense of counterbalancing considerations,
the plan and groundwork of a convinced and effective life.

There is one unfailing test of real greatness both in life and
literature, and that is depth of feeling. The cynics who stand
upon the pinnacle of literary renown, men like Lucian and
Voltaire and Anatole France, have poured delicate ridicule upon
the popular beliefs of their time, but delicacy and ridicule
do not of themselves embalm a reputation. What is deepest
in these three great men of letters is a serious and all-pervading
concern for the high claims of human reason, a belief in good
sense and tolerance and clemency, coupled with a detestation
of the cruelty, the fanaticism, and the superstition which
debase human nature ; and it is this real depth of sentiment,
clothed in language of brilliant and witty perspicuity, which
gives to their writings an enduring claim to respect.

'Great thoughts', says Vauvenargues, 'spring from the
heart.' The literature of mere elegance, of wit out of relation
to feeling and character, evaporates like dew under a hot
September sun. What preserves formal beauty is the pulse
of living interest in living things. 'Not by learned labour
amongst past ages, not by fancying into life again exploded
beliefs and forgotten ways of life was the Divine Comedy
written, but by living more intensely than others the life of
the time, feeling more keenly what others felt, hoping more
ardently, imagining more distinctly, speaking more eloquently.' [1]

Great examples are made to be followed. The force of

[1] Seeley, *Lectures and Essays*, p. 152.

conviction which inspires the comprehensive doctrine of the rationalist philosopher or religious poet far transcends the compass of ordinary characters ; but convictions originally feeble and interests originally faint are capable of being strengthened and multiplied by a steady discipline of brain and will. It is part of the duty to self and society to endeavour so to discipline and multiply them. For if the world is to be redeemed from vulgarity and emptiness, it will be by the efforts of men and women who have schooled themselves to throw heart and mind into the eager, burning issues of their age, facing the disappointments, vanquishing the drudgery, confronting the preliminary effacement of the thought, but never losing faith or slackening the cords of purpose in their endeavour to right the wrongs and relieve the sufferings which they see around them.

We speak of self-cultivation, but what is self ? A focus of relations stretching out through kith and kin to every point in the orbit of experience. It is impossible here to treat with any approach to completeness a subject large enough to fill a whole library of folios. It must be sufficient if two aspects of this process are lightly touched on—our duties to the old and our duties to the young.

Those who are acquainted with Anglo-Indian life are quickly made sensible of the impoverishment of a society bereft of old persons and children and composed exclusively of efficient men and women in the full tide of vigour. Not only is the wholesome refreshment and piety which comes from the combining of different generations in the same family temporarily snapped ; but the little adjustments of temper and bearing which arise out of the communion of the aged, the middle-aged, and the young, are lost as well. There is a certain lack of elasticity ; a sense of deprivation and sacrifice which is palpable. The value of maintaining the coherency of family life in face of all difficulties is nowhere so readily appreciated.

There is a quaint passage in the Laws of Plato to the effect that ' if a man makes a right use of his father and his grand-father and other aged relations he will have images which above all others will win him the favour of the gods.' The idea that the old age of our kinsfolk is a possession or treasure which may be used or misused, squandered or employed, and that the moral worth of a man is evidenced by the way in which he discharges his obligations of piety to the old, is common to the philosophical speculations of antiquity. Indeed, it is not surprising that in a society in which the average duration of life was so short, special value should have attached to the counsels of age. The few who survived the perils of youth and early manhood stood out with a peculiar eminence.

' Without the old,' says Cicero, ' cities would be altogether impossible.' [1] The ballast of elderly experience was necessary to the safety of the ship of state.

The requirements of modern hygiene have greatly extended the average length of life in civilized countries, and white hairs are now as plentiful as in the days of Cicero they were rare. Or rather, perhaps, it should be said that there has been an upward extension of youth, men and women retaining into advanced age habits of bodily and mental activity which in harder and earlier times would have long ago left them. In general, however, the broad lines of a man's intellectual make-up are settled before the age of forty. He may modify some opinions, soften some prejudices, fill in the framework of his mental landscape with more detail ; but unless he be a creature of quite unusual spring and elasticity he makes no great change after forty.[2] It follows that in times of rapid

---

[1] *De Senectute*, xix. 67 : *Mens enim et ratio et consilium in senibus est : qui si nulli fuissent, nullae omnino civitates essent.*

[2] ' Most men begin to be old fogies at the age of twenty-five.' William James, *Talks to Teachers in Psychology*, p. 166.

movement like the present the cleft between the real mental horizons of two successive generations is apt to be startlingly wide, so that father and son, mother and daughter, seem almost to speak a different language and to inhabit different worlds. Such discrepancy, carried to a high point in sensitive and intellectual natures and illustrating within the circle of a single family the pain which attends all human progress, is a great theme for tragedy ; and in the revolutions of taste, thought, and manners in which Europe has recently been involved such tragic contrasts must be not infrequent.

The moral to be drawn is that the cultivation of that natural piety to the old which Plato preached is more necessary in a moving than in a stationary society. The wider the gulf between the generations, the greater the need of moral engineering to bridge it. To neglect the old is not only to cut oneself off from a beautiful moral relationship, but to miss the inner significance of progress. The world does not advance like a motor-car by a series of explosions. There is no one point of time before which we can say, ' All was Folly ', and after which we can say, ' All is wisdom '. The movement is continuous, each generation contributing its share and making possible the events which follow. The neglect of this wider truth, the recognition of which is essential to any comprehensive grasp of the conditions of social welfare, was the great flaw of much of the revolutionary philosophy of the eighteenth century. Here are some wise words coming from the founder of Positivism : ' The evil influence of revolutionary philosophy ', writes Auguste Comte, ' is singularly exhibited in Condorcet's work in the form of an inconsistency which must strike every reader. The human race is there represented as having attained a vast degree of perfection at the close of the eighteenth century while the author attributes an entirely retrogressive influence to almost every doctrine, institution, or preponderant power throughout the whole past. Whereas the total progress accomplished can be nothing else than the result of the various kinds of partial progress realized since the beginning of civilization.'[1]

The fallacy which is here criticized receives another form in the paradox that all education is a vast impertinence. The argument is that every generation must be allowed to make up its own mind and not to have its mind made up for it. At bottom, this is the argument of the anarchist, who pleads that the attempt of one human will to influence another is in itself criminal. The reply is that men are so constituted by nature that they cannot avoid acting on others and being acted on in turn, that such reciprocal influence is what is meant by life in society, and that the question for the educationalist is not whether a child shall be influenced from outside or no, but from what quarter and in what form that influence shall come. To contend that it should never come from parents or elders but always from coevals is simple lunacy.

No wise man will disparage the power of education. Most of the progress of the world is due to it. Recent excavations in Crete and in Egypt show us that the manual skill of the human race has made no progress. Gems were carved as delicately and with as fine a taste and exquisite a precision in early Minoan days as now. Carving was as finished under King Tutenkhamen as under King George V ; and as for the human intellect, even Glasgow University has not improved on Aristotle and Plato. We are neither cleverer, nor stronger, nor gifted with a higher degree of manual skill than our distant ancestors ; and if there has been organic evolution, its progress has been so gradual that even now the accumulation of variations is not clearly perceptible. Such progress, then, as has been achieved has been the result not of organic but of

[1] H. Martineau, *The Philosophy of Auguste Comte*, vol. ii, p. 59.

social evolution. It has been the result of education and the accumulation and transmission of knowledge and invention and the organization of industry. It is to these forces, and not to any change in the physical and intellectual power of man, that we attribute the present state of civilization and its difference from the conditions which are described in the Homeric poems or may be inferred from the monuments of ancient Egypt.

In this process of social evolution the school has played, if not a decisively predominant, at any rate an important part. It has been the chief medium by which knowledge has been transmitted from one generation to another, and each successive generation has been equipped with the implements to fresh discovery. And it has also been employed to imprint upon the young definite conceptions of religious and patriotic duty. In the writings of the Greek philosophers nothing is more emphatically insisted on than that the education of the young should be adjusted to the spirit and character of the polity.

Two questions arise here. How far should a system of education aim at imparting a definite conception of civic obligation? And how far should it concern itself with putting the young into possession of those branches of human knowledge which are most definitely connected with social and political problems? Should we attempt to impress certain political and social doctrines on our children? Or should we encourage them to interest themselves in political and social facts? Or should we do neither of these things and allow the civic education to come later on when mind and character are mature?

There is, I think, little difficulty in answering the first of these two questions. In a broad sense all education should aim at good citizenship. It should have for its principal object the inculcation of a sense of duty to others. Man is a political animal, as Aristotle observed. He is equipped with qualities which imply a social reference. He has ears to hear with, eyes to see with, fingers to touch with, a mind to think with, and the gifts and qualities which he possesses are only intelligible and can only find their highest field for exercise in social intercourse with his fellows. To educate children to be selfish, to teach them that the end of existence is either pleasure to be snatched on any terms and without reckoning of social cost, or conversely an ascetic and self-centred detachment from the world, is clearly a perversion, because it starves the better side of human nature. 'The nobler a soul is the more objects of compassion it has,' says Bacon in the wonderful eighth book of the *De Augmentis*.[1] To educate away from compassion or from any of the great human virtues is clearly to base education on a vicious plan. It follows that a narrow sectarian education, abounding in exclusions and sweeping condemnations, and very closely circumscribing the circle of the elect, is to be condemned. Whether the proclivity be religious or economic or political makes very little difference. A school in which the teaching is characterized by a violently anti-semitic bias, or a violently anti-capitalistic bias, or a violently anti-French or anti-German or anti-vaccination bias, is clearly a bad school. To nourish premature antipathies on matters admittedly controversial among honest men is no part of the educative function.

Moral indifferentism is a danger on the other side. To love the good and to hate the evil, to admire the beautiful and to dislike the ugly, are clearly essential qualities of a citizen's education. Nothing is morally indifferent. But to what extent are we entitled to assume that one form of polity is morally superior to another, or that our own country is morally superior to all others, or that one form of social organization has a higher degree of ethical soundness than any others? Ought we to educate for the polity in any specific sense?

[1] Bacon's Works (ed. Ellis and Spedding), vol. v, p. 44.

The answer to this question cannot, I think, be an absolute affirmative. It must depend upon the moral quality which such an education implies in any particular case. Assume a society of cannibals, or of debased cut-throats, or of selfish materialists, assume a polity governed by the principle that the coarser forms of economic service are to be performed by rightless men, or that in the conduct of foreign affairs a particular nation is rightless and for ever disqualified from equitable consideration ; clearly an education in the spirit of such a polity would be a bad education. The truly civic education would be an education of emancipation, of protest.

History, of course, furnishes the most striking example of such an education of protest in the story of the early Christian Church. The education of these early Christian communities was an education away from the polity. It was anti-civic, anti-Roman in a very fundamental sense, loosening the ties of allegiance to the State in peace and war, as the Absolutist Conscientious Objector, making a sacrifice of his personal comfort for the ideal of a warless world, was anti-civic in the immediate and obvious sense of the term. But what is it that affords the justification for the education away from the polity ? It is, I think, the belief that it is based upon higher moral conceptions and is calculated to foster a higher type of character than the conventional education of the State. An education adjusted towards a change of polity effects nothing of value unless it is based upon a regeneration of the human conscience. The complaint made by Renan in his later days against the French Revolution was that the change from monarchical to republican institutions had not been founded on a regeneration of the human conscience. It had not made the individual Frenchman better, or more humane ; but had been compatible with great cruelties and excesses, and an unabated spirit of political intolerance.

That in the broader sense education should be civic is beyond controversy. An education, informed by an ethical purpose, is an education having a civic result. But we have still to consider whether there should be in the courses of education devised for the young a specific bias in the direction of particular political ideals. Should the young be taught a political catechism? Should they be directly taught to love their country and to admire its constitution? Should they be given the general outlines of economic and social science? Ought the object of a public education in Britain to be the education of British citizens in certain standards of civic duty conceived as being characteristically national?

In the catalogue of the House of Commons Library made in 1828 there were precisely eight books on Political Science and Political Economy, a lesser number than that devoted to Heraldry, one of the few forms of exact knowledge which has no civic utility. The works of Ricardo and Malthus were not in the collection. There was a fairly good collection of books relating to the history of the United Kingdom, but very little on foreign history. Now this is very significant of the kind of culture which was traditional in England at that time, and was thought to be adequate to the needs of an English gentleman in the House of Commons. A broad education in the humanities of Greece and Rome was then the staple of a university education, and the House of Commons was principally recruited from Oxford and Cambridge. Political science and political economy were nowhere subjects of general academic study. They were not set for the Degree Examinations. It was safe to neglect them. An apt quotation from Horace would do more to establish a parliamentary reputation than a knowledge of Adam Smith or a profound acquaintance with the mysteries of the foreign exchange.

All this is changed now. Social and economic problems have

become so insistent, fill so large a sphere in the political prospect, obtrude themselves so continuously into the arena of debate and excite such violent emotions when they do, that no statesman can afford to neglect them. The time of a Cabinet is, indeed, largely absorbed in economic considerations, and no government could go into action without a full complement of business brains on the Treasury Bench.

Nevertheless, it does not follow that school-children are wisely educated upon economic or social studies. Some years ago Mr. Arthur Acland introduced into the Evening School Code of the Board of Education a syllabus of instruction on the Life and Duties of the Citizen. It consisted of statements of fact concerning the rôle played by different functionaries such as the policeman and the rate-collector, together with appropriate moral observations as to the need of public spirit and a sense of public responsibility. A considerable number of text-books were at once produced by enterprising publishers, all of which were reviewed at the time by Mr. Graham Wallas, who pronounces that ' they constituted perhaps the most worthless collection of printed pages that have ever occupied the same space on a bookshelf ', and that the lessons which were founded upon them ' failed to stimulate any kind of interest in the students '.[1] The experiment was a failure. Young people want something more stimulating to the imagination than desiccated information about the details of local government. The real way to create the civic spirit in the young is by showing them the examples which history affords of lives lived and deeds done for the common weal. The more direct and specialized the civic training, the less effective will it be. From this point of view nothing is more to be regretted than the growing tendency among working men, desirous of repairing their lost educational opportunities in after life, to prefer

[1] *Human Nature in Politics*, p. 191.

an arid training in the details of economic history or of some economic dogma to a broad and generous discipline in the great imaginative writers whose thoughts have moved the world and entered as an inspiring force into its nobler and more disinterested movements.

Let it, however, not be supposed that some civic lessons of a practical kind cannot be appropriately and successfully taught to children. The war-savings movement is a case in point. Here a social object, of the very greatest importance, not only for the effective conduct of the war but for the spread of the investing habit among the people, was forwarded in a most effective and natural manner by missionary work among the elementary schools. The children were taught the value of thrift, encouraged to practise it themselves and to enlist the interests of their parents, and the theoretical lesson was given an immediate and practical point by the issue of shares within the reach of a child's savings, and bearing an attractive rate of interest. The great multiplication of government bond-holders in the last ten years is very largely due to the schools, who have thus rendered an invaluable service to the social stability of the country.

Other civic lessons, besides the all-important lesson of thrift, may from time to time be usefully brought before the mind of children. The President of the Board of Education in England is constantly being assailed by excellent persons who desire him to give special prominence in the school curriculum to some aspect of truth or policy to which they attach a special importance. The Navy League urge that a very special place should be given in the education of British children to the rôle played by sea-power in history, and more particularly to the importance of keeping the British Navy as a bulwark of national security. Temperance reformers desire that children should be taught that alcohol is an evil; apostles of the League of

Nations that they should be instructed in the Covenant and principles of the League; strong imperialists that they should be well founded in Imperial Geography; while Socialist, Communist, and Proletarian Sunday Schools have their own particular receipts for turning out citizens.

That children should know something about the hygiene of food and drink, something about the history of their own country, something about the existence of other countries and of their titles to respect as having contributed to the sum of civilization, that they should not be wholly ignorant of the kind of polity in which they live and that they should be given if possible an admiration for the literature of their country and for the great men who have brought it to its present point of greatness—all this will be generally admitted. What, however, most true educationalists would dispute is the contention that children should be educated in any school of political and economic opinion. Give a child a good sound basis of knowledge as to the larger elementary facts of life; teach him to exercise his reasoning faculties; let him learn how to use a book in a spirit of critical freedom : and then leave him to form his own opinions as to that which is wise and unwise in the sphere of political action from the gathering experiences of life. What greater injury could be done to a young brain than to load it with a number of unexamined shibboleths, each one of which may prove to be a genuine obstruction to the impartial understanding of the concrete and complicated problems of life !

Some such theory as this is, I believe, congenial to the British mind. We prefer freedom to regimentation, and a good broad general education to a sectarian discipline in one or other school of political opinion. We have sufficient faith in the political instincts of our race and in the stability of our institutions to leave to chance much that in other races, less easily circumstanced, is made a matter for serious discipline. The French *lycée*, the German gymnasium, the American Public School are more directly concerned with the education of a specific State sense than are the State-aided schools in Great Britain ; and for this reasons may be assigned rooted in history or in overmastering need. A country like America, invaded by an annual flood of emigrants belonging to every European race and tongue, looks to the public school as the great instrument for the production of American nationality. The school gives the common language, the common culture, the common civic outlook. It makes of Hungarians and Italians and Greeks English-speaking citizens of the United States, gives them an outline knowledge of American institutions, a pride in American freedom, and a sense of American equality. The mission of the school is well understood ; it is to make America one and indivisible.

In countries which have undergone great political crises, the educational system comes necessarily to be viewed in the light of some large political aim. South African statesmen had to ask themselves, when they were plotting South African Union, what kind of polity they wanted and what was to be the relation between the Dutch and the English races ; and their decision is stamped upon the school curriculum. The French *lycée*, with its barrack-like discipline and the military uniforms of its scholars, is the product of Napoleon's mind as it revolved upon the military necessities of the French State. If the Free State in Ireland should throw up a great statesman he would undoubtedly use the educational system of the country to educate the Irish people in the duty of taking active responsibility for the maintenance of law and order in their own country, for no force less strong than national education can restore the sentiment which national education has for centuries set itself to destroy.

A question arises whether, with the growth of historical studies and the consequent development of historical foresight, nations will not be tempted to impart more and more of conscious political ideas into the teaching of the young. The nation which before the war had paid most attention to historical studies and was most given to the flattering task of casting its own political horoscope was Germany. Nowhere was the study of world-history more ardently pursued, or the faith in the Messianic Mission of a chosen people so firmly and generally held. Even pacificists and strong opponents of the Hohenzollern monarchy considered that the sheer superiority of German civilization would ensure its triumphant acceptance by all the backward nations—and all nations were relatively backward—of the world. The doctrine of Treitschke was that Germany was beset by enemies, the most formidable of which was Great Britain, each in turn destined to be conquered by her victorious arms. The colleges and schools felt the influence of this political philosophy. The whole mind of the nation was trained to think of Germany noble, magnanimous, environed by foes, but destined at the appointed moment to achieve its glorious destiny by war, or by a succession of wars, until at last the world-peace was realized under the shelter of the almighty imperial shield. Public speeches, lectures, newspapers, lessons, all converged on the same point—the destiny of Germany and the enemies who stood in the path.

When the defeat came in 1918 the Prussian minister of public instruction issued a circular recommending that the hatred of foreign countries should no longer be taught in the schools, but replaced by a policy of systematic amiability.

The military collapse of Germany must not blind us to the fact that this intellectual discipline in civics was in one respect surprisingly successful. If the object of the system was to produce a patriotic nation, willing to endure infinite hardship for the sake of the fatherland, that object was amply attained ; but if the design was to obtain an intelligent and critical public opinion, we should all admit that the political side of German education before the war was a lamentable failure. The example should serve as a sufficient warning against adjusting a scheme of national education to a preconceived view of the political evolution of the world in the next few decades.

The truth is that statesmen are at a loss to look far into the future. It is sufficient if they find some not intolerable solution for the problems which rush in upon them at so inconvenient a speed from day to day. If we could with certainty predict the different combinations of powers fifteen or thirty years hence, we might, perhaps, allow that knowledge to affect in some degree our public education. But this we cannot do. We must be content to be ignorant of the future, and in our ignorance of the future we shall be best advised if we content ourselves with telling most scrupulously the truth about the past.

IV

THE CLAIMS OF NEIGHBOURHOOD

'Je prefère ma famille à moi, ma patrie à ma famille, et le genre humain à ma patrie.' Telle est le dévise de l'homme vertueux.—D'ALEMBERT.

'I prefer my family to myself, my country to my family, and humanity to my country.' Such is the device of the virtuous man.

THERE is no sentiment better known than Burke's famous aphorism, 'To be attached to the subdivision, to love the little platoon we belong to in society is the first principle, the germ as it were, of public affection. It is the first link in the series by which we proceed towards a love of our country and nation.' The little platoon, whether it be school or university, village, town or county, serves as the seed-plot of that affection towards the common weal which is the soul of patriotism. Burke, it will be observed, does not base patriotism on reason but on emotion. Patriotism may be justified by reason. A man may come to the considered conclusion that on every ground of rational self-interest it is better to be a Scot than an Englishman, and a Briton than a Malayan. But he is not a patriot on reason. His reason may teach him that other countries are greater, more populous, more prosperous than his own; that their institutions are superior, their armies more powerful. Nevertheless, he prefers his own country because it is his own. He does not reason about it—he feels.

The second feature of Burke's theory of patriotism is that it is a natural growth from sentiments of affection inspired by one of the many small segments into which society is divided. Home attachments lead on to local attachments, and these again to nationalism, and ultimately to concern for the affairs of humanity as a whole. The warm-hearted affectionate imaginative man moves from the first in an atmosphere of social pieties, enlarging their circle as his experience develops. If local patriotism has a value it is chiefly as a school for that deeper and more generous sentiment which leads a man to sacrifice his life for his country or for one of the great humane causes of the world. If the *esprit de corps* which is so strong a motive to existence and to the maintenance of honourable standards of activity at school and college is to be encouraged, it is because it is the germ of a virtue capable of application in a wider field. The kind of sentiment which makes men extravagant even to the point of ridicule in praise of their university or their town is a spur to civic action, so precious that if such emotions were to be eliminated from the common-wealth, laxity would invade every branch of the administration and patriotism wither at the root.

Such a theory points to a system of education, some part of which is directed to the inculcation of these local or partial affections. The argument is that if a Glasgow boy does not care about Glasgow, he is never likely to care about Scotland, and that if he does not care about Scotland, he is not likely to care about mankind. A cosmopolitan education given to Glasgow boys would invert the true order of rational develop-ment. It is healthy for them to think of Glasgow as the second city of the Empire, to realize its place in the world of commerce and industry and science, and to care about its future as a deposit committed to their charge. Readers of Maurice Barrès's novel, *Les Déracinés*, will recall the severe stricture which that passionate son of Lorraine passes upon the French national system of education with its uprooting, universalizing tendencies, the masters all stamped with the hall-mark of the Kantian philosophy and bringing down from Paris their heavy standardized intellectual menu, the consumption of which was quite sufficient to occupy the digestive energies of their pupils to the exclusion of any more congenial form of diet. In contradistinction to this severe and uniform discipline, Barrès preaches the gospel of a provincial culture. Let children be given a love of their province. Let them learn to value its traditions, to love its landscape, to feel themselves passionately as Lorrainers or Bretons or Burgundians, and you will have a strong and healthy France. The suction of the big towns, the subdivisions of industry, the growth of locomotion, all tend to uproot men from their native soil, to sap local piety, to weaken the springs of patriotic responsibility, and spread a restless, homeless spirit through the community.

The patriotism shown by all the great European countries during the war shows that there is not much substance in the fear that modern systems of education are in effect diminishing the love of country. There is, however, a sound psychological basis in the doctrine that one of the principal ingredients in patriotic affection is a love of the physical aspects of the country in which we have been reared, of its hills and valleys, its streams and lakes, its pleasant cornfields and fragrant woods. Even where the landscape is wild and the living hard, the home of our fathers exerts its subtle spell and claims an unalterable loyalty.

> From the lone shieling of the misty island
> Mountains divide us and the waste of seas,
> But still the blood is strong, the heart is Highland,
> And we in dreams behold the Hebrides.[1]

Let us admit the political and civic value of these strong local attachments. Can they be overdone? Mr. Chesterton has written an amusing story, *The Napoleon of Notting Hill*, based on the supposition that the passionate feelings which animate one Balkan State against another may be generated with equal force by an urban district. Is there any reason

[1] For the origin and correct form of the Canadian boat song, see E. T. Cook, *More Literary Recollections*, p. 283.

why an alteration of scale should involve an alteration in values? Why should not Notting Hill or Kensington generate as brave a sentiment, as generous a spirit, as high a sense of adventure, as deep a sense of devotion as Britain or France? The Athens of Pericles was not as populous, the Florence of Dante not as large. The reason is that Notting Hill or Kensington are not separate States, as were the Athens of Pericles and the Florence of Dante, but subordinate and alterable parts of a larger polity, and that their public affairs consequently claim only a small fraction of the attention of the citizens who live there. Tow Notting Hill into the middle of the Atlantic Ocean, give it a hundred years of history, let it defend itself against enemies, and then perhaps it might throw up a Napoleon. Be it remembered, however, that Napoleon was not content with Corsica, but had definitely come to the conclusion that the age of small States was past.

A most difficult question to determine with regard to the just claims of localism is whether or not it is right to keep alive a subordinate language. There can be very little question that the sense of Welsh patriotism is heightened by the preservation of a living Welsh language and by the care which is bestowed upon its cultivation. Patriotic Bretons cherish the Breton tongue ; there has been a literary revival of Provençal in Provence, of the Auvergnat dialect in Auvergne ; while the Irish are making desperate efforts to revive Erse. Indeed the Sinn Fein movement in Ireland, upon its intellectual side, has been largely inspired by the belief that Erse, which was the medium for an ancient literature of a certain but greatly exaggerated value, might be made the vehicle for a distinctive modern culture which would enrich the civilization of the world. The general effect of the Peace Treaties has been to give additional strength to this separatist and local tendency.

In the United States of America exactly the opposite view

is taken. The object of the public system of education in the government of the Union is to manufacture American citizens and to make every American child learn to speak and use the English language. By a gigantic system of educational pressure the original languages of the emigrants are squeezed out in the second generation, and a uniform speech spread throughout the land. There can be little doubt that the Americans have been guided by a very wise instinct in ridding themselves from the first of the language difficulty. They have a sufficient crop of troubles, arising from the coloured population and from the varying racial traditions of their immigrants, without adding to these the problem of Babel : and the advice which is sometimes given to American Germans, American Magyars, and American Galicians to cherish and preserve their national connexions with Europe is thoroughly unsound. The true future of America lies in the adaptation of its vast and heterogeneous population to the standards and ideals of the English common law and of Anglo-Saxon liberty. To foster the continuance or to permit the official use of other languages than English would be gratuitously to encourage the forces of disunion within the State.

In general a nation is handicapped by the possession of a subordinate language. No British Government would act reasonably which endeavoured to discourage the knowledge of Welsh in Wales. And yet on what principle of general utility can we defend the employment of so much intellectual force upon a language understood by so small a fraction of the human race? There is only one argument which would justify it. If it could be shown that there was some honourable peculiarity of Welsh genius and temperament which could not be expressed otherwise than through the Welsh speech, so that the disappearance of Welsh as a spoken language would involve a real spiritual loss to Wales and to the world, then the case for the preservation of Welsh would be irrefragable. But I cannot be convinced that this is so. I cannot believe that where the literary genius exists, it cannot find its true expression in any one of the rich world languages. The Celts of Wales and of Brittany have made great contributions to modern eloquence. Chateaubriand, Lamennais, Renan, Lloyd George have obtained a world-wide audience, but they have expressed themselves not in the Celtic language of a province but in a tongue familiar to their civilized contemporaries in every continent. Had they been confined to Breton or Welsh, their audience would have been small indeed.[1]

This, it may be urged, is an argument for putting within the reach of every child one of the world languages. It is not an argument for extruding the provincial language or the *patois*. It is an argument for a bilingual system in education, when the provincial tongue is already in the field; and since every one is the better for knowing two languages, the existence of a provincial language is a positive encouragement to intellectual progress.

To this contention there is an easy reply. It is that if a child is to learn two languages, there is no parent in the world who upon an impartial judgement would not prefer that his child should know two world languages rather than one supplemented by a provincial tongue. Who would deny that English and French or English and Latin provide a better intellectual equipment than English and Erse or English and Welsh? There may be special local reasons or special political reasons which make it desirable that children should learn these smaller languages. It may be, and no doubt is, a source of patriotic satisfaction to know them. It brings the child into

[1] A similar observation applies to the Irishmen, such as Sheridan, E. Burke, Charles Lever, Bernard Shaw, W. B. Yeats, who have kindly employed the English language.

closer touch with the tradition and history of his race, deepens his pride, strengthens his piety, may purify his character. That all these good results may ensue from a cultivation of the small local languages may be conceded. What is, however, to be remembered is that each of these languages imposes a burden and erects an obstacle. The divisions between men are not to be multiplied *praeter necessitatem*.

A distinction may fairly be drawn between the cultivation of the minor languages of the world and the preservation of dialect. Basque stands upon a different footing from Provençal. The first of these two languages, though of immense interest to the philologist, belongs to a different family of speech from any of the greater European languages, whereas Provençal is a form of Romance language very easily acquired by any one with a competent knowledge of Latin or French. It requires very few hours of study to enable a French scholar to appreciate the beauties of Mistral's *Mirèio*, whereas Basque and Finnish and Welsh can only be understood after a long period of special discipline. It follows that the preservation of Provençal as a distinct form of speech and organ of literature imposes a very light disability upon those who are compelled to learn it, in comparison with the handicap of the Celtic or Ugro-Finnish languages. Our conclusion, then, is that the purposeful intensification of local feeling by the study of a language distinct from any of the great families of human speech is a step to which objection may be taken. It is idle to suppose that it does not in itself constitute a handicap, though it may have advantages in point of fact as stimulating some people to intellectual exertions which they would otherwise be unwilling to take.

In general, however, local sentiment is one of the broad civic impulses which the wise statesman will endeavour to foster. If it is not always rational, it is generally real. It was proved by experience in England that a civic university would be more efficient and better supported than a federal university, because the conception of a civic university touched the sentiment of civic pride and civic rivalry, whereas a university the credit for which was spread over several cities was nobody's child. Indeed so strong is local feeling in England that private subsidies to any large amount are surprisingly difficult to obtain for the two national universities, whereas in the case of the civic universities purse-strings are more freely untied. Experience shows that few things are more precious in modern society than the spur of local patriotism.

For this reason there are few questions more closely affecting the common weal than the quality of the men who enter local politics and have the handling of local affairs. Are the conditions of public life in our great cities sufficiently attractive to enlist the services of disinterested or experienced men? Has not the advent of the motor-car detached many of the leaders of industry from close and serious association with the life of the city in which their money is made? And is not this a great evil? Are we not tending to a system of local government in which the main part of the work will be transacted by a permanent and technically skilled civil service, while only the broad direction of public policy is left in the hands of the direct representatives of the ratepayer? Has not the time come when a royal commission should be appointed to report upon this vast new administrative personnel, its method of recruitment, its numbers, its competence, which has grown up unperceived, unchronicled by our social historians, just as in the course of the nineteenth century an administrative service grew up, equally unnoticed, in Whitehall? And as the municipal bureaucracy develops in strength, skill, and importance, will there not be a danger of a sensible relaxation in the public interest in affairs?

On the whole it would appear that the motives which lead men and women in this country to desire to take a part in the conduct of local business are sufficiently strong to ensure the maintenance of a fair standard of competence and honesty. The legitimate desire for influence, the very generally diffused taste for public debate and administrative work, the social prestige attaching to the discharge of public functions, the desire to reform some abuse or to promote some beneficent change, these motives have hitherto been sufficient to enlist a reasonable supply of public virtue in the local services.

One of the dangers to be avoided is the multiplication of elections. In the vehement reaction against autocracy which characterized the early stages of the French Revolution, there was a mania for popular election. The constitution of 1791 multiplied elections to such a point that an active citizen, according to the calculation of Taine, would be compelled to spend half his time electing members to some body or other, if he were fully to perform the duties devolved upon him. The result was easy to foresee. The average citizen being invited to do more than was reasonable, in effect did less than was reasonable. The whole public work of the country fell into the hands of a small and violent minority, and by an automatic and natural revulsion, the constitution which was devised to inaugurate the reign of liberty led by swift and certain stages to a strong and centralized autocracy.

In this experience we find the classic warning against a policy which in the name of liberty and democracy places upon the shoulders of the average citizen a greater burden than he is willing and anxious to bear. It is indeed the principal argument against the scheme, for which there is otherwise much to be said, for an annual and partial renewal of our municipal bodies.

If elections are triennial, a good deal of attention is paid to them, the claims of candidates and programmes are ardently canvassed and busily discussed, and there is for the moment a strong light cast upon the principal issues of municipal policy, the prospect of which is in itself of some value as a deterrent to questionable courses. If on the other hand elections are annual, there is a danger that public attention may be fatigued, that less care will be taken by electors, that the polls will be small, and that the general interest in local affairs will be diminished by the frequency with which it is solicited.

Similar arguments apply to schemes for substituting an elective for an hereditary or nominated second chamber, though here they have less force. It is sufficient to emphasize the point that the capacity of the average elector for taking an effective part and an intelligent interest in elections is limited, though doubtless capable of expansion, and that it is the part of wisdom to recognize his limitations in our electoral arrangements.

The merits and demerits of a system of proportional representation are brought to the same test. Will proportional representation have the effect of keeping up a high general level of interest in affairs by giving to minorities who otherwise might be permanently unrepresented a chance of exercising their due electoral weight? It is argued, and with force, that if minorities go for a long time unrepresented they cease to care, and that such lethargy is a public evil. The evil, however, such as it is, does not assume such large proportions in local as it does in national life, because party lines are less stereotyped and more fluctuating in local than in national politics. On the other hand, the principal defect of a system of proportional representation, that it results in diminished majorities and weakened governments, is less obvious in local affairs, because the executive work of a locality is generally transacted through committees, in each of which the minority receives its share of representation.

What should be the attitude of the citizen towards the government of his locality when the time comes round for the exercise of his vote? One party will probably profess to save the rates and another will be prepared to spend them. One party will raise the flag of economy, the other of social progress. The money question will always be kept well in the forefront of the discussion, and will often be the determining factor; but it is clear that in any intelligent appreciation of civic duty the money aspect of local government is a superficial aspect. The real question to be decided is whether the community as a whole will benefit by the expenditure. And to answer such a question as this properly involves a study of social politics on every side.

Let it be argued, for instance, that economies should be effected in the expenditure upon the schools for defective children, on the ground that to spend more than a very small amount of money upon children who may be expected to make no great economic contribution to the community in return is a waste of public resources which might be more profitably employed. Let it be argued that the education of blind children and crippled children and mentally defective children and deaf mutes is a luxury inappropriate to a heavily taxed and heavily rated country, and that all this side of public benevolence should be curtailed. Let it be argued as part of the same general philosophy of politics, that such public money as is expended on education should be concentrated so far as possible upon those children who by reason of their physical and mental powers are most likely to make an adequate return to the State, and that in consequence a very severe process of sifting should be applied at intervals during the career of the young, so that only the elect should receive the benefits of the higher kind of education. As against such a view as this, what is the reply? The first point to consider is whether it is desirable that the elementary schools of the country should be efficient, and whether they can be efficient if together with the normal children there are grouped children who cannot profit at all, or can only partially profit, by the ordinary course of instruction, and who act as an impediment to the education of their fellows. Then we have to consider whether, since defective children cannot be properly educated in the elementary school and interfere with the education of normal children, they should be educated at all. Is it agreeable to our instincts of humanity that children who have already been heavily handicapped by nature should receive an additional disadvantage at the hands of the State? Is it economical that the community should be burdened with the support of citizens who have received no training whatever which may fit them to make a contribution towards their own livelihood?

There are other arguments, less obvious but of equal force, in favour of special schools for defective children. It is in these schools that the power of education is most signally displayed. To teach the blind to read, the mute to speak, the mentally defective to work with their hands, is the greatest triumph which the art of the educator can achieve over reluctant nature. To the cynic who holds that the only education is that which a man gives to himself, the successes obtained by the modern methods of instruction in an institute for the deaf mute affords the complete answer. Here you have the educator *in excelsis*. He does everything for his patient. It is by his art, and his art only, that channels of communication are opened out which enable the afflicted child to take his proper place in the community, to receive and impart information and ideas and to obtain the corporeal refreshment and elasticity which are derived from the impulses of a mind freshened by movement and external contacts. The loss of this teaching, which in some respects forms the most delicate and instructive branch of the teacher's art, as it is also the most indispensable help to those for whom it is designed, would be a great moral catastrophe to the community. The teaching of defective children, which is necessarily more individual than the teaching of normal children, makes a contribution to the stock of ideas about teaching in general which is far less easily gleaned from the experience of class-rooms filled with normal children doing normal work at a standard pace. The ordinary difficulties of a child are seen here, as it were, through a magnifying glass. And there is no expert in pedagogy who would not assert that his science would be greatly impoverished if this field for observation and experiment were withdrawn.

Such are some of the reflections which would occur to the mind of the social student when he is endeavouring to make up his mind as to the legitimacy of this branch of public expenditure. Reflection of this general kind would not, of course, exhaust the matter. There would be the consideration as to whether economies could be effected without prejudicing the general effectiveness of the work ; considerations as to whether some sacrifice of public good was not advisable in this direction in order to achieve a preponderance of public advantage elsewhere, and in particular as to whether a better balance of social effort might not be obtained by a larger expenditure on prevention and a smaller expenditure on cure ; upon a campaign for instance against syphilis, which is one of the most potent causes of blindness, as against an expenditure upon schools for the blind.

This last query intrudes itself whenever we are called upon to consider any practical detail of social reform. Ought each generation to do what it can to alleviate its own sufferings, or should it reserve part at least of its resources for the benefit of posterity? Is there a case for saying: 'Here is a mass of present social evil which we can to some extent alleviate by a given expenditure of energy, time, and money, but on the whole, greatly as we are moved by sentiments of social compunction to do this, we think that in the long run it is better to treat it as irredeemable social waste, and to concentrate all our efforts upon securing conditions which will reduce and probably ultimately abolish this evil, even though we ourselves shall in all probability not be here to witness the result of our labours?'

I think that the answer to this question would depend first upon the confidence which we are prepared to repose in the efficacy of the preventive measures, then upon the degree to which the spectacle of present misery touches the heart, and finally upon the extent to which the resources at the disposal of society enable us to cure it. To cease educating the blind of this generation on the ground that the funds so employed would be better expended in combating the physical conditions out of which blindness commonly arises would offend the common sense and humanity of the world. We know that the education of the blind brings in an immediate and active return in human happiness and efficiency. We know that by depriving the blind of education we make them a misery to themselves and a burden to the community. On the other hand, although we believe that we can greatly reduce the volume of blindness by preventive measures spread over a generation, we have not the same certainty of effecting our object by a given expenditure, and may reasonably hope that with the further advance of science those who come after us may be enabled to effect larger results by a diminished output of effort.

The truth is that you cannot treat a social problem, however minute, with any intelligence, without raising far-reaching questions of principle. Everywhere man must act upon some theory of human nature and of human destiny, upon some creed, inarticulate it may be and never consciously envisaged, but nevertheless colouring and shaping the mass of his activity. When Miss Hannah More explained that in founding village schools she would do nothing to make the poor discontented with their station, she was acting upon the philosophy of life expressed in the English Church Catechism of the sixteenth century, a document accurately reflecting the state of society which existed during the life of Dean Nowell, its principal draftsman and the genial inventor of bottled beer. When a town councillor urges that the education of children in the elementary schools in his neighbourhood should be confined to the three Rs., he is in effect denying the right of children to anything more than a slave's ration of education, and is assuming that the art of statesmanship consists in the maintenance rather than in the removal of inequalities. When, again, objection is taken to the salary of an engineer or officer of health on the ground that it is superior to that which is earned by the skilled artisan, many large questions are raised, and among them, the value to the world of a relatively leisured class.

The local field of politics may seem narrower than the national or the imperial. The sums involved are smaller, the area covered is more contracted, but within that area issues constantly arise which call for the highest exercise of statesmanship and imply the widest and most far-reaching principles of political or social action.

There has been no lack of energy and spirit in the local politics of this island. The study of such a book as Mrs. Green's *English Towns in the Fifteenth Century* shows how rich was the variety of constitutional form and of political activity in that age of English history of which so little that is good is known, but which is notable as the precursor of the great expansion of national effort under the Tudor sovereigns.

The criticism which can be levelled against our local life is not lack of vigour but want of foresight. The great town took us by surprise. It was a new phenomenon, and perhaps for that reason our forefathers may be excused for having failed to realize its dangers and its opportunities. Town-planning for us came a century too late. We are only just beginning to scheme ahead, not for towns but for whole districts, within which it is anticipated that great industrial development may occur. In Germany and America prudent people have taken warning by our example, and have already shown how greatly the material comfort of a community, not to speak of the aesthetic amenities, may be improved by the exercise of municipal forethought. In the Western and Middle Western States of America a wise prudence has dictated the reservation of wide tracts of land for educational purposes, and the large endowments which result are exercising a great and increasing influence upon the development of secondary and university education in those regions. How different, we may be tempted to ask, would have been the future of English education, if the wealth which Henry VIII diverted from the monasteries had been employed upon the endowment of learning and education instead of on the enrichment of the gentry ?

The statesman will naturally consider how best to develop a spirit of intelligent forethought in the management of local affairs. If the area of administration is too small, if the work of administration is too minutely subdivided, or if again the pressure of the central government upon the local bodies is too severe, it will be difficult for the fountains of local initiative to play with freedom. The administration may be fool-proof ; it may work without scandal and up to a reasonable standard of efficiency; but since there will be no opportunity for any large exercise of the imagination, the town council will be devoid of originality, a humdrum government served by humdrum talents, exciting but a faint interest among the citizens and innocent of those forward-reaching thoughts which give elevation and dignity to public policy. Aristotle maintained that the city should not be so large but that its citizens could hear the voice of a single crier. There are civic functions the adequate performance of which depends upon minute neighbourly knowledge; there are others which call for scope, and postulate a wide area and operations on a large scale. So long as an elementary school was considered as an isolated unit, a local school board of neighbours might be the best instrument for managing it, but as soon as education began to develop and the elementary school came to be considered as part of a system of schools, secondary, technical, and so forth, it became clear that it was necessary to bring into existence a body capable of thinking about education in all its varieties and over a wider area. The Act of 1902, which transferred educational administration from the school board to the educational committee of a county, a county borough, or a borough, was a measure in this direction. So, too, was the Act of 1918, which encouraged local authorities to devise schemes for education in all its branches and to submit them to the Board of Education for approval. It was hoped that educational administration would be rendered more intelligent by the invitation to think ahead and to think about education as a whole, which was then extended to the local authorities; that there would be fewer hand-to-mouth expedients, and a more scientific application of the available resources to the present and future needs of the community. ' A great business ', says Mr. Henry Ford, who should know something about it, ' is too big to be human.' The march of science, which is constantly calling for larger economic units in government, does to some extent dehumanize administration. On the other hand, it gives to administration more power and efficiency, makes it more attractive to talent, and invests it with an appeal to the civic imagination of the many, to which no purely parochial effort could aspire.

The history of the administrative county of London is a case in point. In the ordinary sense of the term there is very little London patriotism. The city is too large, the population too fluctuating, the national or imperial interests too predominating. There is not in London the sense of community which animates the inhabitants of Manchester or Sheffield. How few Londoners could give you the name of the Lord Mayor, still less of the chairman of the County Council? How faint is the interest in the University of London! How small a proportion of the population resident in London regard it otherwise than as a place in which to earn a livelihood or to enjoy society! And yet the size of the administrative county of London, the importance of the problems with which the County Council has to deal, the greatness of the sums which it controls, all these factors do attract eminent ability to the local service of London, and have resulted in the output of a mass of work in the sphere of education and public health which has set a high standard for the rest of the nation. There are, it is true, the inevitable complaints of the overgrown bureaucracy, of the cold inhuman touch, of excessive regulation, defects incidental to the conduct of all business on a very large scale. But then there are the compensating virtues, the great momentum behind reform, the variety of experiment permitted by the available scale of the resources, the highly trained skill of the servants which so great a body is enabled to employ.

From these observations it should not be inferred that

local partriotism is one of the rarest emotions of mankind. It **is,** on the contrary, so natural, it grows up so quickly and easily, it draws, or may draw, sustenance from such slight and insufficient forms of nutrition, that the problem for the states-man is not to excite or create it, but to give it a useful and elevated instead of a foolish and low direction. History, sport, family connexions, but above all the deep-rooted sentiment of preferring a place with which you are connected to a place with which you are not connected, simply by reason of the fact that it is your own county, town, or village, and not another's, contribute to make local patriotism one of the widest political sentiments of mankind. The sense of antiquity may contribute to fortify and deepen the feeling, but it is not an essential condition of its manifestation, for a raw Australian or American town appears to excite as much local pride as one of the historic counties of England which dates back to Anglo-Saxon times. I well recall that in the course of a conversation which I had at Boston in 1909 with Booker Washington, the famous leader of the coloured race, that remarkable man observed that while most white men in the States abused their coloured fellow-citizens, they generally made an exception in favour of the coloured men of their own neighbourhood. The week following I happened to be in Richmond talking to the Governor of Virginia. The colour question, as was indeed inevitable, came up for discussion, and the Southern statesman did not disappoint me by any lack of vigour in his denunciation of the deficiencies of the negro race. He added, however, that an exception must be made in favour of the coloured men in Virginia, who were very much superior in every way to the coloured men in any other state of the Union. So strong is the force of local feeling and local knowledge that it serves as a corrective to one of the most powerful prejudices of the human race.

We are sometimes tempted to forget that in spite of all the improvements in locomotion which have rendered travel so easy and pleasant to persons of moderate means, the vast majority of mankind is condemned by poverty to comparative immobility. How small a proportion of human beings have seen any country but their own? How few have any real acquaintance with more than two or three tiny localities in their neighbourhood? The obstinate spirit of localism is only to a slight degree modified or refined by travel. What is really contributing to break down local boundaries and to enlarge the horizons of men is not the ease with which they can transport themselves from place to place, for it is vouchsafed to but a small minority to do this, but the levelling effect of education, of the newspaper press, of the cinema, of the gramophone, and of all the mechanical inventions of an age of science which facilitate the transfer of experience. When we realize that villagers in the heart of Africa may listen to their chieftain's gramophone, as it gives out patter songs from the London music hall, that a Devonshire farmer, after selling his stock at Barnstaple or Exeter, may step into the cinema hall and behold a crowd in Delhi or New York, and know that the scene unrolled before him is true in every detail to a past reality, it becomes clear that the localism of the future will necessarily be different from that of the past. It need not be less intense, but it will be less blindly exclusive and self-sufficient.

If the question be asked why we should endeavour to serve our locality, or what claim a locality, as a locality, has upon our civic allegiance, the answer, I think, is that the service is rendered not to a place but to a community of which we are a part, from which we derive benefits, and in the advancement of whose welfare we perfect our own characters. Perhaps that is not the whole answer. Perhaps it might be argued that in some cases at least we owe much to the inarticulate appeal of landscape and architecture, and that the natural beauty with which we may have been surrounded in childhood and early youth may be not only the real source of our admiring relation, our homage, and our service, but the basis of our obligation.

> Love had he found in huts where poor men lie,
> His daily teachers had been woods and rills,
> The silence that is in the starry sky,
> The sleep that is among the lonely hills.

Such a claim would seem to be excessive. The wonders of nature may create, as they did in the case of Wordsworth, a sense of obligation towards their Creator, but cannot furnish a special ground of obligation towards those who participate in the enjoyment of them. The art of man stands in a different category. A city crowded with imposing buildings creates a very legitimate sense of obligation to the community whose munificence and taste has enriched the aesthetic experience of its contemporaries and of posterity, and a recognition of aesthetic obligation, though it may often be inarticulate and unconscious, enters, I believe, as an element, more frequently than is generally supposed, in the pride and affection which the citizen entertains for the city of his birth. It follows that in attempting to elevate the aesthetic taste of its members a city is nourishing the sense of civic pride and responsibility which contributes in a general way to the furtherance of its welfare. The pages of the great Florentine historians of the sixteenth century are full of the artistic glories of their beloved city. It is clear that the patronage which the Medicean princes extended so bounteously to the fine arts was to themselves a source of legitimate political authority and to their subjects a continual reminder that they formed part of a noble institution, greater than any individual, and dispensing from the store of its outward beauties a lustre upon all its members. The erection of a good building is a civic act. The greater the architect, the more intimately is the sense of social service interwoven with the satisfaction of his aesthetic impulses. Listen to the words of Sir Christopher Wren, the first of British architects and one of the sovereign men of genius of our race :

'Architecture has its political uses ; public buildings being the ornament of a country ; it establishes a nation, draws people and commerce ; makes the people love their native country, which passion is the original of all great passions in a commonwealth. The emulation of the cities of Greece was the true cause of their greatness. The obstinate valour of the Jews occasioned by the loss of their Temple was a cement that held together that people for many ages through infinite changes. The care of public decency and convenience was the great cause of the establishment of the Low Countries and of many cities in the world. Modern Rome subsists still by the ruins and institutions of the old.'[1]

Nothing is more indicative of the prevalence in the past of selfish greed and civic improvidence than the present aesthetic state of many of our British cities, unplanned, inconvenient, unredeemed by a single noble building, and offering to the eye the monotonous spectacle of mean dwellings and unsightly factories. To repair our past improvidence, to make life decent and tolerable in our crowded cities, to combat vice and disease and ignorance, these are huge tasks, but they do nor exhaust our civic obligations. Beauty is an ingredient in social welfare. In some form or other, whether it be in the shape of painting or architecture or music or of all three arts in combination, the members of a community which professes to be civilized must be provided with access to beauty. One great building reclaims a wilderness of squalor. The artistic reputation of a town has been founded on an organ, a church,

[1] *Parentalia* (ed. 1750), p. 351.

a single old master. If the wealth of individuals is to be levelled down by taxation, if we can no longer rely upon the private patron, we must draw upon public funds for the satisfaction of our corporate necessities. Of these none is greater as an inspiration to character and civic duty than some permanent and imposing manifestation of one or other of the fine arts.

There are indications that the country is slowly waking up to its duties to the arts. There is at least one town in England which actually provides good music at the expense of the rates, and the municipal buildings which have been erected in the last thirty years in our principal towns bear witness to ambition which transcends the considerations of size, cheapness, or convenience. It may be questioned, however, whether enough is done to cultivate and encourage local talent in the fine arts. Where there is a school of art partially supported by the ratepayers, the students might be afforded an opportunity of furnishing decorations to municipal buildings which would otherwise be unadorned. To some extent this is already done. The students of the Royal College of Art have been invited to contribute frescoes, illustrating different aspects of London life, to the new County Council buildings in London. A beginning has been made and an example set which might be widely followed.

The local patronage of the fine arts is beset by the danger, which accompanies every form of local activity, that undue preference will be given to local claims, and that through a lax indulgence to the neighbourly spirit, bad work may be preferred to good. The one rule which should guide civic action in this as in every other department is the stern unbending rule of excellence. It is far better for a town to have good buildings and good pictures and good music, even if they be provided by aliens, than to content itself with an inferior local product. But the more necessary it may be to give artistic commissions to outsiders, the greater is the obligation to secure for the best of the local talent adequate opportunities for development. This end is in the long run most effectually achieved by setting the standard high, even if for the moment local claimants are passed over in favour of artists whose claims are superior. The only case in which locality should be allowed to count is where artistic merits are more or less evenly balanced.

There is something attractive in the notion of a great artistic industry, like the Staffordshire potteries, relying for its designs and artistic proportions upon the arts and crafts of the neighbourhood. But I doubt whether the idea is even now capable of complete realization. An industry fighting for a place in the world market must buy talent wherever talent can be found. It cannot afford to be circumscribed in its choice by the accident of locality. If there is no taste to be picked up in the neighbourhood, it must search for taste far and wide, must be willing to import artists from France or Belgium or Germany, until native, and by preference local talent, has reached the level of training and discernment which the work requires. And even then a rigorous protection of native ability would be open to the objection which is always levelled against a protectionist policy, that it sins against the law of excellence. The truth is, that the best service which an industry can render to its locality is to maintain itself in existence by the quality of its wares and the efficiency of its labour. In so far as localism interferes with efficiency, it defeats its own purpose.

The limits within which local patriotism may be usefully encouraged are therefore traced. Patriotism, local or national, should never give shelter to mediocrity, or minister to the spirit of rigid exclusion. The old critical maxim in the sphere of literature, that you should have preferences but no exclusions, applies with even added force in the region of political feeling. Intermunicipal rivalries are a healthy form of sport so long and only so long as they are regarded by those who indulge in them as a means of getting good work done and of spreading the beneficent contagion of disinterested endeavour through every class of the community. Politics is a very rough business. If you wish to appeal to the average man, you must employ a dialect which he can understand. Tell him that science has devised new modes of electrification, and the information may fall on heedless ears. Tell him that the rival city has adopted them, and he will be alert to follow and outstrip. No one who has had experience of life in a great industrial city can fail to have noticed the healthy and animating influence of this form of competition in the sphere of public improvements.

The great danger of local politics is favouritism and corruption. These are evils so chronic, so insidious, so multiform in their modes of operation that only by increasing vigilance and energy can we be certain that they do not deflect the course of public policy. Experience shows that the ordinary antidotes are often painfully ineffective. The local press, instead of furnishing a free and fearless commentary on affairs, may be in the hands of a commercial group interested in particular financial policies. The debates in the town council may fail to reveal what is going on behind the scenes. Gross jobs may be perpetrated without attracting hostile attention. Public moneys may be squandered, municipal development pushed out in one direction and checked in another to suit a group of land-holding interests who have acquired a corrupt hold upon influential members of the corporation. Adventurers may rise to power by purchasing large blocks of shares in the leading industries, and may then use their opportunity for the furtherance of their private advantage. And these evils are more likely to arise in local than in national government, because the smaller the area, the greater the influence of wealth and the less the influence of independent criticism. The moral is obvious : no citizen of good, wise, and high character can afford to be entirely passive. He has a duty to his city; he has obligations to the public opinion of the community to which he belongs. If he cannot afford the time to serve upon local bodies, he can at least come to a definite conclusion as to the character of the men who exercise power in his locality, as to whether they are thieves and time-servers or honest servants of the public good. And when the time comes to register a vote he can give a considered judgement for the clean and disinterested handling of the corporate affairs.

V

PATRIOTISM

'Wherever there are Annamites God causes the bamboo to grow.'—
ANNAMITE PROVERB.

Puisqu'il s'était offert pour la France, il s'était rapproché de Dieu qui
reconnaît Son Fils dans le sacrifice des hommes et s'émeut à sa vue.—
R. BAZIN, *Charles de Foucauld.*

'Since he offered himself for France he came near unto God, who recognizes
His Son in the sacrifice of men and is moved by the sight.'

IF ever there was an opinion supported by the witness of
the noblest minds of history, it is the belief in the value of
patriotism as a source of civic well-being and exalted personal
character. Our own conception of patriotic virtue has been
so largely fashioned by the Greeks and the Romans, it owes
so much to Thucydides and Plutarch and Livy, and has come
down to us laden with so many historical associations, that it
is somewhat difficult for us to stand outside the zone of the
peoples whose intellectual heritage, like our own, is derived
from Greece and Rome, and to examine with cool impartiality
the sources and value of a sentiment which we take for granted
as high among the moral goods of mankind.

One observation, however, may be confidently made. In
a world of warring communities, patriotism has a clear utilitarian value. What sentiment could more usefully assist a
community, menaced by jealous neighbours, to maintain its
existence, than that powerful feeling of common fellowship,
which binds together the members of a family, a clan, or a state,
in resistance to the outer world? We may question the survival
value of sleep. We may challenge the survival value of aesthetic
appreciation. The survival value of patriotism is very obvious
and is printed on every page of history. Indeed, the success

of Rome against its enemies is to be attributed pre-eminently to the moral appeal which the Republic made to its citizens, to the sacrifices which it demanded and received, and to the strong commemorative instinct, rooted in the family pride of the great patrician families, which preserved the memory of heroic deeds as an example and inspiration to succeeding generations.

The fact that patriotism is a useful preservation of states is not the source of its power. The value of patriotism for the individual is not utilitarian. A man is not a patriot on calculation ; he does not argue that upon a hedonistic balance it pays him to be patriotic and that it pays the State that he should be patriotic. Such ideas may enter the consciousness of the intelligent patriot, but they do not make up its essence. Whatever may have been the quality of the motive two thousand years ago, it is now ideal, not utilitarian, a sentiment, as Mr. Santayana has finely said, which ' associates a man working and dying with an immortal and friendly companion, the spirit of his race, a spirit which he received from his ancestors tempered by their achievements and may transmit to posterity qualified by his own '. [1]

The Italian poet D'Annunzio, writing the apology for his seizure of Fiume, explains his creed in the following flight of lyrical eloquence. ' We disobeyed no one, because we obeyed love. My religious feeling poured itself out beyond all the dogmas taught and all the rites handed down by tradition. Religion was for me the persistence of the race and the virtue of the blood.' [2] And he proceeds to speak of ' Italy which alone is great and alone is pure '. Now this effusion is clearly nonsense. It is untrue that Italy is the only great country, for she has many rivals in greatness. It is untrue that the blood of the Italian people is pure, for the present race of the Italians are

[1] *Reason in Society*, p. 183.   [2] *Per l'Italia degli Italiani.*

a mixture of Etruscans, Latins, Celts, Teutons, Greeks, Albanians, and Slavs. It is absurd to argue that the persistence of the Italian race could be furthered by an enterprise which was certain to result in the loss of Italian lives. And, finally, it is an empty paradox to say that ' nobody was disobeyed ', because in point of fact the Italian Government was disobeyed, the Allies were disobeyed, and the public law of Europe was openly flouted. To erect a lyrical impulse into the supreme law of life is to challenge the very basis upon which civic order is founded.

On the other hand D'Annunzio's apology, divested of its extravagances of thought and statement, does truly state the emotional essence of patriotism. The patriot feels the call of the blood, and is inspired by the vision of the greatness of his country. Asked to give a rational account of his creed, he may lapse into palpable mythology and show himself to be walking in a world of ethnological or historical illusions. His preference for his own country may be no more logical and no more defensible than the mother's preference for her child. It may be a natural function like breathing. It is sufficient that it is his own. The images which the thought of country may summon to the mind are not the important or decisive thing. They will vary indefinitely in quality and multitude according to individual endowments. To one the notion of country will come with the familiar smell of fried-fish shops ; to others with the vision of air-washed moorlands or the tinkle of mountain burns ; to others with crowded historical memories of the manifold achievements of his race ; to others, again, with the clear and cameo-like memory of friends and companions.

Memory is so treacherous and uncertain a philtre, that we cannot predict even in our own case what at any moment of high emotion may be the special aspect of a complex whole which will pass through the sieve and be represented to the field of consciousness. Nor does it particularly matter. The force which moves the will is the resultant of an accumulation of obscure stresses and instincts working below the threshold of rational life and often surprising the reason by the unexpected energy and vehemence of their appeal.

But when we have given full weight to the instinctive character of patriotic emotion, we have done nothing more than assert that patriotism is human. There are other human emotions, equally instinctive, equally strong, which require a good deal of rational discipline before they can be made serviceable to society. Is this so with patriotism? Are we entitled to say that the patriotic instinct is always good, or does it, like the purely animal instincts, require a good deal of moderation and adjustment before its true social value can be realized?

A moment's reflection is sufficient to show that patriotism has this advantage over the animal instincts. It is essentially altruistic. The patriotic man in so far as he is patriotic acts and thinks not for himself but for his country. Nor is the moral quality of his will dependent upon the kind of country which inspires his love, nor even upon the policy which that country pursues. The sacrifice of self to imagined social good may be as complete and as noble on a small as on a great stage, the lustre of self-surrender as brilliant in a hopeless as in a victorious cause. Neither the antiquity of a state nor the splendour of its past history, nor its present power, nor the span of its future ambitions, affects the ethical quality of the personal emotion by which its life is defended. Portugal may inspire as high a form of patriotism as Spain; Uruguay as Germany, Switzerland as the United States. External accidents of geography or polity may determine the particular ideal which a man sets before himself, but in themselves have no bearing on the problem whether a man's patriotism is blind or enlightened, time-serving or heroic, on a low grade of instinctive imitation, or the fruit of a gracious, original, and imaginative mind.

Nevertheless, great exemplars of human virtue have their influence. It is easier to educate the raw impulse of patriotism until it becomes a reasoned and elevated sense of companionship with the best traditions of the race, in a country with a great history and a living present, than in a country whose historical memories are shabby, or obscured, or whose political destiny has been wound up. There are some parts of the world—India is a notorious example—where the commemorative instinct is very faint. Great cities are allowed to fall into ruin. Archives are not preserved ; there are few chronicles or histories. Generation after generation of man is allowed to fade away into oblivion without a trace left upon the sands of time. In such countries, where there are not even family memorials, as in ancient Rome, there is no past to which to make appeal as a source of political idealism for the future. Politics are not the main interest. Man is regarded as a passing shadow, this human life as a bubble on the ocean of eternity, the little activities of the human swarm as the passing shimmer of the moonlight on the mango grove, ironic witness of the distant and eternal calm of the spirit's orb. In such countries the patriotic impulse is naturally low. There is no patriotism, for there is no sense of country ; only a deep feeling of the nothingness of man in face of the tremendous forces of nature and the all-pervading spirit of God. For India patriotism is an import from the west ; it is adopted as part of the paraphernalia of western civilization with our assemblies and franchises and political notions of government. But it is not indigenous, and it can only fully thrive by taking on oriental and religious forms. Outside the narrow circle of the unreligious it becomes extreme, fanatical, mystical. The image received by the cultivated Indian from his college reading in Shelley and John Stuart Mill passes into an oriental dream of deified man. Tilak, the radical agitator, is received in the Central Provinces with divine honours. He is no longer the able and zealous expositor in the English language of English notions of liberty and self-government. He is more than human ; he has divine properties. He is raised up to exercise absolute sway over his kind. The new wine passed into the old bottles produces all kinds of strange ferments. There is a taboo against western things. The inbred feeling of caste, deepest of all things in India, asserts itself with redoubled force against the alien and his impure ways. All kinds of obscure, atavistic emotions, rooted in the religious rather than in the secular life of the past, work in the inflamed and turbid consciousness of the bazaar. The hatred of a foreign and unclean thing is probably the most important of these various influences.

At certain periods of their history western nations have shown a similar deficiency in the patriotic sense. Michelet, who was born in 1798, used to speak of Germany as the India of Europe, denoting by this phrase that the Germans were so absorbed in metaphysical and mystical speculations as to be only faintly interested in the problems of material power. A nation of poets, dreamers, and musicians, without political gifts, without political ambitions, subdivided into a number of petty states, and only at rare intervals conscious of any common German feeling, such was the picture of Germany which presented itself to the mind of a French historian writing towards the middle of the nineteenth century. There could be no sharper contrast than the Germany described by Michelet and the Germany preached by Treitschke and exhibited to the world in the course of the last generation. In the span of a single lifetime a thorough discipline in patriotism had converted a naturally docile population from being one of the least politically-minded races in Europe into an acceptance of the State as being the source of all authority, and the be-all and end-all of life. There is, perhaps, no clearer instance in history of the power of education to produce a spirit of sustained patriotic fervour in a people who for centuries had been conspicuous for the low temperature of their public emotions.

The idea of patriotism is so firmly connected in the public mind with the idea of war that it is worth while to consider whether this connexion is an accident or a necessity. In time of war, patriotism is at fever heat. Men give their all for the country. The moral standard is exalted by the spectacle of suffering and sacrifice in the common cause. People who have never consciously thought of their country as a whole, or of themselves as called upon to make voluntary sacrifices for their country's good, are seized with a patriotic frenzy and infected by the general contagion of public service. Many men and women reveal under such a stress unsuspected depths of emotion and heroic power. More especially at the beginning of a war, before the inevitable lassitude and disillusion have set in, there is a great exhilaration of the public temper, the excitement of action mingling with the zest of novelty and the prospect of panoramas of life widely different from the dead monotony of ordinary industrial existence. As the war proceeds, the sense of exhilaration wears away and gives place to a mood of dogged resolve, or of mutinous revolt against the fundamental unreason of an ordeal by force ; but so long as a war lasts, it gives scope for the exhibition of many noble human qualities, and upon the whole tends to exhibit man at once in his highest as well as in his lowest and most savage aspect.

It has often been contended that the many virtues encouraged by war, and by the preparation for war, are of such ethical value, that if war did not exist, it would be necessary to invent it. Moltke thought of war as a great purifying influence, and as an antidote to materialism and sloth and egoistical narrowness.[1] From time to time, in his view, war was necessary for the cleansing of mankind. The ancients took much the same view. They applauded the institutions of Sparta, because they were specifically planned for the education of the martial virtues. And though the precepts of Christianity are opposed to war, the teaching of the Churches throughout the ages has laid stress upon the value of those elements in human character which are fortified by the prospect and exercised by the practice of the military art.

It will at once be admitted that most of the virtues, summarized by the name of patriotism and powerfully evoked by war, are in reality capable of being developed by any form of wholesome emulation. The desire to put one's own country ahead of other countries in the arts of peace is a powerful and wholesome social motive. It is not necessary, in order to obtain the inspiriting advantages of emulation, that society should burden itself with the waste and ruin of war. Those advantages may be gained at a cheaper price. There may be emulation in commerce, emulation in education, emulation in public hygiene, emulation in art and science, emulation in the skill and wisdom with which the claims of the different classes of society are harmonized by custom or legislation ; and such emulation may be the source of great exertions. And quite apart from international rivalries of this stimulating kind, there is the salutary competition of school with school, city with city, county with county, calling with calling. What an American psychologist has called the ' rivalrous ' disposition of man has a wide field for its development in the normal life of a modern community at peace with its neighbours. Peace, no doubt, brings plenty in its train, but not necessarily luxury or plethoric

[1] For a wonderful retort, see Guy de Maupassant, *Sur l'Eau*.

sloth. Whether or no such evil results follow a long period of peaceful development will depend upon factors of will and character which may vary to infinite degrees. That peace may bring such evils in its train is indisputable ; but to speak of them as the inevitable consequence of peace is clearly a confusion of thought.

There is, however, one human virtue as to whose future, if war were outlawed, as the Americans say, and became henceforward impossible, there might be some doubt. I allude to the virtue of courage. It will be remembered that Adam Smith, in a famous passage of the *Wealth of Nations*, argues that it is the duty of government to prevent the growth of cowardice, even though the martial spirit of the people were of no use towards the defence of their country. ' A coward,' he observes, ' a man incapable either of defending or of revenging himself, evidently wants one of the most essential parts of the character of a man. He is as much mutilated and deformed in his mind as another is in his body who is either deprived of some of its most essential members, or has lost the use of them, and to prevent this sort of mental mutilation, deformity and wretchedness which cowardice necessarily involves in it, from spreading themselves through the great body of the people necessarily deserves the serious attention of government.' [1] The conclusion which the great economist drew is that the whole community should be trained to gymnastic and military exercises. Besides, where every citizen has the spirit of a soldier a smaller standing army will be requisite, and the dangers to liberty, be they real or imaginary, which are commonly apprehended from a standing army, are diminished.

In so far as physical courage depends upon physical health, the standard can be maintained by the proper combination of public and private hygiene and physical training. In so far

[1] *Wealth of Nations*, Bk. v, c. i.

as it depends upon moral qualities, these are the fruit of nature and nurture in the widest sense and are no exclusive or necessary consequence of the intermittent accident or continuous prospect of wars. That high courage can be shown both on land and sea independently of war is a commonplace of observation. The miner, the railway driver, the sailor, the doctor, the parliamentary statesman, each in his own way, may be called upon for the highest exercise of human courage. What war does, and what peace cannot do to the same degree, is to furnish to the whole manhood of a country a simultaneous opportunity for the exercise of this not uncommon though admirable virtue. But there is little ground for the apprehension that the stock of courage in the world would be sensibly diminished by the cessation of war. The lesson of the late war was to prove the contrary, and to show that physical courage, so far from having been injured, had been powerfully assisted by the advance of intelligence, education, and moral cohesion. No troops have ever received so much punishment without yielding ground as the highly educated armies of the most advanced western countries in the late war. Every past record of valour was eclipsed. And the reason was to be found not in any special discipline, not in any formed martial habit (for the new armies of Britain and the Dominions were as courageous as any of the veteran troops of the Continent), but in the very high degree of national pride and civic spirit which results from a sound system of popular education acting upon a wholesome people.

It would not, therefore, appear to follow that war is a condition of patriotism, or that a country which fails to offer frequent opportunities of a violent death in its behalf must cease to inspire the love or devotion of its citizens. If this were true we should expect the Swiss to be a worse patriot than the Mexican, and the love of country to be entirely extinct among the Icelanders, who are, as we know, as devoted to their wild and barren island as any people in the world. The citizen of the United States does not boast about his wars. He boasts about his institutions, and is apt to look down upon Europe as the cockpit of senseless rivalries and pestilential feuds. When Dr. Johnson said that patriotism was the last refuge of scoundrels he was primarily alluding to a contemporary political faction which claimed for itself the title of Patriot; but the observation has a wider reference. It emphasizes the truth that no virtue is so easily or commonly simulated by unworthy people for selfish ends. The misfortune of patriotism as a virtue is that it is always in fashion. Nobody dares to say that he is unpatriotic; everybody cloaks his political action under the guise of patriotism. If you happen to sell beer or spirits, it is because beer is a food as well as a drink, important to the welfare and physical prowess of the nation, and that brandy is, as Dr. Johnson observed, the drink for heroes. Corset-making, as we have recently been apprised, is a prominent key industry essential to national security and deserving to be sheltered against the competition of the French. In times of war the patriotic sentiment is shamelessly exploited by scoundrels to serve their private ends. Even in the House of Commons, politicians who refused the call to arms take up the cause of the ex-service man, plead his grievances, and angle for his votes under the high name of patriotism. It is, indeed, of all the great qualities of mankind that which has been most vulgarized by abuse.

It is, then, a question of great importance for society that this feeling of patriotism should be purified of alloy. How to give to a whole population a love of country, which shall be genuine, unaffected, based upon an intelligent appreciation of the real titles to esteem which the country may possess, freed from all suspicion of ostentation, of ill-measurement or illusion, and compatible with a just estimate of the claims and contributions of other lands, this is one of the fundamental problems of popular education.

One method of patriotic instruction is certainly false. Historians are often tempted into teleology. They assume that the whole history of mankind has been a steady and conscious preparation for the achievements of the race whose exploits it is their mission to celebrate. To Hegel the purpose of the Divine Reason was fulfilled in the organization of the Prussian kingdom. America was an impertinent irrelevance. Other philosophers have maintained that the discovery of America was facilitated by Providence in order to spread the Catholic Faith. In a people singularly ungifted for politics, the idea of the Messianic Mission produced extraordinary aberrations in speculation and practice. Learned fanatics maintained that everything great in the world had been achieved by men of the Teuton stock. Christ was a German, Dante was a German, St. Thomas was a German. So widespread was the megalomania pervading German minds between 1870 and 1918 that even German pacificists, bitterly opposed to the Hohenzollern monarchy, held that nothing could resist the native force of German superiority.

This type of exaggeration always leads to trouble. No nation has anything to gain by involving itself in a cloud of political illusions. Sooner or later the rude hand of circumstance tears aside the veil, and the facts have to be faced in all their rough unpleasant incongruity. The floor of history is white with the bones of the self-elected favourites of Providence. Empire has succeeded Empire; proud and brilliant civilizations have passed away, leaving little behind them but the scattered and scanty fragments of bygone splendours which reward the spade of the modern excavator; prophet after prophet has been falsified by the event. The illusion of preeminence in the field of national affairs is no more advantageous than it is commonly found to be in the private life of the individual. Self-measurement and self-examination, exact and remorseless, are precious elements in the wise conduct of national as well as of individual life.

It has sometimes been urged that the world would be relieved of the evils attendant upon excess of patriotism if it were made to learn out of a common history book. Let us all go to school with the same master is the contention, and we shall think the same thoughts about our past and be led out of the pestilential swamp of unprofitable historical rivalries into the serene atmosphere of scientific and balanced truth. In so far as this is a plea for the teaching of world-history upon a scientific plan, as part of a general course of education, it is a step towards a better and more rational understanding of the world in which we live. To know the history of one nation only is to have a very limited and mutilated apprehension of the real nature of mankind. Some notion of general progress, even if it be drawn in the barest outline, is an essential. Too much, however, must not be expected from the prevalence of a common fund of ideas as to universal history. Such a fund is no novelty. For many centuries Christian Europe was content to accept the general scheme of history which Bossuet derived from the book of the prophet Daniel. The succession of Empires, the predestined triumph of the Universal Catholic Church, the ultimate frustration of heresy, such was the teaching given from a million pulpits and instilled in a million schools during those ages of European history when humanity was almost continuously torn asunder by the turmoil of war. There is little reason to hope that a common code of historical doctrine would of itself avail to extirpate international animosities in the future, seeing that it has so signally failed to achieve this result in the past. If the Christian Churches have failed to soothe the passions of man, are we to expect that a text-book of world-history will be more successful? This is no reason why such a text-book should not be attempted. The ramparts of human reason against the elemental tides of passion will always be weak, and it is safe to predict that from time to time they will crumble in the future as they have crumbled in the past. But is this a ground for failing to keep the dykes in repair? The more formidable the flood, the wider its power of devastation, the clearer is the call for labour on the barriers.

It is sometimes said that the progress of science and education will avail to dry up the flood. That is a vain expectation. It neglects the ugly fact of human nature which dissociates energy from circumspection. The energetic exercise of the human faculties seems to demand as the preliminary condition a limitation of vision, and it is energy, not vision, that rules the world.

The advent of democracy has not fundamentally altered this condition of things, for though it has spread education and enabled several millions of favoured men and women to enjoy a far wider experience of past and present than was given to all but a small handful of the elect in antiquity, it has, on the other hand, imposed such heavy burdens upon its public men that sheer energy outweighs many of the finer qualities of mind. To the rude half-blind vigour of democratic politics the large charity of historical science is a useful counterpoise. The value of an intelligent teaching of history as a factor making for an enlightened as opposed to a fanatical spirit of patriotism is, therefore, not to be underestimated. To fortify character, to train judgement, to provide a discipline in evidence, as well as to transmit such knowledge as may give to the student a reasonable view of the world in which he lives, and of the course of events which have brought it to its present position, these are the prime objects of historical teaching. Upon the quality of the historical teaching given in the schools, more than upon any other branch of instruction, will depend the quality of a nation's patriotism. If the historical teaching is narrow and Chauvin, so will be the public feeling ; if on the contrary it is conceived in a spirit of fairness, if it offers a continuous invitation to balanced verdicts and to the scrutiny of accepted prejudice, if it does not attempt to gloss over failures which bring discredit on the nation, or to disparage its real achievements, then its lessons will enter as a wholesome, and perhaps even at times of crisis as a decisive influence, into the public opinion of the country. If a religion of hate is taught in the schools, the well-springs of public opinion are poisoned at the source. Fortunately there is little need to preach this lesson to a nation so good-humoured as the British ; but Irish public opinion, which has been nurtured upon histories of persecutions and rebellions not impartially told, and American public opinion, which until recently was unduly influenced against this country by a very one-sided presentation of history in the eighteenth century, have both been seriously affected by patriotic perversions of historical facts. There is no justification in making foreigners out to be angels ; but their point of view should be presented fairly. Otherwise the historian is untrue to his mission.

It is not a necessary condition of patriotic feeling that a State should be successful in war. On the contrary, it has happened more than once in history that the moment of deepest political humiliation is that in which national emotion is most deeply stirred, and the national will to retrieve the fallen fortunes of the country strung to the highest pitch. The battle of Jena was interpreted in Prussia not as a military disaster only, but as a signal that the whole social and political life of the Prussian State needed regeneration ; and a not dissimilar reaction followed the catastrophe of the Second Empire in France. Nor is the intensity of patriotic feeling very much affected by the size of states; and it would be difficult to decide which of the two had a greater measure of pride in the institutions of his country, the ancient Spartan or the citizen of the United States.

On the other hand, a national calamity may be of so destructive a character as to sweep away all the familiar political and social landmarks and to leave the inhabitants of the vanquished country void of any sense of direction and empty of the State-sense which had been their historical heritage. Such a fate seems to have overtaken many inhabitants of the newly-fashioned German and Austrian Republics. They are stunned by the weight of their misfortunes, and cannot adjust themselves to their new position. In the prevailing uncertainty and indecision, civic faith and resolution crumble, and men surrender themselves to thoughts of private advantage and lose interest in those grand issues of national policy which were formerly their passionate concern.

A similar result may ensue if a people from whom great sacrifices have been demanded feel that they have been betrayed by their Government and led, through bad management or treachery, to a desperate and uncomfortable situation. There is a sudden feeling of despair. The extreme tension of the war once relaxed, men give themselves over to their private woes. They are disgusted with politics, and the extent of their past devotion to the State is a measure of their present aversion. They have lost the sense of zest with which, while the tide of hope and success was running high, they discharged their appointed functions in the public economy. To a nation in such a mood it seems as if the whole elaborate machinery by which State life is carried on is a cruel device for cheating man of his private happiness. They are sick of the State, and they do not greatly care what fate it may encounter. That such a mood was very widely prevalent in Germany before the French entry into the Ruhr seems to be placed beyond all doubt. There was a loss of faith, the more demoralizing by contrast with the intensity with which the belief in the omnipotence and wisdom of the shattered system had been held.

'Il faut à l'humanité,' says Renan, 'pour faire de belles choses un peu de métaphysique, graine qui détermine la fermentation.'[1] In the great moments of human life, when sublime resolutions are taken, the impelling motive is always transcendental. To die for one's country, to perish for an idea, to surrender life or all that gives value to life for some cause felt to be advantageous to human happiness, what sensible proof exists that in taking such actions as these the certain loss will be compensated by the uncertain gain? We are told that we should die for our country, but what is our country but a metaphysical abstraction? The soil of Britain will not be grateful to us. The climate will not amend its fickle ways. To those who survive us in Britain we shall be a memory fragrant perhaps at first, but becoming fainter and fainter as the years proceed, until to the distant generations of our race we shall be but the shadow of a shadow. To die for posterity, but what has posterity done for us? To die for humanity, but what assurance have we that all the lives laid down for humanity in the long centuries of human history have lightened one hour of human toil, or uprooted one infirm or ignoble impulse from the human heart? To serve the great end for which mankind was created, but what end is that? To be eaten of worms? To be whirled round the sun till the day foretold by our physicists arrives, when human life upon the planet will once more be extinct, when Homer and Aeschylus, Shakespeare and Milton, all the divine spirits who have

[1] *Fragments intimes et romanesques*, p. 44.

cheered and consoled humanity on its painful voyage, will be as if they had never existed, and there will be neither voice to speak nor ear to hear nor brain to understand, nor memory to transmit? When our ashes will be dissolved into dust and no trace be left of the curious and unquiet race of animals who, for a brief spell of time, lived and suffered upon the crust of the dying planet? With the aid of a little metaphysics man waves aside these misgivings, and surrendering all that he counts precious for a cause, fulfils his idea of self-perfection in sacrifice.

It is a commonplace of observation that a war stimulates patriotism and is succeeded by a period of heightened national and militarist feeling. So great is the force of human unreason that at the very time when it is most to the economic interest of mankind that barriers should be overthrown in order that the ravages of war should be repaired with the least possible delay, we find on the contrary that nations are carried away by nationalist feeling to raise their tariff walls, to prohibit or limit emigration, and to try to make themselves as comfortable, as secure, and as self-sufficient as they can behind the ring-fence of their national boundary. This is the common tendency which is now being very signally illustrated by the practice of many of the greatest States in the world. And the example of the United States of America, which, in order to protect its workers' wage and to diminish unemployment, has restricted emigration and stiffened its tariff, raises the question whether patriotism may not be described as an enlarged form of selfishness.

An even more important question is involved in this steep and formidable aggravation of national feeling. Is it not likely, if unchecked, to lead to a new series of wars, wars for raw material, wars for food, wars for power, wars for a place under the sun? Have we not reached a period when no form of patriotism is or can be deemed enlightened which is not affected by cosmopolitan considerations ? Can it be regarded as altogether safe, quite apart from considerations of regard to the common history of humanity, for great half-empty countries to practise a policy of rigid exclusion ? Or again, assuming it to be the case either that the iron or the coal or the oil or any other of the great staple commodities upon which national prosperity is founded becomes the monopoly of a single power or of a group of allied powers, would not that fact in itself constitute a danger to the peace of the world, failing some arrangement for distribution which was generally satisfactory ? Indeed, the more powerful a nation becomes, the greater its responsibility to the world.

It will, no doubt, be urged that every race is justified in protecting its own type by such means as it can find to hand. Even though there be very little to choose between two types, as for instance between the German and the Swede, or the Magyar and the Slav, it would generally be regarded as justifiable by historical convention for any one of these races to resist fusion with any other. And *a fortiori* is a race justified which seeks to protect itself from being swamped by a markedly inferior type of the human species. A nicer question arises when the danger to a race springs not from the competition of an inferior but from that of a superior race. Ought the true patriot to welcome such competition, to court the loss of the old inferior type of nationality in view of the advantages offered by the superior and invading type ? Ought he to say : ' Here is a race different from my own, stronger, more vigorous, capable of wider combinations, possessing finer gifts. It is the path of true wisdom to submit to its direction, to sink our own national individuality in that of this stronger and more vigorous nation, and to accept with a light heart the offer which destiny has made to us ' ? Perhaps it is idle to ask such a question, seeing that no patriot so situated would be likely to ask it. He would assume that his own race was as good as any other; and his assumption would be wrong.

It is then a matter for very careful consideration whether we have not now reached a stage of evolution in which it is necessary that our notions of patriotic duty should be revised, whether it is possible to maintain in full vigour the old exclusiveness, whether war has not become so great a menace to civilization that greater authority should be attached to such machinery as may be contrived for averting it; whether, in fact, we are not passing into a phase of history when the purely national aspect of civic duty will be felt to be insufficient, and will require more and more to be supplemented by wider conceptions.

VI

PROBLEMS IN POLITICAL OBEDIENCE

' Both the public and the private good of States as well as individuals is greater when the State and not the individual is first considered.'—PLATO.

THERE has probably been no age in human history in which national passions have been so fierce and yet the duty of patriotic allegiance so keenly criticized as the present. It is not my present purpose to discuss the causes which have led to the growth of nationalism, first in Europe and then in Asia, and have in recent years intensified the fissiparous tendencies of the human race. No one, however, can doubt that national passions are stronger now than they were in the eighteenth century, and that their strength constitutes a standing menace to the peace of the world.

At the same time, the legislation of the civilized countries of the world bears witness to a sensible relaxation in the stringency of the old doctrine of patriotic allegiance. The mediaeval theory was that nobody could put off his country. It was expressed in the maxim ' Nemo potest exuere patriam suam '. Wherever a man travelled, wherever it might please him to settle, he carried his nationality with him, an inalienable and imperishable possession. An Englishman might elect to live in China. He might marry a Chinese wife, concentrate his property in China, exchange Christianity for Buddhism. He would still remain to the end of his life a British citizen, owing allegiance to the British state. Such was the mediaeval doctrine, rooted in the feudal conception of the relation of lord to vassal, and supported by all the sentiment of a relatively stationary society. The idea of exchanging one allegiance for another by a process of naturalization was entirely foreign to the jurisprudence of our ancestors. An English citizen was an English citizen for all time. Indeed, it was not until 1870 that the principle of nationalization found a place in our statute book. For a long time forces had been gathering strength to explode the old doctrine. The discovery and settlement of the American continent by European races opened up an era of general travel and displacement which produced as a necessary consequence a marked relaxation of national ties. The pressure of population upon the means of subsistence in Europe, the erection into a cardinal axiom of statecraft of the doctrine that means should be found of disposing of superfluous population by emigration, the growth of a rational as opposed to an emotional view of looking at politics, and the weakening of monarchical and religious sentiment, these causes in varying degrees have contributed to displace the old idea of inalienable allegiance in favour of a new conception of an allegiance founded on individual choice.

The moral issues arising from this relaxed notion of allegiance are often of a most perplexing character. A patriotic Scot settled, let us say, in the Transvaal ten years before the South African war, and enabled to thrive under the laws and institutions of the Dutch, suddenly finds that the land of his adoption is drifting into a serious quarrel with the country of his origin. How is he to act? He is contented with the government of President Krüger; he does not believe that it is so black as it was painted by the Uitlander Press; since he has prospered on his farm, and, indeed, risen to affluence under the laws of the Transvaal, he has every reason to feel gratitude for the protection which has been extended to him. He is conscious of no curtailment of liberty, civil or political. He gets on with his Boer neighbours, who are farmers like himself, more easily than with many of the cosmopolitan adventurers who are flocking in to make their fortunes from the gold mines. He has taken up Dutch citizenship, and he believes that the real motive behind the attack upon the Republic is the desire to annex it, and not, as was reported, any concern for the safety of women and children. On the other hand he is a pure-blooded Scot. His instinct is to side with the British Empire, with men of his own race, even though he thinks that the British Government has been persuaded to a course which he believes to be wrong. It is a very painful election. Eventually he decides to act on reason rather than on instinct, to repay his debt to the land of his adoption, to risk his life for his opinion, and to take up arms for the side which he thinks has the better cause, against the call of that deep traditional feeling which comes to all of us from race and home.

In the case which I have assumed, the Scottish settler in the Transvaal takes arms with his fellow-burghers against the country of his origin partly because he has accepted citizenship in the Transvaal, but partly also because he thinks that on the substantial point at issue the Transvaal is right and the policy of the British Government is wrong. If the attitude assumed by the Scottish settler can be defended, as I think it can, on ethical grounds, should we be prepared equally to defend the action of a British citizen, who, coming to the same conclusions on the rights and wrongs of the particular quarrel, decided to join the Boers against his country?

The answer surely is in the negative. The British citizen is in the full enjoyment of the rights and privileges which such citizenship confers. He has not taken on the citizenship of another country. Having a full liberty to migrate to America or to Africa he has chosen to remain in Britain, though he is fully aware of the fact that under the operation of our party system the acts of a British Government will not always be to his liking. The South African War breaks out. He violently and honestly disapproves of the policy which led to it ; his conviction that upon the particular issue the Transvaal is right and Britain is wrong is quite as strong as that of our imaginary Scottish settler. What is his duty? It is clearly to make the fullest use of the right which the laws of his country give him, to express his opinion publicly, and to endeavour to convert his fellow-countrymen to it. Assuming that his end is political justice, he would, were he a sensible man, argue that the best method of achieving that end is by influencing the opinion of his own countrymen rather than by outraging their sentiments. To take up arms against his own country would be an act of defiance calculated to defeat the very end in view, which is the conversion of his countrymen to a different frame of mind. Moreover, it is the conversion of his country and not its defeat in war which he may be assumed to desire. He does not wish his country to be destroyed or humiliated ; he wants it to change its mind and to come to view its international obligations under a different light.

An act is an example. If a man decides to take up arms against his country, he must desire others to do so too. If he thinks that it is his duty to fight his country, he must consider that it is equally the duty of others, not of some others, but of all others, who are placed in like circumstances with himself. ' Act on a maxim ', says Kant, ' fit for law universal.' It is impossible to hold the position that what is right for me is not equally right for one situated as I am.

If a man takes up arms against his country because he believes that it is fighting in an unjust cause, it is an affirmation of his conviction that the injustice of the State revokes allegiance and justifies the extremity of physical resistance. No moralist would deny that there are limits to the obedience which the State can require of its members. The notion that the State is sacrosanct, that it can do no wrong, that it must be supported and defended no matter what iniquities it may perpetrate, that the one and only law of citizenship is ' My country right or wrong ', is utterly contrary to the dictates of the individual conscience. Just as a Member of Parliament, as Burke has taught us, owes to his constituency, not his vote only, but his judgement, so the citizen owes to the State the free and honest exercise of his moral faculties, and, if he believes a policy to be wicked or tyrannical, must not hesitate to declare his view. Nothing in the long run is so injurious to the civic sense as the timidity which restrains the members of a community from giving vent to their real opinions and from taking risks in order to make their opinions effective. Indeed, one of the principal troubles in Catholic Ireland consists in the lack of moral courage, and the general detachment from any sense of political responsibility, which now appears to characterize the bulk of the population. If men would come out into the open, say what they think, and back their opinions by sustained effort, the troubles which have distracted the Catholic south would long ago have disappeared. Here true civic courage consists in giving support to a government ; but in the case which is more familiar it consists in attacking it. To challenge a government to the point of civil war is, however, so grave an act that it can only be justified by most exceptional circumstances, and after the fullest and most disinterested consideration. More particularly is this the case when the Government which is complained of provides the ordinary openings through Parliament and the press for the free declaration of opinion. A resort to force, before every constitutional method has been exhausted for obtaining the change of mind which is desired, is an impatient renunciation of that faith in the power of reason which lies at the root of good citizenship. If the Government of your country embarks upon a war of which you disapprove, your duty is to promote a movement for peace, and to employ such influence as you may possess in impressing upon the mind of your countrymen the best method of redressing the wrong which has in your opinion been inflicted upon an innocent nation. *A fortiori* is it your duty to exhaust the weapon of persuasion before resort is made to force when the rock of offence is not the entry of your State into an unjust foreign war, but the passage of an unjust statute which may be amended or repealed.

The complexion of the question is altered if the constitution of the State is so ordered that all freedom of political speech and action is denied to the private citizen. The right of resisting a tyrant has been debated in all ages. A people kept down by force has, it is contended, the right to liberate itself by force. If the force is supplied by an alien power, the case for resistance is strengthened inasmuch as such a government lacks *ab initio* the element of consent which in varying degrees is present in the governments of all organic states. Here there are only two tests which can be applied to determine whether or no the resistance is justifiable. There is the test of ethics and there is the test of expediency. Let us consider first the ethical test, i. e. Is the moral idea which animates the rebel higher than that which informs the Government? and let us assume that the relations of government and governed are as follows : The Government is alien ; it is the result partly of conquest, partly of passive acceptance, the rule of an oriental people by a distant western island. It is a government which may be described as a paternal despotism, gentle, administering even-handed justice, enlightened, the source of great moral and material improvements. Originally rapacious, it has by swift and progressive stages reached the position of regarding its power as a trust to be executed for the benefit of the peoples under its charge. All idea of vulgar exploitation has vanished. Its officials are incorruptible, able, expert, laborious. It is the means of communicating to backward communities the ideas and culture of the most progressive and active portion of humanity. It has battled against famine and plague ; has built railways, irrigated deserts, founded schools and universities, maintained the peace among warring communities, and raised millions of its subjects to a level of civilization and material comfort far higher than any to which they would have attained under other stars. It is, however, an alien government. In the last resort it rests upon alien guns and alien bayonets. Though it has granted certain liberties of speech and action and even admitted its subjects to certain spheres of political power, it retains in its own hands jealously and firmly the keys of ultimate authority.

It cannot be denied that the moral idea underlying such an exercise of imperial authority is high. Whatever criticisms may be levelled against its original credentials, such a government, assuming the description which has been given of it to be substantially correct, is performing a service to humanity. It is in essence a tyranny, but an educative tyranny. Though at certain points it may be regarded as oppressive, its main action is one of liberation, seeing that it provides a shelter from the numbing blasts of material catastrophe to millions of its subjects, and at the same time introduces them to the ideas upon which the progressive civilization of the west has been founded. To its opponents it may respond with truth that it is applying to the onerous task of government high gifts of prudence and political experience, and that, if it be to the interest of the world that the backward races should be raised by those who are more advanced in the arts of peace, nowhere is there a better example of such a work honestly and thoroughly undertaken.

The reply to this line of argument might take one of two forms. Men of moderate and reasonable temper, living under such an alien dominion, might say, 'We appreciate the excellence of your institutions and achievements. You have given us much that we value. You have brought us your ingenious material inventions; you have schooled us in your modern system of education; you have introduced us to the marvels of your science and the glories of your literature. You have taught us to feel that what is good for you is good for us. We observe that you lay great stress upon the value of political freedom. Indeed, your greatest writers of prose and poetry have sung its praises, and your own political history represents a long and steady progress towards it which we understand to be a just and sufficient theme for national self-glory. The crown, therefore, of your work among us must be the full grant of our liberties. You must withdraw as soon as it is clear that we can manage for ourselves. Liberty is more precious than efficient government. We want to feel that the laws are our laws; we want our young men to learn in school and college that they may aspire to a high place in the political system of their own country, and that their own country occupies an independent place in the political system of the world. It is, therefore, our policy to force you to enlarge our liberties by steady degrees, until they become so complete that we may be regarded in substance, if not in form, as the masters of our own destiny.'

Another school of thought more vehement and drastic might argue as follows : 'We are Easterns, you are Westerns, and as one of your poets has said :

East is East and West is West, and never the twain shall meet.

The attempt to impose your western civilization upon our eastern land is, and must be, injurious to the soul of our people. You bring us food, but it is such as our systems cannot digest. Your parliaments, your press, your notions of western liberty are alien to the temper and spirit of our people. Some of our own people have been captivated by your notions, well enough perhaps for you, but repugnant to our deepest instincts and oldest and most sacred traditions. We have no value for efficiency. The speculative philosopher who earns a pittance in your western universities is, according to our scale of values, higher in the order of being than the most progressive merchant, the most vigorous public servant, the most eloquent parliamentarian. Your whole rule, therefore, is founded on a falsehood. You are doing what you think is best for us, that is educating us in your western ways and away from our own eastern modes of thought and feeling, when what we really want is to be orientals true to type and not bastard sons of the west. We therefore repudiate you and all your works. The more benignant your government, the more able and disinterested your civil servants, the more dangerous do we consider you. We propose to do our best to evict you by force. No matter whether your defeat be followed by fifty years of bloodshed or anarchy. The prize is worth the contest and the sacrifice—an oriental land governed by oriental tyrants in the old oriental ways without the profane intrusion of vulgar hustlers from the west.'

It is clear that between the first two political philosophies there is no real ethical distinction. The ideal is substantially identical, that is a civilization in which an eastern race profits by the fruits of western culture, and is organized upon a western plan. The difference which divides the two schools of thought may be whittled down to a question of time and opportunity, the western government holding that the process of education has not yet been advanced to a stage at which further political concessions can be safely made, and its eastern critics asserting that concessions are long overdue ; or it may go a good deal deeper and involve a contrariety of opinion as to the ultimate capacity of the eastern race to profit by complete independence.

But the kind of society which is contemplated both from the eastern and western angle is the same. On both sides it is agreed that the interfusion of eastern and western ideas and practices has been an advantage, and that it should continue. There is on both sides an acknowledgement of the same political values. Governors and governed alike assent to the proposition that the institutions of a free society, assemblies, newspapers, universities, schools, are good for man, be his skin white or coloured. Compared with this agreement upon essentials, the divergence of view as to time and opportunity, or again as to the ultimate fitness of the oriental race for full emancipation, is comparatively unimportant.

Far otherwise is it with the third type of opinion. The ideal of the Oriental wrecker, who desires to recall a vanished world, to snap rudely and finally the ties which bind east to west, careless of consequences, and in full anticipation that for many years to come the results of the revolution will be terrible, is one for which it would be difficult to find a moral justification. It is no defence to say that a form of polity and civilization which is the unaided result of native qualities is morally superior because it is indigenous and unaffected by foreign influence. On such a plea one could justify a reversion in Britain to the jurisprudence of the Anglo-Saxon Codes, and in Germany to the ethics of the Nibelungs. The claim that a foreign influence, whether religious, or ethical, or scientific, or political, should be rejected simply on the ground that it is foreign is a repudiation of elementary good sense. What does it involve? It assumes that nations can reach their highest perfection in a life of isolation, that the solidarity of the human race is a myth, that one people has nothing which it can give to another, that a nation can never correct its errors in the light of alien precept, alien example, and alien knowledge, that the progress of intercommunication between nations, leading, as it inevitably has led, to interfusion and blending, is a calamity and not a benefit, and finally that morality is limited by latitude and longitude.

Such a view in other words negates every ethical principle. It is also contrary to the plain lessons of history to assume that conquest is a necessary evil. The Greek conquest of Asia Minor, the Roman conquest of Gaul, the Norman conquest of England, the spread of European civilization in North America by settlement and conquest have unquestionably resulted in a clear balance of good over evil for the human race. Nor does the legitimacy of a government depend upon its origin. The only title-deed upon which a government can rightly rely is the quality of the service which it renders to the governed.

There is a second test which should be applied before resort is had to the extreme measure of political defiance. The would-be rebel should ask himself whether it is likely that his rebellion will succeed, and whether if the chances of fate are heavily weighted against him, he will not be increasing the sum of human unhappiness by raising the dust of a futile disturbance. It is not sufficient that he should be convinced of his own moral superiority to the government which he desires to dethrone. He should also have some clear idea of the kind of government by which he desires to replace it, supported by a reasonable expectation that his efforts will be crowned with success. The truth is that every government has a kind of justification. It satisfies certain needs. Otherwise it would not exist. It is also true of every government, that being a human contrivance for meeting human needs and fulfilling human appetites and interests, it is never anything but a machine for second-best expedients. So while all governments do some good and fulfil some need, all governments disappoint. The would-be rebel should, therefore, make a preliminary allowance for these two considerations. He should reflect that the government which he seeks to overturn cannot be altogether bad, and that any government which he can set up in its place cannot be altogether good. He may effect some improvement ; if he be a passionate idealist he will expect the improvement to be great ; but if his idealism be qualified by a knowledge of history, he will not expect a government of angels in a world inhabited by men. These considerations make for caution, not for political quietism.

To these arguments for caution there is added the uncertainty which always attaches to the issue of extreme political courses. It is a commonplace of political experience that no Act of Parliament works out exactly as its framers intended. Human foresight is never quite adequate to the inexhaustible casuistry of life. Some combination of circumstances arises, unforeseen and perhaps incapable of being foreseen, which either deprives a particular provision of its anticipated value or causes it to work actual detriment instead of good. And if there is this element of lottery even in the sphere of humdrum domestic legislation, by how many degrees is not uncertainty increased when we come to deal with a projected rebellion against the State itself ! What warrant have we for thinking that the momentum of passion and prejudice, which is necessary to carry such a movement to a successful conclusion, will die away when success is reached, and yield pride of place to cool reason and the equitable consideration of balanced interests ? The more uphill the struggle, the more fierce the resistance, the greater is the likelihood of the formation on a large scale of that special type of human character which is formed in revolutionary epochs, and has always been found sterile of benefits to the human race, a character rendered hard, suspicious, and narrow by the perils and vicissitudes of life, and lost to all intellectual elasticity by the violence with which it has committed itself to the catchwords and formulae of the age.

These considerations, however, must not be pushed too far. They make for caution, not for quietism. The early rebellious manifestations of the Italian *Risorgimento* were, judged by the calculus of ordinary human prudence, quite desperate. They were ill-planned and they were put down with the greatest ease. Should we therefore condemn them? Not if we are prepared to applaud the whole movement of the *Risorgimento* and to rejoice in its success. If we take that view, if in the issue between Italian nationality and foreign dominion we side with Mazzini and Cavour and Garibaldi, and think that Italy deserved to be free and that the world has benefited by Italian freedom, then we must applaud the men who took the first initial risks, desperate as those risks undoubtedly were, in a great and generous cause, and not condemn them because they paid the forfeit of their ill-success. The justification of these early risings must be founded on the moral value which we attach to the movement and the degree to which we think that a premature and abortive insurrection helped rather than hindered its ultimate triumph. It is sometimes a necessary condition of victory that the advance troop should be sacrificed.

Another variant of the same ethical difficulty is provided by the case of passive objection. A Congregationalist minister objects to being rated for a Church school, and declines to pay. A pacificist objects to serving in the army in time of war, and declines to serve. In each case the objector puts himself to some inconvenience by his resistance to the demands of the government. In each case he bases his justification upon the rights of conscience, claiming that the government is asking him to do something unjust, and that it will offend his conscience to obey. In the one case it is considered a criminal thing in a government to tax one of its subjects to advance a form of religious education of which he disapproves ; in the other case it is held to be a crime to co-operate with a government in waging war.

Now it is clear that the principle of passive resistance might easily be carried to a point which would make all civilized government impossible. If everybody felt himself entitled to resist any law of which he disapproved, no laws would be obeyed. If A., a Baptist, is justified in resisting a law which promotes denominational education, B., an atheist, is equally justified in resisting a law which promotes undenominational education. If A. refuses to pay a tax which helps the Church of England, B. may refuse to pay a tax which supports the army. The existence of a civilized government assumes that the individual conscience is tender but not too tender. Not a year passes without parliament enacting laws which are thought wrong by quite a considerable number of people, who, nevertheless, resign themselves to obey the law until they can procure its amendment or repeal.

It may, however, be urged that a law which touches the religious conscience stands in a special category, and that when the State invades the province of religious belief, its action may be rightly resisted by the individual. On ethical grounds it is difficult to establish such a distinction. A law may be objected to, on valid grounds, as tending to encourage drunkenness, betting, or prostitution. Is it to be contended that the evil, let us say, of an education in the tenets of the Church of England, is so much greater than the prevalence of these three vices, taken singly or in conjunction, that a law to establish denominational education may be rightfully resisted while laws tending to promote drunkenness, betting, and prostitution, stand in an altogether different category and must be accepted? On ethical grounds it is impossible to establish a difference in kind between one kind of law and another, and to conclude that the State may be rightfully resisted in the one case and not in the other. From this, however, it should not be concluded that the individual conscience is rightless as against the State, or that occasions do not arise when the law may be rightfully resisted. In every age idealists have suffered for their creeds and the world has been the better for their suffering. The early history of the Christian Church is full of such examples of resistance to State law founded upon inner illumination and upon a view of life utterly out of harmony with the prevailing political conceptions of the age. And every great religious creed has its roll of martyrs. The justification of martyrdom, however, rests upon a basis far wider than that which belief in some form of supernatural religion affords.

It does not, indeed, depend upon religious profession in the narrow sense of the term. An atheist may go to the stake for his non-belief as honourably as a theist for his belief. The value of these protests of the individual conscience consists in the fact that there are no virtues more precious to human society than intellectual honesty and moral courage, and that the exhibition of these virtues in their most heroic form serves as a reminder to the race that there are things which good men prize more than comfort and security and life itself.

The mention of the early Christians reminds us that one of the forms which their protest against the existing order of society most commonly took was refusal of military service. The Absolutist conscientious objector during the war, who in some cases was a Quaker and in other cases was devoid of any definite religious belief, took up the view shared by the early Christians that war is always wrong and that it is sinful to participate in it. A belief for which a man is willing to suffer imprisonment, contumely, and ruin has all the qualities attaching to a religious creed. But is it for that reason justified? Readers of Hobbes's *Leviathan* may remember that that protagonist of absolute government admitted one notable exception to the omnicompetence of the State. The Leviathan (i. e. the State) was debarred from requiring a man to serve in the army. Indeed, there can be no more extreme claim than that the State should be empowered to go into every home and to pick out the valid men to fight in a war. It is a tremendous assertion of State authority, a most violent interference with individual liberty, to enforce military conscription upon the subjects of a State. And when the resistance to military service is based not upon the political ground that it interferes with freedom, but on the ethical ground that all war is wrong, and that for the lack of such individual protests the wrongfulness of war will continue to afflict mankind, the claim of the conscientious objector seems very strong.

Let us put the case in its most favourable light. Let us assume a man utterly devoid of vanity or self-seeking, of high personal courage spiritual and physical, distinguished by the fidelity and zeal with which he devotes himself to the duties of a citizen, and yet possessed by the idea of the wrongfulness of all war, and perfectly ready, if required to do so, to endure every physical torment or public obloquy for his belief. Let us assume in fact a saint, modelled on the type of the early Christian martyrs. Is he acting the part of a good citizen in resisting the law of his country, and if so, is the State justified in punishing him?

The Absolutist of whom I speak would contend that he was obeying a higher law than that of the State. He would contend that so far from setting a bad civic example he was acting upon a maxim fit for law universal, seeing that if all men were equally enlightened war would become impossible, and the world would be relieved of an intolerable burden of unnecessary suffering. I think that we must admit that such a man, acting upon such motives, is ethically justified, that he is acting as a good citizen should act, and that he is sacrificing his own personal comfort to what he believes to be the permanent advantage not of his fellow-citizens only, but of the whole world now and in the times to come.

And yet while the individual may be right in following in this high matter the light of his conscience, the State may be equally right in punishing him. There is first of all a point of logic to be considered. Why is war condemned? Because it involves the use of physical force. But it is clear that society is entitled to use physical force to protect itself against internal foes. It apprehends the thief, it imprisons or executes the assassin, it breaks up disorderly crowds. Behind the law there is always in the last resort the sanction of physical force. But if force is legitimate against internal enemies, why is it illegitimate against external enemies? Is it really to be contended that no State, however innocent, is permitted to protect itself against attack? Would it, for instance, be a reasonable position for the friend of humanity to take up, that in the event of a concerted and unprovoked attack of the more barbarous portions of the human race upon those countries which are most advanced in the arts of peace, it would be to the interest of mankind to allow barbarism to prevail in the contest? There was once upon a time an occasion when, owing not to pacificism but to sheer military weakness, this actually happened. The Roman Empire was overwhelmed by the barbarians, and for centuries the brightest lamps of civilization were eclipsed throughout Western Europe. With so awful an example before us, can we agree that it is never right to repel force by force? That force is no remedy may be admitted. Mere force never cures human ills; its application belongs to the science of preventive not to that of curative medicine. But is the passive acquiescence in the use of force by others a remedy either? The argument is that a country without an army or a navy, a country inhabited by a population of pacificists, will be safe.

Nobody will attack it, because it will neither cause disquietude to other States nor afford to an enemy the opportunity of earning military prestige at its expense. We must not dismiss this contention without examination. In point of fact States do in certain stages of civilization enjoy a certain measure of protection by reason of their military weakness. They are not attacked because they are a menace to no one. But let us suppose that the State, which has disarmed itself on principle, possesses advantages either territorial or commercial which are coveted by its neighbours, will disarmament prove a sufficient shield and buckler of defence? Historical analogy is not encouraging. The military weakness of the Polish kingdom was no protection against the partitions of the eighteenth century. The military feebleness of the aboriginal inhabitants of the American and Australian continents, so far from repelling the settlement of white intruders, was an actual invitation to it. Nor has a thoroughgoing contempt for the military art secured for China immunity from the presence of hostile armies.

The argument of the Absolutist may thus be countered by the plea that it is neither strictly logical nor conducive to a practice calculated to extinguish war. He might and indeed probably would reply that he cared little for logic or for success, that whatever might be urged in favour of the application of force on the comparatively minute and occasional scale demanded by the necessities of internal police, the use of force in war was indefensible, and that as for success, if everybody in the world were converted to pacificism there would be peace, just as if every one were converted to virtue there would be virtue, and that it is no more an argument against conscientious objection to say that it will not be generally imitated than it is a valid ground for objection to virtue that the world will always be plentifully supplied with knaves.

Every one must feel the moral force of this rejoinder. Still it will not follow that the State is debarred from punishing the conscientious objector to military service, however virtuous his record and pure his intention. We have to assume that the State is justified in its quarrel; that it is fighting for some ideal end, and that there is some moral issue involved in the conflict which would be advanced by its victory and retarded by its defeat. Or at least we must assume that such is the view of those who are directing the policy of the Government. On these assumptions the State calls upon its members to take up arms. Equity permits no exceptions, no favouritism. The service is terrible and dangerous. The sacrifices demanded are almost without limit. Only a small proportion of those who go to the war take any joy in fighting or in the military life. It is impossible to maintain content and discipline in the armed forces, if it be understood that a tender conscience procures exemption from personal risk without dishonour or penalty. However much it may be desired and desirable to procure for real cases of religious conviction a complete exemption from penal consequences, it may be found impracticable to do so in view of the state of public opinion. The conscientious objector is then made to suffer in the interests of that firm discipline without which the military end of the State cannot be attained, and if the end be approved in the tribunal of justice, the means indispensable to the end must be approved also.

Apart from the two cases of individual resistance to the State which have been considered, there is an aspect of resistance in general which deserves attention. It is said that minorities must expect to suffer, and it is clear that no minority can be in as favourable a position as a majority. For this reason it is the more important that minority views should receive all the consideration which they can obtain, and the smaller the minority, the stronger is the case, viewed from the standpoint of the minority in question, for giving to the minority view as startling and impressive an advertisement as possible. From this angle, the campaign of the conscientious objectors was successful, though the moral effect of the movement was largely impaired by the very considerable admixture of cowardice and sham which entered as a debasing alloy into the pure ore of the pacificist gospel.

If, however, the question is asked which of the two is the better citizen, the man who on strict grounds of conscience declines to obey the law of military service, and the man who, while equally conscientious and equally desirous of peace, submits himself to it, can there be any doubt as to the answer? It is true that the act of the conscientious objector, like every act proceeding from a pure and disinterested motive, has a social or civic value, though that value is singularly diminished by the fact that refusal of military service *ipso facto* exempts the objector from the risks and hazards of war. Even then if the act of refusal be intrinsically courageous, it has necessarily the appearance of being cowardly, and fails therefore to exercise the good influence attaching to conduct which is generally regarded as disinterested and brave. And the civic value of the act, assuming it be founded on the conviction of the sinfulness of war, suffers a further discount by reason of its intrinsic inconsistency.

If war is a sin, then the State has no right to maintain military or naval establishments and to tax its subjects for their support. And if it be sinful to submit to military conscription, is it any less sinful to acquiesce in voluntary service? How can it be argued that it is wicked to serve in person, but venial to hire another to serve in your place? Upon the hypothesis of the intrinsic sinfulness of war, it is just as sinful to contribute to the support of a voluntary army as to serve in a conscript army. In each case you are participating in sin. The only difference is that in the one case you risk your person and in the other case you do not. It follows that the conscientious objector who has paid taxes without demur or cavil for the upkeep of the military establishments of the State in time of peace is acting with inconsistency if on the outbreak of war he refuses to serve in person when required to do so by the law. Consistency demands a protest all along the line, a protest against war taxes and war establishments and against all the forces contributing to war, including those newspapers which advocate warlike policies. To protest only when war breaks out is to protest too late. Is not the citizen already an accomplice in war by the mere fact of his acceptance of institutions which postulate the possibility of war and are framed upon the assumption that the State may be called upon rightfully to fight? And if the attitude of the conscientious objector to military service be thought out, does it not imply a very thorough and far-reaching challenge to the life of the society of which he is a member?

There are some who base their refusal, not upon a general view of the sinfulness of war, but upon a personal and insuperable aversion from the taking of human life. This instinct is so deep, so imperious, so much a part of their nature and nurture, that they cannot submit to its violation. They would rather die. They do not reason. They say, 'Abhorrence of taking life is the deepest thing in me.' This form of religious belief is, of course, very well known in India, where one important community objects not only to the taking of human life, but to the taking of all animal life. Even a fly or a mosquito is sacred. Better endure the horrors of typhus than the black sin attaching to the extermination of a louse.

Such scruples, however overdrawn we may think them to be among Oriental peoples, are clearly in themselves humane and honourable, and the note of a civilized society. So far from a man being a worse citizen by reason of his deep personal repugnance to the shedding of blood and to acts of physical violence, he is clearly the better for it. A statesman may have all the brilliant gifts with which a man may be arrayed by a bountiful nature—eloquence, promptitude in action, devouring energy, inexhaustible fertility in resource—but if he prefers war to peace, he is no statesman, but a danger to society. Respect for human life, aversion from violence and brutality, are not only essential parts of private morality, but furnish an important part of the ethical foundation upon which the structure of any civilized State is erected. There is then everything to praise and nothing to condemn in this feeling of repugnance to the taking of human life. The more widely it is spread throughout any community, the less likely will that community be to enter lightly into a quarrel or to be defaced in its domestic life by the cruelties of the savage nature. The entertainment of these personal feelings, how-ever, furnishes no adequate ground for the refusal of military service, but adds to the merit of undertaking it. Indeed the acceptance of military service in spite of this overwhelm-ing personal sentiment is the supreme triumph of moral self-discipline and heroism. To hate killing from the bottom of the soul, and yet to be prepared to kill in a just quarrel at the call of your country, is the simple perfection of civic virtue. Sacrifice and self-discipline can go no farther.

The case would be somewhat altered if there were reason to expect that this humane repugnance to the taking of life would be permanently obliterated by the experience of war and replaced by the heart of a savage. A man has a right to resist what he feels to be morally degrading. He has a right, for instance, if the State were to order him to change his religious conviction or to murder his father or to forge cheques, to say, ' No, I would rather die.' But does war carry with it a necessary degradation and coarsening of humane feeling? Is it true to experience to say that those who have waged war acquire an appetite for blood? Is not experience just the other way? There are, indeed, some fine temperaments which respond to the fascination of the higher aspects of war, and there are coarse and savage natures whom war suits. They like the appurtenances of war, the lack of personal responsibility, the excitement, the opportunities of pillage, and the fighting. But this is not the sentiment of the majority of civilized men. They go into a war reluctantly : they endure what they have to endure : and, though nothing is more infectious than brutality or more depressing than the speed with which human nature becomes callous to physical pain, they come home with their original feelings of detestation and horror greatly strengthened by bitter experience. The best missionary for peace is the man who has tasted the anguish of war without becoming infected with its intellectual interest.

In general it must be said that aversion from war is a sentiment so rare among the white races and so much to be encouraged in every community, that a State is wisely inspired in according toleration to pacificist doctrines in time of peace, so long as they do not take the form of subverting the loyalty of the army, and that in time of war as much toleration should be permitted as is compatible with national safety.

We are here led on to consider the right of the individual to express his opinion freely. It may be premised that no individual has an absolute right as against the highest interest of the community of which he is a member. Individual rights are always conditioned by public advantage. Accordingly, when we are discussing the right to freedom of expression, we are in reality discussing the extent to which it is to the public interest that such freedom should be permitted. On the other hand, there is no public interest apart from the happiness of individuals. The State is not an organism apart from and independent of the individuals who compose it, nor is a policy capable of justification unless it can be shown to produce an increment in individual welfare and happiness. When therefore we say that individual rights are conditioned by public advantage, we are in effect laying down the principle that the rights of one individual are necessarily conditioned by the rights of other individuals, and that in a rational ordering of the State the interest of each is so adjusted as to harmonize with all the other individual interests concerned. Holding these principles and applying them to the case under considera-tion, we can say at once without fear of contradiction that it is to the general advantage of the community that there should be a free expression of individual opinion. Freedom should be the rule, restriction the exception. The arguments for freedom have been so often stated, they are so familiar a part of our common political prudence, that they require very little elaboration here. Unless a large measure of individual liberty is permitted in the sphere of thought and expression, all the intellectual and many of the moral virtues of the com-munity wither and decay. The discovering movements of thought are inhibited, the salutary discipline which comes from the cut and thrust of discussion is lost, the immense social value attaching to the utterance of sincere but unpopular opinions disappears, submerged by the insipid and monotonous levels of a servile and State-made convention. The latter years of the reign of Louis XIV and the whole period of the Napoleonic Empire furnish an illustration of the spiritual loss resulting from the suppression of freedom by the force of autocracy. It is better even that the most extreme and ridiculous opinions should be published to the open air of the world than that they should be driven under the surface to fester and poison the secret springs of action. If there is wild doctrine flying about let it be represented in Parliament, where it can be dealt with in debate. There is no better advertisement for hasty, bizarre, or passionately one-sided opinion than the honourable label of persecution.

On these and other broad grounds of political prudence, liberty should be the general rule. It is so in Great Britain. A man under our law is free to publish what he chooses, subject to the liability that a jury of his countrymen may find him guilty of an offence against the law of libel, blasphemy, sedition, or official secrets. It would not be lawful in this or any other country to incite to crime. Obscene publications are unlawful as contrary to public decency; there are other minor limitations, but in general there is a wide latitude accorded to the expression of private opinion. Save for the comparatively trivial exception of stage plays there is no licensing. A man can publish what he likes when he likes, subject to the risk that he may be violating the law. It is sometimes in the public interest that this risk should be boldly incurred.

It does not follow from the general desirability of encouraging the free expression of opinion that it is to the public interest at all times and in all circumstances to publish information however exact, or opinions however sincerely believed to be true and valuable. The ordinary commerce of life would be impossible if every one were to say exactly what he thought of every one else. Reticence is the best part of social tact. The men who express themselves most freely have generally least of value to express, and there is a good deal of sound human experience in the educational maxim, that little children should be seen and not heard. Indeed the whole process of education involves what the Catholic theologian is apt to describe as the economy of truth. The skilled teacher imparts to his pupil as much of the truth as his disciple can absorb. He omits important aspects, he discards necessary qualifications, he presents his lesson in a form simplified and adapted to the stage of intelligence attained by the learner, fully conscious of the fact that what he is imparting is not the whole truth as he knows it, but as much of the truth as the learner is able to take into his experience. And it is on similar grounds that most of the imagery employed in popular religious teaching is defended by intelligent theologians. The imagery is not doctrine but literature ; belongs not to the category of scientific truth, but to that of aids to ethical emotion.

The duty of the citizen to tell the truth must not then be interpreted as a direction to scream it from the housetops in season and out of season. If everybody were to insist upon telling everything he knew to everybody he met, only the deaf mute could be accounted happy. Speech has its responsibilities as well as property, and of all the blessings vouchsafed by Providence to man there is none more acceptable to the commonwealth than a happy and liberal use of the gift of silence.

VII

THE CLAIMS OF RACE

'The subtlety of nature is greater many times over than the subtlety of the senses and understanding.'—BACON.

'An exact determination of the laws of heredity will probably work more change in man's outlook on the world and in his power over nature, than any other advance in natural knowledge that can be clearly foreseen.'—W. BATESON.

EVERYBODY who takes an interest in social questions at all is familiar with the fact that a battle has long been engaged between two schools of scientific thought as to the relative influence of heredity and environment in the determination of human character. One school lays stress on inheritance, the other on physical and social surroundings, and the first of these two schools of thought has greatly advanced its position in popular esteem by Weissmann's disproof of the inheritance of acquired characteristics and by the active and valuable work which has been done during the past generation by so many scientific explorers in the field of eugenics.

Perhaps the opposition between the two contrasted views can be best displayed by a pair of quotations. ' Of all vulgar modes of escaping from the consideration of the effect of social and moral influences on the human mind, the most vulgar is that of attributing the diversities of conduct and character to inherent natural differences.' That is the deliberate opinion of J. S. Mill, given indeed before Weissmann's investigations, but long after Darwin had made the world familiar with the conception of natural selection and the struggle for existence. And here, in seeming opposition, is the verdict of Professor Karl Pearson, who has done so much to impart statistical precision into eugenic speculations. 'We are ceasing', he writes in 1903, 'as a nation to breed intelligence as we did fifty to a hundred years ago. The mentally better stock of the nation is not reproducing itself at the same rate as it did of old ; the less able, the less energetic, are more fertile than the better stocks. No scheme of a wider or more thorough education will bring up, in the scale of intelligence, hereditary weaklings to the level of hereditary strength. The only remedy, if one is possible at all, is to alter the relative fertility of the good and bad stocks in the community.'[1]

Nobody can doubt that we are here faced by a question so important that the whole texture of our thoughts about the commonwealth may be affected by the reply. We are as citizens concerned with the maintenance of the standard of our race. Who, indeed, would deny that we have a duty towards our race? Not, indeed, a duty to shield it from admixture with foreign stocks, for such admixture is often advantageous, but to preserve it from debasement, and this not in any narrow or sectional interest, but because it is to the advantage of humanity as a whole that every race should be as vigorous, as intelligent, and as well conducted as human contrivance can devise. And if it could be shown that the predominant influences making for vigour, intelligence, and morality lie in the sphere of heredity and not in that of environment, then it follows that a great deal more attention must be given to the thesis of the eugenists by the legislatures of the world than has hitherto been accorded to it. And this in effect is what the eugenists expect of the politicians. They ask them to consider every social question in the light of its bearings on the problem of race cleansing. Old age pensions, workmen's insurance, immigration laws, compulsory educa-

[1] *On the Inheritance of the Mental and Moral Characters in Man. Biometrika*, vol. iii, p. 159.

tion, pensions for widows, the general scheme of taxation, trade unionism, the family wage, feminism, women teachers in the elementary schools, there is hardly a social problem which may not directly or indirectly have some influence upon the maintenance of an adequate racial standard. The eugenists do not, indeed, claim that these questions should be regarded solely from the point of view of the breed. They acknowledge that immediate economic and immortal ethical considerations must have their weight, but they maintain that whenever a clear case can be made out that certain social customs or legislative enactments are dysgenic in character, public opinion should be mobilized against them.

The claim that the citizen should pay attention to the question of heredity is no novelty. In all the political speculations of Plato and Aristotle it is regarded as an important part of statesmanship so to regulate the age of marriage as to ensure, so far as this can be done, the prospect of healthy and vigorous offspring. Moreover, great attention was paid by the ancient philosophers to the control of population. A State must be neither too large nor too small, but if possible a limited civic aristocracy based upon servile labour and carefully bred with a view to the good and complete life. Nor was such doctrine uncongenial to the family pride of the Romans.

> Fortes creantur fortibus et bonis ;
> Est in juvencis, est in equis patrum
> Virtus, neque imbellem feroces
> Progenerant aquilae columbam.

Belief in the sovereign qualities of race has indeed been the creed of all the aristocracies as of the humbler folk who for centuries of human history were content to serve them.

With the development of democratic opinions in the eighteenth century it became fashionable to disparage the weight of those hereditary influences to which the ancients

attached so much importance. The equality of man was proclaimed, the differences between race and race attenuated or
ignored. In the sanguine mood which preceded the French
Revolution no bounds were set to the degrees of human
perfection which might be reached with the aid of wise laws
and enlightened institutions and expanding knowledge. If
the African negro could be raised to the level of European
man, how frail and low were the barriers which sundered
European society, and how easily removed! Listen, for instance, to the words of the least visionary of all the great
thinkers of that age. This is what Adam Smith writes in the
Wealth of Nations (Book I, c. 2):

'The difference of natural talents in different men is, in
reality, much less than we are aware of; and the very different
genius which appears to distinguish men of different professions,
when grown up to maturity, is not upon many occasions so
much the cause as the effect of the division of labour. The
difference between the most dissimilar characters, between
a philosopher and a common street porter, for example, seems
to arise not so much from nature as from habit, custom, and
education.'

The modern professors of eugenics will have none of this
optimism. They ask us to face the fact, which is now plain
to all, that different races are differently endowed by nature,
some being relatively high and others relatively low in the scale
of civilization, and that within every race men and women
differ from one another in natural inherited ability, and that
no matter what education is supplied, these natural differences
will persist. They argue with Weissmann that acquired
characteristics are not transmissible by inheritance. What is
transmitted is a germ plasm which is 'so carefully isolated
and guarded that it is almost impossible to injure it except
by treatment so severe as to kill it altogether'.[1] If, for instance,

---

[1] Popenoe and Johnson, *Applied Eugenics*, p. 63.

a susceptibility to tuberculosis is a character of the germ plasm, it will be transmitted down the ages so long as human vehicles for the transmission of that germ plasm exist, quite independently of the fact whether any parent in the line of descent has or has not fallen a victim to the disease. Preventive hygiene, the spread of sanitary education, and other social contrivances may help the individual to keep the enemy at bay, but they cannot affect the race. The enemy remains immortal. The son starts neither helped nor hindered by the life experience of his ancestors.

How far this innate basis of mind and character which is transmitted in the germ plasm from generation to generation is a vague mass of plastic tendencies, or how far it contains much that is specific and differentiated, is a matter upon which science as yet speaks with no decided voice. Professor McDougall is inclined to attach considerable importance to the views of a distinguished medical psychologist, Dr. C. G. Jung, who has revived the theory of innate ideas, and holds that they seem to be supported by such well-known phenomena as the apparently spontaneous and untaught moral reactions of children which seem to be in some manner or degree preformed or hereditary in their constitution.[1] It is too soon to say how far Dr. Jung's theory of the inheritance of specific moral and intellectual tendencies (which must surely be very difficult of rigid demonstration) is likely to gain general acceptance among men of science. Sufficient be it to observe that were it accepted the claims advanced for heredity as a predominant influence in the determination of human qualities, already greatly enlarged by the conclusions of Weissmann, would receive a further extension.

From such biological premises, with some aid from the consideration of the passing away of earlier civilizations, the

[1] *National Welfare and National Decay.*

eugenists proceed by easy stages to demonstrate the numerous shortcomings of the social philosophy which prevails in our modern democratic age. Talent is hereditary : virtue, so the American statistician reports, is generally associated with talent. There are good human stocks and there are bad human stocks. It is the tendency of modern civilization to encourage the multiplication of the bad and the extinction of the good. It should be the task of statesmanship to reverse this process.

The argument is supported, as is now generally known, by a great mass of impressive testimony. There is evidence as to the inequality in the mental calibre of races and of classes within the same race, evidence as to the comparative scarceness in any race of talent or even of respectable ability, evidence as to the strong probability that distinguished men will have distinguished relations, evidence of the evil effects of a bad strain manifesting themselves generation after generation. The genealogies alike of able men and of the mentally defective are called into contribution with great effect. And it is obvious that the matter is not one of purely academic interest. There is a real note of alarm in this eugenic literature, and more especially in that part of it which proceeds from America, where the problem of race preservation, in view of the infusion of poor immigrants from eastern and southern Europe, has become a matter of acute and painful importance. This is what Mr. Lothrop Stoddard, a clever American writer, tells us : ' One million seven hundred thousand young men were examined in the recent American army tests, all physically fit. Less than one out of twenty ($4\frac{1}{2}$ per cent.) possessed really high intelligence.' And again : ' The army tests show that intelligence is being steadily bred out of the American people. Forty-five million or nearly one-half of the whole population will never develop mental capacity beyond the stage represented by a normal twelve year child.' And intelligence is bred out, because the stronger breeds, owing to their higher social standards and larger scale of economic needs, have fewer children than the weaker breeds, and because the weaker breeds are in turn protected from destruction by the fostering agencies of hygiene, police, and education which a humane civilization supplies. ' Never perhaps ', concludes the writer, ' have social conditions been so dysgenic or destructive of racial values as to-day.' [1]

The evidence as presented and interpreted by this school of social inquirers is understood to point to another conclusion, which, if true, is of great social importance. It is contended not only that intellectual distinction is a quality attaching to a comparatively small number of human stocks, but that broadly speaking the grades of intelligence in a modern democratic society like England and America coincide with the present social stratification, the very stupid stocks being at the bottom, the very clever stocks at the top, and the stocks of intermediate intelligence in the middle of the economic scale, so that somehow, whether by natural or social selection, innate merit succeeds on the average and in the long run in attracting its proportionate economic reward. Further, some statistical evidence has been accumulated for the purpose of showing that the contribution made by the lower class in society to culture exhibits a progressive decline, the families of craftsmen, artisans, and unskilled labourers contributing a larger proportion of distinguished men in the Middle Ages than in the nineteenth century, and a larger proportion in the first half of the nineteenth century than in the second.

It is easy to see the kind of political and social argument which may be based on such premises. The sacrifices required

---

[1] Lothrop Stoddard, *The Revolt against Civilization*, p. 64; and see E. A. Rose, *The Old World and the New*, p. 303.

of the middle and upper classes in order to maintain a minimum of comfort and decency throughout society must not be so great as to deter them from early marriage and large families. The ladder from the bottom to the top must not be too complete or easy to climb, otherwise there may be a danger of the good stocks in the lower ranges of society prematurely exhausting themselves through the sterilizing process which everywhere follows upon social success. Charity can be carried too far. Poverty, grim as the doctrine may seem, has its eugenic value, helping as it does to hasten the extinction of stocks which are unequal to the burdens of modern civilization. And if the poor are always with us, it is by one of those merciful-cruel dispensations of Providence by which, like Death itself, the onward march of humanity is secured.

> Thou shalt not kill, but do not strive
> Officiously to keep alive

is a counsel recommended to the careful consideration of the statesman.

Moreover, to the degree to which this doctrine is accepted in its full scientific rigour and with its large aristocratic implications, a shadow falls upon the even surface of modern democratic practice. If heredity counts for so much, environment for so little, if the limits within which education can effect improvements are in any case so narrow, and if the capacity for intellectual improvement tends to vary directly with social status, is not the democratic community tempted to spend too much upon the education of its poor and too little upon that of its wealthier classes? Does it not again fall into the error of providing a similar intellectual diet to intellects radically dissimilar? Is it not tempted to lay its educational plans upon the hypothesis that every stratum of society is equally rich in diamonds, whereas the facts prove that the lower you dig, the fewer diamonds you extract? And was not the older plan of educating children according to their respective stations in life truer to the inexorable facts of nature? The eugenist is tempted to condemn Macaulay for recommending the education of the peoples of India in Western culture, and the Americans for their introduction of compulsory education into the Philippines.

Recent investigations have thrown some doubt on the solidity of the biological thesis upon which so much of this great scaffolding of social and economic argument has been erected. The theory of the non-transmission of acquired characteristics is, I understand, less generally accepted than it was ten years ago. But for my present purposes, it will be convenient to accept Weissmann's doctrine as unassailed and unassailable, and to consider how, if this be so, we, as citizens, anxious to do our best for the community, would be well advised to shape our course.

The first observation which occurs on the biological part of the case is that we know nothing of the extent to which the potentialities and tendencies sheathed in the germ plasm respond to differences of environment. They may be sensitive to external stimuli or they may be insensitive. They may oppose a rigid front to the varying play of circumstances or they may assume Protean forms under the shifting stress of life's experience. The biologist can tell us nothing. Yet if the biological argument is to be employed as the foundation of a far-reaching social policy it is surely necessary that we should be more closely informed as to the power of environment to mould these innate tendencies. The whole cogency of the social case depends upon the environment having little power, but this is exactly what has not been demonstrated. What has been demonstrated (always assuming that we follow Weissmann) is that the germ plasm descends intact and uninfluenced by what has happened to the mind and body of its bearer during life; not that the potentialities contained in the germ plasm have been uninfluenced for each individual by his life's experience.

And it is the degree of susceptibility to this influence which is the important thing to determine. Let us take the simplest of all illustrations, a large family, children of the same parents, each member of which is exposed from childhood onward to a different social, intellectual, and physical environment. To what extent will the common stock of innate tendency reproduce itself in each brother and sister? Will the differences be more prominent than the resemblances or the resemblances than the differences? Or take another instance. Mozart was an infant prodigy. At the age of four he was already a wonderful musician. The story of his achievements as a child seems a miracle, but it is true. And he came of a musical family. His father was an excellent musician and a good and capable man. His sister was an accomplished artist. He married and had children, but none of his descendants appear to have distinguished themselves either as musicians or in any other rank of life. Now in what proportions did heredity combine with environment in the formation of Mozart's genius? In preponderating proportions one would imagine, in the case of so great a prodigy. And yet can we be sure what would have happened if Mozart's father had received no musical education, or if the sensitive child, instead of being born and bred in an atmosphere of exquisite sympathy and among the most musical people in the world, had been transported in infancy to a rude log hut in the Canadian prairie far from musical instruments and musical thought and the encouragement of musical *virtuosi*? Even in Mozart's case we cannot affirm with certainty that environment did not count for much.

Then can we rely upon intelligence tests such as those

recently employed in the case of the American army as affording an exact measurement of inherited gifts? Is it not probable that young men who have had the advantage of an education continued through adolescence will tend to respond more rapidly to such tests than coevals of equal ability who have been compelled to spend several years on a farm or in a shop? The human brain is strengthened by use, and rusts with disuse. Even tests taken in early childhood cannot, it would seem, furnish exact evidence of unqualified hereditary powers. The character of the child's experience, its physical condition at the moment, the nature of the external stimuli which have been supplied to it from the moment of birth, must enter into the account as disturbing factors.[1]

While then such statistics as those to which we allude are valuable as showing the uneven distribution of intelligence as between different races or as between different sections of the same race, and also as exhibiting everywhere the great preponderance of low over high intelligence and the differential advantage derived by the clever from their education, they are less valuable as indications of the distribution of socially valuable stocks. The great majority of mankind are economically poor. The great majority of mankind are intellectually stupid. It follows that the chief result which leaps to the eye after any tabulation of the results of intelligence tests on a comprehensive scale is the huge number of the stupid poor. What the meaning of this stupidity is, in what proportion it is due to innate limitations of intellect, and in what proportions to defective opportunity, is less clear. Nor do we learn in what number of cases it may be regarded as an indication of a germ plasm, the continuance of which is against the interests of society as a whole.

[1] For some valuable remarks on the non-reproduceable part of our acquisitions see W. James, *Talks to Teachers in Psychology*, pp. 116–43.

Is then the science of eugenics, apart from such counsels as it may give on the art of healthy living, bankrupt of social direction? We do not think so. There seems to be a general agreement among men of science that some stocks are in reality tainted, and that the taint is exhibited by symptoms which are clearly cognizable. There are the congenitally defective who have a high degree of fertility; there are some families with a special liability to tuberculosis, others with an hereditary susceptibility to alcoholism, others again with the taint of the terrible infection of syphilis. It is surely in the general social interest that such infected stocks should not be perpetuated.

Can any further directions be laid down? No doubt there are outside these narrow limits varieties of the human kind whose multiplication is undesirable. But our knowledge is far too imperfect to enable us to discover what varieties these may be. On this point I owe to Professor Bernard Bosanquet a judgement, which he rightly describes as of great importance, derived from Professor Bateson's work on Mendel's *Principles of Heredity*.[1]

'To the naturalist it is evident that while the elimination of the hopelessly unfit is a reasonable and prudent policy for society to adopt, any attempt to distinguish certain strains as superior and to give special encouragement to them would probably fail to accomplish the object desired, and would certainly be unsafe.

'The distinction is created probably by the fact that whereas our experience of what constitutes the extremes of unfitness is fairly reliable and definite, we have little to guide us in estimating the qualities for which society has or may have a use or the numerical proportions in which they may be required. But especially important are the indications that in the extreme cases unfitness is comparatively definite in its genetic causation, and can, not infrequently, be recognized as due to the presence of a single genetic factor. There is as yet nothing in the descent

[1] *Social and International Ideals*, p. 149.

of the higher mental qualities to suggest that they follow any single system of transmission. It is likely that both they and the more marked developments of physical powers result rather from the coincidence of numerous factors than from the possession of any one genetic element.'[1]

This is a very wise caution. We are not entitled by the present state of our knowledge to carry the naturalist's view of human society beyond a narrowly restricted territory. After centuries of human experience, the laws which govern the emergence of genius, the rarest and most valuable of the gifts of man, still remain in the darkest obscurity. We do not know how to breed genius. We cannot tell what forms of genius we may specially require. We can frame no sort of estimate as to the proportions in which unskilled labour should stand to directing ability a hundred years hence. But we are certain that the race is improved by the mating of healthy parents. We know that children should be born and nurtured under wholesome conditions, and we know in broad outline what these conditions are. Further, we have ample ground for thinking that by the action of public opinion, supported in some cases by legislation, certain extreme and painful cases of congenital defect may and should be removed.

One other point of special importance to the British and American peoples remains to be noticed. Experience seems to show that the union of white men and women belonging to races far below them in civilization is rarely successful in producing a vigorous stock. There have been individual exceptions to the rule, but so infrequent as not seriously to invalidate it. And the question therefore arises whether the recognition of such a law imposes any positive duty upon a white race which is through the circumstances of political or economic life brought into contact with civilization of an altogether lower order.

---

[1] Mendel's *Principles of Heredity*, p. 315.

It would be rash to dogmatize. Who would be prepared to say that on balance the world has lost by the unions which have taken place between the European and coloured inhabitants of the United States, or between the British and the Hindus, or between the Spanish conquerors of South America and the native Indian population? No student of economic history would deny that these mingled breeds, though rarely capable of originative power, may, and indeed do, perform a useful albeit humble rôle in the economy of society. In North America, for instance, it is believed that such success as the coloured population has attained in the higher ranges of business can invariably be traced to an admixture of white blood, and that if this admixture is bad for the white half of American society, it has brought some compensating benefit, at least upon the intellectual side, to the coloured. Nor should we forget that an absolute taboo upon the union of the white and coloured races would have deprived the world of the incomparable genius of Alexander Dumas.

Still it is a reasonable ambition on the part of the higher race to discourage, by such sanctions as racial pride and public opinion can supply, any gross disparagement of its purity. A half-breed race involves a new problem, which often assumes very difficult forms, and the world is so full of trouble already that difficult problems are not to be multiplied unnecessarily. Moreover, it is most exceptional that such unions should be either inspired or swayed by the motive of spiritual comradeship which is part of the civilized conception of marriage; or that a white man, so uniting himself, should not by that very fact lose caste not only with his fellows but, what is far more important, with himself. The true relation between races far removed from one another in the scale of civilization but condemned to endure together under one flag was described in a happy phrase by Booker Washington: 'The fingers of one hand, always separated but always co-operating!'

The foregoing argument has assumed that it is a definite part of civic duty to aim at the maintenance of a certain racial standard, and to give effect to that aim both by such improvements as hygiene and education may introduce into the general environment and also by the elimination, in a few extreme and clearly marked cases, of tainted stocks. It is not, however, everybody who accepts this principle. By the Roman Catholic Church the idea of race-cleansing through the elimination of unfit stocks is regarded with distinct hostility, and to many good men who are not members of the Roman Catholic faith, the naturalists' view of human society seems animal and at variance with ethical dignity. They say, 'We do not like the idea of treating the human race as if it were a stud farm. It may be true that your present proposals are comparatively mild. It may be true that you are at present only concerned with preventing either by legislation or by social pressure the multiplication of a few extreme types of the mentally and physically degenerate, but that is simply because you are too ignorant to proceed farther with safety. If biological science would provide you with a recipe for producing males or females, for producing calculating boys and violinists, for producing every grade of human stupidity and cleverness *à choix*, would you not upon your principles be compelled to accept it? If you propose to use your present imperfect knowledge to control parentage and birth, will you not *a fortiori* be compelled similarly, but on a vastly increased scale, to employ that larger knowledge for which biological science is in search? *Principiis obsta.* Far better trust to natural selection for the elimination of the unfit, than accept a principle which may, if science has its way, lead to the construction of one of the greatest systems of tyranny over the individual life which the wit of man has devised.'

On this matter people are apt to feel extravagantly, and this may be an extravagant way of putting the case, but there can, I think, be little doubt as to the general tenor of the reply. It would be first that the best ethical opinion of every age has accepted the view that physical soundness, which is most often closely allied with moral health, is one of the good things of life which it is reasonable and right for a good man to desire for himself, for his wife, and for his children, and which it is equally reasonable for the State to seek to promote among its citizens, and second that while it is therefore well to keep physical considerations in view, as we do in our whole policy of public hygiene, we recognize that they are not the only considerations which count, and that they may have to be correlated with other needs and subordinated to other calls. Let me illustrate the first point by a simple instance. Supposing that a young man were conscious that he belonged to a family of inebriates, that all through his family history so far as it was known to him the same fatal tendency to inebriety had broken out with the same distressing consequences for the happiness and wellbeing of the home, and suppose that with this knowledge in his mind, he had come to the resolution to abstain from marriage and so to bring his ill-starred line to a close, would this determination be praised or blamed by good men? Can there be any doubt as to the answer? Every man of good sense and good feeling would say of such a resolution that it was absolutely right and proper, and dictated by true civic feeling. But if it be moral for an individual to abstain from marriage on definite eugenic grounds, how can it be immoral for social opinion to support such abstinence or for the State to promote it? Inexpedient it may be; dangerous even it may be, to attempt to frame a general prohibition in such cases, but no clear thinker will conclude that it is immoral or inherently incompatible with the principles of high-minded and provident statesmanship.[1]

[1] Monsignor Brown, a distinguished Roman Catholic prelate, tendered the following opinion to the Commission of Enquiry into the declining birth-rate, 1913 : ' No human authority has any right absolutely to prohibit any individual against his antecedent will from contracting marriage, as such prohibition would be contrary to the Natural Law, e. g. the State cannot lawfully forbid the marriage of the poor or the physically defective.' —*The Declining Birth-rate, its causes and effects*, p. 391.

VIII

THE ETHICS OF WEALTH

'Where ignorant armies clash by night.'—M. ARNOLD.

ADMITTEDLY there is no more important branch of civic duty than the adoption of a right attitude towards the problem of wealth. How ought the citizen to regard wealth? How ought he to employ it? What powers and privileges should he assign to the State over private property? In what ways should he endeavour to limit the undue influence of sinister interests in the conduct of public affairs? These questions lie at the root of political thinking, and no political philosopher from Plato downward has been able to avoid attempting some answer to them.

What then is wealth? The economist answers that wealth is that which has value, and that of value there are two kinds, value in use and value in exchange. He tells us that while all things which have a value in exchange have a value in use, it does not follow that all things which have a value in use have a value in exchange. Fortunately for the happiness of mankind, some of the greatest blessings which we enjoy have no exchangeable value. They are either so abundant or else they are so individual that they are not bought and sold over the world's counter. We do not buy the blessings of breathing the air; we do not sell the blessing of a good digestion: the one because it is furnished in unlimited quantities by the bounty of nature, the other because it cannot be transferred by its fortunate possessor to another. Nor is there any direct and certain ratio between the value which the consumer obtains for a commodity and the price which he is compelled to give for it. We obtain commodities at a sacrifice lower than that which we should be willing to endure rather than go without them, and when this happens we reap what economists have happily called a consumer's surplus.

These elementary considerations are only recalled to mind because they illustrate the fundamental truth that wealth in itself has no existence. Wealth is always relative to human needs, human temperament, human faculties. What value should we attach to the National Gallery, were the human race simultaneously smitten with blindness? What deaf mute would purchase a piano or a gramophone for his own pleasure? What unlettered and hungry rustic would not willingly exchange a First Folio for a dish of beans and bacon? What shipwrecked crew on a desert island would not prefer a good crop of bananas to all the gold in the Bank of England? With every change of taste and circumstance wealth passes into non-wealth, non-wealth into wealth. When peace succeeds war, swords are converted into ploughshares. Some years ago the silk hat industry was flourishing in England. Now it is only kept alive by the patronage of the Jews and the requirements of the Synagogue.

It is usual to measure the wealth of a nation by statistics as to its exports and imports, its revenue returns, its bank deposits, and the like, and returns of this kind are useful as furnishing a rough indication of national prosperity. It is clear, however, that such returns furnish no clue as to the quality of the demand seeking satisfaction in the goods which have been the subject of economic exchange or as to the amount of happiness which these exchanges have secured. Further, some of the most important elements in national wellbeing, such as climate, health, national temperament, are left out of such an account.

Moralists have, therefore, rightly pointed to the very

limited and unsatisfactory character of the conventional economic measurements as indications of real wealth. They have pointed out that it is important to consider not only how much is produced and exchanged, but what is produced and exchanged; that there is all the difference in the world between a base demand for base things and a liberal demand for liberal things; and that it is therefore a prime object of civic concern that economic demand should be educated by liberal forces and guided to rational ends. Satire is familiar with the spectacle of the vulgar *nouveau riche*, the man who having come into a fortune by some lucky stroke, without having acquired liberal tastes and a sense of civic responsibility, throws away his money without obtaining real satisfaction either for himself or others. But what is true of an individual may be true also of a State. Here, too, there may be a vulgar, uncivilized, illiberal use of national resources, and a wrong turn given to the currents of economic demand. It is easy to supply fictitious instances. Let us imagine a State whose exports mainly consisted of opium and its imports of strong drink, or one whose chemical industries were solely employed in the manufacture of poison gas, or one again whose population was so debased in morals and taste that there was no demand for literature which was not vulgar and lascivious, for architecture which was not uselessly ostentatious, or for music above the standard of the music hall. In all these instances a great deal of labour and capital would be employed in producing what to the cultivated and sensible citizen, the φρόνιμος of Aristotle's *Ethics*, would be rightly characterized as nonwealth, because it failed to satisfy the reasonable wants of a reasonable citizen in a reasonable community.

If then there is no such thing as absolute wealth, no wealth out of relation to human wants, and if it is also true that the conception of what constitutes wealth differs according to the stage of civilization reached in any given community, so that what is regarded as wealth at one stage becomes valueless at another, does it not follow that wealth is never an end, but always a means to an end? And that that end must be conceived in terms of the individual, must be some state of the individual soul or character, and that whether that state be termed happiness or the good life, it must in any case be worth having from an ideal point of view?

It may seem a paradox to say that wealth must be conceived in terms of the individual, for in our ordinary speech we speak of a wealthy State. But the wealth of a State consists of the wealth of its individuals. A State has no capacity for absorbing wealth, apart from the individuals who compose it. A State has no eyes to see with or ears to hear with, no stomach requiring to be filled, no human whims or fancies requiring to be gratified. The wealth of a State is and must always consist in the power of individual human beings to obtain satisfaction for their wants. And when we ask whether a State is rich, we should not be content with an affirmative answer unless we are satisfied that its inhabitants are happy.

It does not, however, follow that because all wealth is essentially individual, the individual has an unqualified and exclusive right to such portions of wealth as he may happen at any moment to enjoy. 'I have a right to this property,' you say. 'It is mine to do with as I like.' On what, however, is this right founded? On inheritance? But no property would be quietly inherited without the protection of the State, which regulates by its laws the course which property should take upon the death of its owner, and secures that each inheritor should succeed without let or hindrance. On purchase? But how can purchase confer a better right than that which was enjoyed by the seller or legitimize the acquisition of stolen goods? By original acquisition? But what is involved by acquisition? Do you acquire a portion of nature by walking over it before any one else, or surveying it, or by plucking blackberries on it? Or must you, in order to derive your right of acquisition, mix your labour with it, as Locke suggested, and if so, in what amounts, with what intensity, and over what period of time? It will be seen that the question is not devoid of difficulty. Most people would say that a man has a right to the proceeds of his labour, and would agree that no system of society could be prosperous which was founded on any other hypothesis. Indeed, one of the cardinal errors of the Bolshevik rulers of Russia is that under their dispensation the reward of labour was so uncertain and precarious as to paralyse the productive energies of society and to plunge it into an abysm of desperate poverty and confusion. But the question to be considered is whether the individual right founded on individual labour is or can be absolute and unconditioned.

The answer to this question must be that no such absolute or unconditioned right does or can exist. If a man has such a right to the proceeds of his bodily labour and to that part of nature with which he has mingled his bodily labour, this right can only proceed from a right equally absolute and unconditioned to his own body. But has a man a right to his own body? Clearly only in so far as he makes no such use of his bodily activities as may be injurious to the society in which he lives. If a man should use his body to forge a cheque or to wreck a train, society sends him to prison. If he uses his body in such a way as to obstruct the thoroughfare, society, through the instrument of the policeman its agent, orders him to move on. If he mixes the labour of his right fist with the eye of his neighbour, society withholds its sanction. If the State does not prosecute private tippling, it brings down the weight of its displeasure upon the citizen who is found drunk and disorderly in the public thoroughfare.

But if we are bound for these reasons to acknowledge that the right of the individual to his own body is not absolute but conditioned, the same argument applies to all rights founded on bodily labour. They, too, are not absolute but conditioned. They are conditioned by the fact that man is a member of society, a social animal, receiving benefits from the human family to which he belongs and owing duties to it in return for benefits received.

A very little consideration should suffice to put this contention beyond all doubt. Every organized State levies taxation from its members, and every tax is an invasion of the rights of property. It may be argued that in a democratic State the tax is conceded by Parliament, but it does not follow that every member consents to it or regards it as just and reasonable. It is, however, generally regarded as just and reasonable, nay more, as inherent in its very nature and constitution, that the State should have the right of taxation. No sane man contests that; but once the admission be made, what becomes of the absolute and unqualified right to private property? It is clear that it is limited by social convenience.

The same conclusion may be reached by another route. One of the greatest facts of history has been the spread of the European races over the American, Australian, and African continents. It is not seriously denied that the expansion of Europe, despite the crimes and disorders by which it has unhappily in some cases been accompanied, has resulted in an increased surplus of benefit to the world. It has, however, been accompanied in all these cases by the dispossession of native peoples of a lower type, who roamed freely over the land before their rights were challenged and overthrown by the stronger and more energetic races of Europe. Can it be pretended that this process is wholly illegitimate; that the right of ownership has no relation to the performance of function, and that a nomad race of aboriginal savages can, by the fact of prior possession, establish an inalienable claim as against the rest of humanity to vast tracts of territory whose wealth they have neither the wish nor the science to develop i

If then private property has rights, these rights are not grounded on circumstances independent of social convenience, but upon social convenience itself. That property should be lodged in the hands of individuals and that these individual owners should be given by law every motive to develop and improve their property consistently with the rights and interests of their fellow men is a contrivance founded on social utility. Just before the South African Union was accomplished a remarkable inquiry was held into indigency in the Transvaal. It was discovered that thousands of Dutch settlers had fallen into such a state of poverty and demoralization as in some instances to have even lost the art of milking cows and to be dependent for their livelihood upon ill-grown mealie crops, and this state of indigency was directly traced to the fact that the land was held upon the communal system and that no single farmer had any interest in working for the production of a crop from which he and his family were to derive no exclusive or preferential advantage. The committee of inquiry, after a careful survey of the situation, concluded with a remarkable recommendation. They saw no other remedy than the introduction of the system of primogeniture.

The truth is that when we speak of the rights of property we are generally thinking of the right of any individual owner to maintain the property to which he is lawfully entitled against any person or persons who may desire to infringe upon his property. As against the unlawful claimant the right of the lawful owner is absolute; but it is absolute not because it is a right anterior to society and independent of social convenience, but for the very opposite reason, because it is so completely founded upon reasons of social convenience that it is enshrined in the law and protected by all the sanctions at the disposal of the State.

Is it, however, always or inevitably the case that the institution of private property works out to the public advantage? There is certainly no modern State which does not from sound reasons of policy curb the rights of private property at a hundred points; but some thinkers and some States have gone farther and have been so much impressed with the evils of private property as to prefer some form of common ownership.

Of the thinkers who have held this view none is more illustrious than Plato, who preaches in his *Republic* the doctrine that the guardians or ruling class in the State are to hold wives and property in common. In advocating so extreme a view as this Plato is pleading for pure government, rather than expounding a theory of economics. He is asking himself the question how the State can be liberated from sinister interests, not how it may become affluent and prosperous. And in the last analysis he finds that the principal contamination infecting the Greek politics of his own day proceeded from one of two sources, either from the selfish desire of the ruling class to augment their fortunes, or from their desire to make use of political power in order to advance the interest of their families. Wealth and Family, in other words, were the perennial sources of political corruption, and if these two root temptations could be removed from the governing class, politics would be cleansed of an inveterate and deadly evil.

The problem which Plato raises in this audacious manner is one of enduring interest. How is Government to be kept clean of sinister interests? How is policy not to be deflected by powerful combinations of men organized for the pursuit of wealth without reference to the larger aspects of social well-being? How is the statesman best screened from the temptations which assail human nature to make use of his public position for private ends? There have been communities, like Paraguay under the Jesuit rule, which have for a time approximated to the Platonic ideal by the pursuit of methods not identical with but approximating to those recommended by Plato. But in general, human experience has not conduced to Platonic methods. Where Government has succeeded in eliminating the two evils of nepotism and private avarice, the result has generally been achieved either by a rigorous code of professional conduct, aided by special circumstances and fortified by a healthy public opinion, or by entrusting the control of affairs to a public-spirited aristocracy beyond the reach of temptation. In reality the State in which the Platonic ends were most completely attained was British India during the exclusive rule of the Indian Civil Service. The members of that service were indeed married, but they were unable to push their family interests in India : they held property, but not in the country which they assisted in governing. They were inspired by a high code of professional honour which prevented them from accepting presents from native princes or in any way turning their public position to private advantage. It may be doubted whether an administration more austerely uncorrupt has ever ruled a great country.

Modern objections to the institution of private property are based upon reasons very different from those which led Plato to adopt his famous theory of Communism. The existing economic system of society is attacked by socialists and communists alike as leading to an unequal distribution of wealth, to waste, to monopoly, to the oppression of the poor by the rich. The argument which is most frequently heard is that if individuals are to be free to amass and to transmit wealth without interference from the State, great inequalities of fortune will result, and that one consequence of these inequalities will be the diversion of labour and capital from the production of necessaries for the poor into the manufacture and distribution of luxuries for the rich. It is not contended that there is in itself anything vicious in luxuries. Indeed the luxuries of to-day become the necessaries of to-morrow ; but it is urged that so long as there exists a class in society insufficiently supplied with the necessaries of a bare existence, labour and capital should not be diverted from the primary task of increasing the volume and lowering the price of necessaries, and further that inasmuch as the demand for necessaries is more stable than the demand for luxuries, employment is rendered unnecessarily irregular by a system which gives direct encouragement to luxurious expenditure, and would be stabilized by a system under which expenditure of this kind would be reduced to very narrow dimensions.

And there is another form of waste to which reference is frequently made in these discussions. There are forms of expenditure incidental to private competition which do not directly contribute to human well-being and are therefore wasteful. There are, for instance, the huge sums spent in advertisement, and there is the capital invested in small businesses which are crushed out in the struggle. It is contended that in the socialistic state such forms of waste would be eliminated or reduced to a minimum, and that on economic grounds therefore a system of competition is to be condemned.

What should be the attitude of the good citizen towards these two forms of alleged waste? One obvious argument in favour of a society in which material fortunes are evenly divided is that such a distribution tends to increase happiness, since it is fair to assume that the power of any given unit of wealth to produce happiness varies inversely with the amount of the fortune of which it forms a part. A five-pound note, which may be a great matter to a domestic servant, is a comparative trifle to a millionaire. A society, then, which is characterized by very abrupt oppositions of fortune is not likely to be so happy as one in which fortunes are more or less evenly divided. It may be more interesting; it may provide more stimulus; it may be able in a small class to develop types of excellence which cannot be reproduced under conditions of greater economic monotony, but it will not be so happy. The very wealthy will be unable to convert part of their fortune into terms of personal happiness; they have more wealth than they can absorb, while there will be many who will have less than they need to maintain a decent existence.

No unprejudiced mind can refuse to allow that there is great substance in this argument. In a State like Denmark, where wealth and education are very generally diffused through the community, there is probably less discontent and misery than in the poor quarters of an English or Scottish town. But the argument for equality cannot be pressed with mathematical rigour. Human beings are not cut into mathematical patterns. They differ in temperament and intelligence and character, in their aptitude for work and their capacity for enjoyment. Certainty and safety may bring comfort to cautious middle-age, but the world is not composed only of grey-heads. To the young, life is an adventure, spiced with delightful hazards, and opening out to healthy ambition horizons without limit. How then would a society organized upon a footing of drab mathematical equality accord with the temperament of youth? How would it satisfy the gambling appetite common to mankind and peculiarly inveterate, as we learn from Tacitus, in the Teutonic race? How would it maintain the spirit of initiative and enterprise on which the material progress of society depends? Nobody can contemplate without pain the thought of human beings living under conditions which are physically, morally, and intellectually disabling. But can any one contemplate with pleasure the grim monotony of a world covered with houses of a uniform size, inhabited by families of uniform fortune, and offering to all its members, whatever their ability, whatever their force, whatever their service, that low, certain, and uniform rate of reward which is obtained by dividing the total economic product of society by the number of those who are entitled to share it?

The strong argument in favour of equalization must then be accompanied by certain qualifications. We may agree that no society can be regarded as properly constituted in which families are brought up under conditions of disabling inequality. We may rightly demand of our legislators that a certain minimum standard of life should be provided for every member of the community. In Great Britain, where education is free up to the fourteenth year and pensions are provided for the aged, and the State makes a contribution to workmen's insurance, a good many of the elements of such a national minimum are actually forthcoming. But the provision of a satisfactory national minimum postulates an adequate fund from which that minimum must be paid. It implies that labour and capital are employed to the best purpose in the most productive undertakings, and since human nature requires a spur, and most men are as indolent as they dare to be, it implies that wide avenues are opened out to economic ambition and that penalties are attached to stupidity and sloth.

The modern socialist is prepared to make concessions to the infirmities of the human soul. He admits that a formal mathematical equality in the division of wealth is neither possible nor desirable, and is willing to tolerate an adjustment of remuneration to social desert. The kind of society which he desiderates will then admit of a certain degree of inequality, but the inequality will be bounded by the fact that the State will be the sole owner of the land, the raw materials, and the instruments of production. Every citizen will be a State servant, will be paid a State salary, which he will expend in the purchase of State-made goods. The immense fortunes of the captains of industry will disappear, for the great businesses will be managed by civil servants, salaried upon the relatively modest scale appropriate to the members of the public service.

There is nothing immoral or peculiarly revolutionary in such a conception of society. The community already controls many natural monopolies and interferes at a thousand points with the economic freedom of its members. It regulates railway rates and the supply of water and lighting and tramways ; it expropriates for purposes of public utility, restricts rents during a housing shortage, subjects factories to various forms of supervision, and through the instrument of taxation annually transfers large sums from the pockets of the rich for the promotion of advantages, such as those of elementary education or old-age pensions, which are exclusively enjoyed by the relatively poor. Why, it is argued, should not the State travel farther upon the road upon which it has already proceeded so far to the manifest advantage of the community ? Why should it not take over the mines and the railways and the shipping ? Why should the drink trade be left to private enterprise ? And agriculture to the careless amateurish ways of the sporting or absentee proprietor ? And house rents to the rapacity of the slum-owner ? No new principle need be invoked. We are more than half socialized already, and if the postal service can be run at a profit as a Government concern, why not the steel trade ?

The argument is sometimes stated as if the world were

necessarily divided into two sharply opposed schools of thought, one favouring individualism and the other nationalization, and that an individualist could not also be a nationalizer or a nationalizer an individualist. This is not so. Every individualist must admit some nationalization, and every nationalizer must admit some individualism. It is not a question of all or nothing. Each case for nationalization must be judged upon its economic and social merits. It is possible to hold that the State could supply the public with a better railway service than the existing companies without being committed to the view that the Government would be equally successful in the management of a very complicated industry like the mines, the prosperity of which depends not a little upon skilful marketing. And again it is quite conceivable that a temperance enthusiast might in the assumed interests of sobriety support the nationalization of the drink traffic, while holding stern individualist views on the mines and railways. Finally, an economist would be justified in drawing lines of demarcation between industries which were of the nature of natural monopolies and industries which were essentially competitive, and again between industries for export and industries ministering to the domestic market only, and in submitting that the Government management of a competitive industry for export is subject to peculiar difficulties and must be argued on its own merits.

No doubt there are general arguments relevant to the whole case—as that an individual owner gets more work out of his men than a public body, or that a Government is necessarily less alert and efficient than the successful business man who has survived the fierce stress of competition, or that no public body ever escapes the dilemma, either of somnolence if uncontrolled, or if controlled, of contracting a senile timidity incompatible with the taking of those great risks which are the soul of a fortunate business enterprise. And no doubt it is well to examine each case in the light of these and other general arguments drawn from human psychology and confirmed or rebutted by the broad facts of human experience. But the argument primarily belongs to the sphere not of morals but of economics. And as each case comes up for consideration, the first question which arises is whether State management will yield a larger dividend.

If there will be less to divide, the case for collectivism falls to the ground, for the safeguarding of the worker against oppression and ill-usage can as well be effected under the régime of private property. The strength of the collectivist case does not lie in the moral region, but in the numerous evidences of economic waste and inefficiency incidental to the régime of unrestricted individualism in industry. Eliminate that waste, says the collectivist, and the national dividend will be increased. Increase the dividend and the national minimum will rise. Raise the minimum, and you will add to the stock of happiness and virtue in the nation.

Whether the dividend will in fact be increased by the abolition of private property in the means of production is what most economists have gravely doubted. The capitalistic system can no more be abolished than the weather. Wherever wealth is saved for future production there is capital, and the abolition of capital would be equivalent to a formal declaration for starvation and barbarism. In truth nobody but a lunatic would suggest the abolition of capital. What the collectivist complains of is not capital but the private ownership of capital. And it is as easy to criticize the present industrial system which proceeds upon the basis of such ownership as it is to find fault with the deficiencies of the British weather. Still the question must be asked : Will nationalization bring an improvement in the dividend?

It is not a conclusive argument for extending the collectivist principle to point to the manifold evils incidental to the régime of private property. The institution of private property is doubtless subject to many drawbacks, but it has in revenge incontestable merits. As Arthur Young observes, ' private property turns sand into gold', and the fact that everybody aspires to have something which he can call his own is a proof that it is an institution deeply rooted in the soil of our common nature, an enrichment of human personality as well as an incentive to economic effort. Why then abolish private property before it has received all the improvements of which it is capable ? Mill asked this question, and it is a question which still awaits an answer. Monopoly must be combated. Privilege must be combated. And in so far as private property assumes the odious shape of monopoly or ministers to the invidious eminence of privilege, it calls for the supervising and regulating hand of the community. But why, when our real aim is to prevent the oppressive or wasteful usage of private property, should we rid ourselves of the manifest economic advantages which attach to it ? Is the nationalization of the drink trade the only solution of the temperance question, the nationalization of the mines the only means of securing effective management and reasonable wages for the miners, the State-ownership of land the only avenue to a revived agriculture ? There are certainly good grounds for thinking that the abuses of which complaint is justly made may be treated by methods which will be less likely to diminish the national dividend, the augmentation of which is the basic condition of an improved level of life for the community as a whole.

But even should this treatment be applied and receive all the success which it is capable of yielding, can we confidently reckon upon any great mitigation of human misery without some regulation of the birth-rate ? In particular communities or at particular stages in the life of a community such regulation may be unnecessary. The birth-rate may be stationary or it may be declining or it may be increasing but nevertheless be outpaced by the growth of economic production. But the problem of population can never be negligible in the calculus of the national conditions which make for human happiness. A declining birth-rate among the more vigorous and intellectual stocks in any given society, coupled with an increasing birth-rate among those stocks which are least capable of making an effective contribution to national welfare, may easily frustrate the good results attendant upon a long series of provident reforms.

Again, the loss of its export trade may confront a manufacturing nation with the grim alternative between a drop in the birth-rate and a drop in the standard of living. Or other contingencies may arise equally disconcerting to optimism. We may indeed rely upon the free play of natural forces to adjust the population of the world to the bare means of supporting it, for famine and disease are never very far in the background. But no experience permits us to assume that a benignant Nature so arranges the ratio between the wealth of the world and the number of those who claim to participate in it as to provide for every claimant the material essentials for a decent and civilized existence.

It is a truism that wealth should be justified in happiness. Not that happiness and wealth are identical, or that wealth has any direct or numerical relation to happiness, for the happiest members of the community are often among the poorest, but because unless wealth be so justified it possesses neither meaning nor purpose. What, for instance, can be more unmeaning than the mere appetite for monopoly? Mr. Havemeyer is reported to have said that it was his ambition to refine the sugar of the American people, and Mr. Gates to have observed that it was the ambition of the organizers of the American Steel and Wire Company to control the wire output of the world.[1] But how will the American people be the happier by reason of the fact that Mr. Havemeyer refines their sugar and controls its price and becomes the sugar dictator over a great continent? And what increment of happiness will accrue to the world from the realization of the ambition of Mr. Gates, the organizer of the American Steel and Wire Company? These grandiose ambitions for economic monopoly, irrespective of the social necessity of the wants to be satisfied, irrespective of the standard of life secured for the workers of the industry, irrespective of the general welfare of society, are simply vulgar. Mr. Havemeyer and Mr. Gates may be admirable employers of labour and patriotic citizens (and we have no ground for thinking otherwise); but if they possess these virtues, it is not by reason of their declared ambition but despite of it. A monopoly, however efficient, is always a danger to the State. Let us never then glorify the man whose avowed end in life is the creation of a business trust.

There is nothing anti-social in the possession of great wealth honestly acquired. What is anti-social is its perverse employment. It is one of the most distressing features in the present industrial situation that class suspicion has been developed to such a point of folly, that even the noblest uses of great wealth are decried as efforts to obtain an illegitimate and oppressive advantage. If a great firm establishes a school for the education of the young people in its employ, it is represented as attempting to enslave the intellect of the workers. If the firm, rendered anxious by the discomfort of its operatives, appoints a welfare worker to promote their interests, it must expect to meet with a similar tempest of disparagement.

And yet the solution of the present difficulties between

[1] James Mickel Williams, *Principles of Social Psychology*, p. 74.

capital and labour largely consists in a quickened sense of the responsibilities of wealth on the side of the employer and of a heightened sense of partnership on the side of the employed.

How is such a sense of partnership to be generated? There is something necessarily inhuman about a big business, and yet scale cannot be neglected as an important element in financial success. Equally there is something inhuman in a limited liability company directed in the interest of absentee share-holders who never come face to face with the operatives by whose labour they stand to profit. Nobody, however, would suggest that the principle of limited liability is otherwise than good, seeing that it enables the small savings of small men, which would otherwise have been unproductively expended, to be invested to the advantage of the community. Nor will any one who has had an opportunity of comparing the rate of industrial progress of two neighbouring cities, in the one of which industries are left on the old proprietary basis while in the other they have been converted into limited liability companies, doubt which of the two systems yields the better industrial results. In the one case the prosperity of the city is at the mercy of heredity and its accidents; in the other case it is free to buy the best managing talent in the market.

It follows that the humanization of industry is not to be found in a reversion to the old types. They have disappeared or are disappearing, and no power can revive them. Here and there small industries will flourish, but the great mass of the working population of the world will not be enlisted in them. They will be regimented in great factories, the specialized human pieces of a huge and complicated system of machinery revolving under the impetus supplied by the confluent force of thousands of separate and unseen rills of capital. It is idle to suppose that we can revert to the older system under which capital and craftsmanship were combined. We must take it for granted that most businesses will be big, that they will trade upon borrowed capital, and that the capitalist, entrepreneur, and workmen will continue to possess distinct and separable though interdependent interests in the concern.

Great good may no doubt be effected by enlarging the spirit of co-operation and mutual confidence on the lines which are now so generally advocated in the press and upon the platform. Let the employer, it is said, put all his cards upon the table. Let him show his workpeople exactly how the firm stands, what are its overhead charges, in what quarters it has to face or to fear competition, what are its profits or losses, and at what price it must sell in order to keep the ship afloat, and his workpeople, being taken into full confidence, will be reasonable in their demands. Quarrels are the fruit of suspicion. Suspicion is the child of ignorance. Dissipate ignorance and confidence will necessarily ensue. The more fully the operative is initiated into all the secrets of the business in which he is engaged, alike on its technical, its commercial, and its economic side, the more intelligent, zealous, and willing will be his service, and the less will he be disposed to regard himself as the victim of exploitation. No one will contest the value of such remedies. No one will deny that industrial harmony implies humane intercourse and that this in turn assumes a frank exchange of knowledge about common affairs and common interests. Nor again will the statesman undervalue the help which may come from a more enlightened and public-spirited way of looking at the ordinary business of life than that which most commonly prevails. ' Business ', writes Mr. Henry Ford, ' exists not for profit but for service ', a noble maxim which if it became the predominant motive regulating the conduct of affairs would solve many troubles. What men principally object to is not work but drudgery (or toil which carries no message to the mind), and to give to the masters and men in a great industry the idea that by their labours they render a real service to the community is at once to rob toil of half its irksomeness.

Something more, however, is required than a bond of social service and the will to economic co-operation, if our industries are to be placed upon a basis compatible with the promotion of humane and efficient standards. The world will not be healed by gentle manners and kind thoughts and educated ideals alone, so long as any great fundamental social injustice is allowed to persist; and at present there are in the modern constitution of British society two points of fundamental injustice, the one bitterly and generally realized, the other not the less real because nine people out of ten do not suspect its existence. The first injustice is the lack of security against unemployment, the second is the lack of education for adolescents.

The lack of security against unemployment may seem a comparatively small matter to persons who are well sheltered from the caprices of economic weather. They may argue that even in bad times unemployment only affects a small proportion of the population, and that of this proportion an appreciable quota is contributed by the work-shy or unemployable. But this method of reasoning is quite misleading, for it fails to take account of the psychological influence exercised by the possibility of unemployment upon those who are in fact employed. If unemployment came only to the idle and the worthless, it might be a benefit instead of a scourge. But unemployment is a spectre which dogs the path of every worker, however steady, however capable. The bankruptcy of an employer, the failure of a foreign harvest, some fault in management or change in the current of demand, may at any moment throw him upon the labour market, the sport of economic circumstances which no zeal, no labour, no skill of his own is available to counter or control. It is this underlying anxiety which gives to the social struggle its character of fierceness and unreason, which leads to the deliberate and organized attempt to slow down production in order to spread employment, and has imposed upon British industry the heavy fetters under which it now labours. It is difficult to over-estimate the moral, economic, and psychological effects which would ensue upon the elimination of this social malady. Security for the worker would relieve the springs of industry from a burden of lead. It would remove one of the chief obstacles which is now opposed to the expansion of ability and the full development of human effort. It would clear the industrial atmosphere of the thick clouds of suspicion which at present obstruct the true vision of social progress. It would bring in its train more wealth, more happiness, more content to the whole world of wage-winners.

If this forecast should seem to be overdrawn, let the sceptic examine more closely the psychical effects which are now produced by the spectre of unemployment. Let him realize how large an ingredient in the present widely diffused sense of social injustice is constituted by the spectacle of undeserved poverty and the expectation of undeserved impoverishment. Let him reflect upon the deep antagonism which this sense of injustice must necessarily cause against the social system of which it appears to be a part. Let him consider the kind of public opinion which is likely to be generated in a class constantly exposed to the peril of sudden and undeserved degradation ; and then let him realize how this opinion translated into trade-union regulations must necessarily tend to the restriction of industry, the increase of labour costs, the curtailment of national wealth, and the further aggravation of human misery.

It is then a cardinal requisite of social progress that this

evil of unemployment should be removed. Even in Great
Britain, where the problem is hardest, it is not unmanageable.
A sound system of insurance by industries would dispose of
85 per cent. of the unemployment in this country at a cost
which would be repaid over and over again by the removal
of a malignant source of unrest and bitterness, and by the
revival of the old and salutary belief that it is the duty of
every worker to give to his work the best that is in him.

It would not be relevant to the present discussion, which is
concerned with the civic attitude towards the problem of
wealth, to enlarge upon the second of the two social evils to
which allusion has been made. The neglect of adolescent
education is a curious and irrational feature of modern
industrial life which will excite the surprise and contempt of
a more enlightened posterity. It is sufficient here to observe
that the Western world has not yet recovered from the
demoralizing influences of the industrial revolution, that young
people instead of being primarily regarded as subjects for
education are still regarded primarily as subjects for industry,
and that until this erroneous and debasing conception is
effectively shattered, no great progress will be made toward
securing that communism in culture and knowledge which is
the only means by which the State can attain unity and the
conditions of modern industrial life be made compatible with
the claims of human self-respect.

To many critics of contemporary industrialism these are
not the defects which really matter. In their view the fundamental injustice of modern society consists in the divorce
between ownership and work. So long as private property
performs a social function and its owner employs his wealth
as an aid to production, private property is justified; but
ownership detached from function, the receipt of profits and
dividends without a share in the human toil and struggle by

which those profits and dividends are earned—that is the accursed tumour, the excision of which from the body politic is the condition of moral and economic health. There are, then, according to this philosophy, legitimate and illegitimate forms of private property. Pure interest is legitimate because the lender of capital is entitled to the market price for a commodity essential to industry, but ' quasi-rents ' derived from good fortune, ground rents in towns, mining royalties, and monopoly profits, being ' functionless ', have no justification and should be abolished.

More particularly is attention directed to the recent development of joint-stock companies and the growth of shares.

' Of all types of property ', writes an eloquent exponent of this doctrine, ' the share is the commonest and most convenient. It is a title to property stripped of almost all the encumbrances by which property used often to be accompanied. It yields an income and can be disposed of at will. It makes its owner heir to the wealth of countries to which he has never travelled and a partner in enterprises of which he hardly knows the name.' [1]   And those who think with Mr. Tawney hold that there will be no substantial increase in the industrial output of the country until the wage-earner is satisfied that he is not working to enrich a class of idle absentees, who, by reason of their holdings, claim to exercise a control over the direction of his industry.   It is admitted that the national dividend (about £40 per head in 1914, and that in Great Britain, one of the wealthiest countries in the world) is lamentably small ; it is avowed that owing to the psychological condition of labour it is a good deal smaller than it might be, but the contention is that until the toll taken by the mere property-owner be eliminated this deplorable under-production must continue. When that central injustice is removed, the workers

[1] *The Acquisitive Society*, by R. H. Tawney.

will approach their task in a different spirit. They will evolve high canons of civic and professional duty and confront their daily toil as if it were a branch of honourable public service.

These views are not the fancies of the cloistered brain. They are very widely held. The official Labour Party holds them. The number of workers in this country who have been sedulously taught and have now come to believe that the existence of a share-holding class, controlling by reason of their holdings the course of an industry of which they know nothing, is a flagrant violation of the elementary principles of social justice, may probably be numbered by the million. And it is clear that an opinion so widely held and so directly challenging the moral credentials of one of the most prominent and essential features of the system under which production is now carried on is a formidable fact. For the elimination of the abuse, if abuse it be, can only be obtained by a violent social convulsion.

A great deal of the ethical argument which lies behind this criticism of modern society may be accepted without a moment's hesitation. We should all agree that ownership divorced from a sense of social responsibility is a bad thing. We should agree that industrial work should everywhere be carried on in a spirit of social service. We should not dispute the moral or economic evils which flow from sharp contrasts between excessive wealth and extreme poverty, nor the reality of the injury which the luxurious expenditure of the rich is apt to inflict upon the poorest members of the working class. Given equal output, a system under which ownership and management are conjoined would generally be recognized to be more wholesome than one in which capital is contributed from one quarter, management from another, and manual toil from a third. Most students of social welfare would be glad to see experiments made in what is sometimes described as syndicalism. Why, they ask, should capital always employ labour?

Why should not the workers in any industry band themselves together to employ capital? And as for many of the forms of property, such as ground-rents in towns, to which objection is taken, they are prepared to consider how any evil which may arise from them may be redressed by alterations in the fiscal system of the country or the laws of inheritance. But the elimination of the share-holding class? How far is this required by the principles of social justice? Here an altogether different order of considerations arises.

It is not disputed by any reasonable socialist that saving is an economic virtue. Nobody is foolish enough to deny that if there is no saving there is no capital, and if there is no capital there is no industry. What the socialist who knows his case is most anxious to prevent is luxurious expenditure, which is incompatible with saving. What he does not always see is that if he discourages saving he encourages luxurious expenditure so long as there is anything left to spend. Some saving then there must be, and under our present dispensation the savings small and large of rich and poor alike can, with the minimum of trouble to their owners, be employed in the furtherance of industry and the extension of employment. It is then admitted that the investor, however self-regarding be his motives, confers some benefit on society. He might have spent; he has preferred to save. The argument, however, assumes that the investor is a 'functionless owner', and it is this functionless ownership which must be abolished as inconsistent with fundamental ethics. Now who are the shareholders in Great Britain? They are some millions of people belonging to every rank and station of society. A few are undoubtedly very rich, but since there were in 1910 only twelve thousand persons in Great Britain who possessed incomes of five thousand a year and upwards, and these twelve thousand persons did not possess more than 8 per cent. of the total wealth of the country, it is clear that many of the shares are held by persons of moderate or slender means. Of these it is safe to assume that by far the greater number are engaged in earning their livelihood, and that the investments which they are enabled to make are the result of socially valuable work in some other field. Indeed the absentee shareholder, so far from being a drone, may be engaged in making a contribution to social welfare far exceeding in value that of the whole body of operatives to whose industry he contributes a share of his savings.

Nevertheless it is urged that *qua* shareholder he is functionless, and that it is as shareholder pure and simple that he is now to be regarded. Save that he contributes his share, how, it is asked, does he help the industry? He takes his dividends, be the conditions of the worker what they may. A tax collector, irresponsible to Parliament, uncontrolled by the press, he claims his pound of flesh as of right and in utter carelessness of the tragedy and comedy of human life which is played out behind the transaction. How can the dependence of business upon capital subscribed under these conditions be otherwise than unwholesome? The managers tend to think more of their responsibilities to the shareholders than of their duties to the men. In the eyes of their employers they stand or fall by the rate of dividend which they can earn for those who are at ease, not by the conditions which they can provide for those who work. So by reason of an inherent lack of ethical quality in our industrial system we are compelled to witness a degeneracy in the fibre of our people. The wage-earner, feeling himself to be the victim of an inhuman and invisible force, which robs him of that which is properly his, works no more than he must. The last spark of professional pride in good workmanship disappears. Confidence is undermined. A feeling of intense and bitter suspicion poisons the atmosphere.

The remedy proposed is the limitation by law of the rate of interest : in other words, the abolition of profit.

The remedy is worse than the disease. Industries do not always make profits : they make losses as well. They are subject by their very nature to every species of risk, and if they are to attract the capital which is necessary for their support, they must be prepared to pay for risk. Some thinkers go so far as to acknowledge this necessity, but suggest that risks may be classified, and that while payments may be permitted in the case of one class of risk, they should be prohibited in the case of another. We believe that no such classification of risks would be found practical, and that the first result of any attempt to interfere with the earnings of capital by legislation would be to impel the investor to place his money in other countries where such restrictions did not apply. The consequences of such a diversion of the stream of capital would be a fall in the demand for labour, a spread of unemployment, and an intensification of those evils of ' ca'canny ' which it is desired to cure.

Let it not, however, be supposed that there is nothing in the industrial situation created by limited liability companies which deserves anxious attention. The new machinery for rendering capital readily available does, unless uncorrected by other influences, tend to make businesses large and inhuman. For this reason a special social obligation rests upon the investor. He cannot, indeed, be expected to familiarize himself with the circumstances of every industry in which he may have a pecuniary interest, nor indeed, without a great deal more study than he would in most cases be able to give, would his opinion of those circumstances be of the faintest value ; but three requirements can fairly be made of him. First, that he should not invest his money in any business of an anti-social character or known for the bad conditions under which its workers are employed; second, that he should regard a large and profitable holding in any concern as carrying with it an obligation of inquiry and humane interest; and third, that deriving an income from industrial investments he should regard himself as in a peculiar degree bound to support well-founded proposals for the amelioration of the conditions under which industry is carried on.

The general growth of a spirit of social compunction and the great advance which has been made during the last fifty years in correcting the harshest features of competitive industrialism would seem to show that these obligations are even now not wholly disregarded.

Writers speak glibly of 'the liberation of industry from subservience to the interests of the functionless property owner', as if it were not to the interest of industry that there should be a general pool of capital, from which drafts may be made as occasion demands. What they really mean by this magniloquence is, not that industry should cease to command capital, not that capital should cease to be paid, but that there should be a limit to its remuneration, and that the investor, who can claim now to exercise a certain function of direction and control in the business which he helps to support, should be henceforward voiceless; that the property in fact, in respect of which he does now exercise a function, should henceforward be deprived of any function whatever. Well and good if all investments are gilt-edged. But on what principles of justice can it be expected that a man should embark his savings, with the risk of loss, in a speculative undertaking the conduct of which is entirely removed from his cognizance and control?

What the equities of the case demand is not a philosophy which shuts its eyes to the ugly fact of business losses, not legislation which will drive capital out of industry, but a just partition of the national dividend between labour, capital, and management, and what is often neglected, the consuming public. If dividends be outrageously high, as may be the case in some widely syndicated industry enjoying the security of the monopolist, then worker and consumer may have a grievance calling for remedy. But is society, even in its present industrial vesture, incompetent to provide redress? In a free-trade country the consumer does not languish for long in the clutches of exploiting monopoly. The worker, too, is not without his weapons of offence. Moreover, public opinion, which counts with increasing force with every advance in democratic control, would support the demand that the worker should receive a share in the increased prosperity of a firm which had thus established itself in a place of dominance and security.

Finally, we cannot altogether exclude the question of the magnitude of the national dividend when we are exploring the claims of a proposal which would certainly jeopardize its increase. We learned just before the war on very high statistical authority that the total output of the country is so small that even if it were evenly divided it would yield no more than an average net income of £162 for an average family of $4\frac{1}{2}$.[1] 'What matter?' replies the iconoclast. 'The smaller the output, the more important that none of it should run to waste!' But surely the miserable yield of nature to the efforts of man is relevant to the whole question! What torrents of controversy over the equities of distribution, what heartburnings among employers and employed, what huge losses in labour time, and all over a dividend so pitiably inadequate that even if the extreme demands of the most advanced socialist were instantly conceded, no very appreciable difference would be made in the hard lot of the workers in the most opulent

---

[1] A. L. Bowley, *The Division of the Product of Industry*, p. 49.

country in Europe! Let it be at once admitted that some shareholding is excessively rewarded. The excess measured in figures amounts to so insignificant a total that it is hardly worth while to overturn the whole industrial system in order to remove it, especially as economic competition, collective bargaining, and public finance constitute forces fully adequate to reduce it within reasonable dimensions. It is then of vital consequence that some attention should be paid even by moralists to this matter of the dividend. As it is the world squabbles about comparative trifles, while the all-important issue upon which the material conditions of our social welfare depends goes unregarded. We are like allies in a war who quarrel over the spoils before they have won the victory.

IX

NATIONALISM AND INTERNATIONALISM

' Je ne juge les hommes que par les résultats.'—NAPOLEON.
' I only judge men by results.'
' Tout État, si j'ose le dire, est un vaisseau mystérieux qui a ses ancres dans le ciel.'—RIVAROL.
' Every State, if I dare say so, is a mysterious ship anchored in heaven.'

No conception is more familiar than that which has formed the theme of the preceding lectures. We all acknowledge that we are bound to obey the laws of our own State, and that we have obligations to society which it is part of our duty to discharge. How these obligations may be most accurately defined, what should be the true relation between the State and the individual, may be matters for discussion. But nobody really questions the fact of political obligation. Nobody challenges the right of the State to claim or the duty of the individual to render obedience to laws enacted by the general consent of the community. Everybody admits that of all the evils which can afflict a State none is greater than civil war and revolution. Most people would consider the art of statesmanship chiefly to consist in avoiding these evils, and no one would hold that a State could be described as truly civilized in which the course of justice was impeded by terrorism and the civil disputes of the subjects settled by the arbitrament of force.

Not that the civilized State does or can dispense with the use of material power. However pacific the atmosphere, however docile the population, however benignant the governing authority, there is somewhere in the background the sanction of force. There is a police, there are prisons, there is a militia or regular armed force which may be invoked, on occasions, to suppress disturbances and maintain the peace. But this force is not at the disposal of caprice or passion. It is the servant of law, and law is or should be the passionless expression of social reason, the means by which the better will of the community receives authoritative expression, the vehicle of the moral purpose of the State.

But when we pass from the national life to international relations, we are conscious at once of a great difference of atmosphere. Here there is no acknowledged authority, served by an international police, disposing of international sanctions, and administering justice as between States. What Hobbes said of individual men in a state of nature, 'Homo homini lupus', appears almost literally to apply to States. In spite of all our progress, States are still, to a large extent, as the founders of international law assumed them to be, in a state of nature towards one another, every State regarding its neighbour as a potential enemy and framing its military plans on that assumption, and every State jealously scanning the political horizon for the clouds which sweep up so suddenly and have often been found in the twinkling of an eye to obscure the clearest sky. The difference between international politics and home politics is something akin to the difference between voyaging on land and voyaging at sea. On land the sudden squall may temper the summer heat to the pedestrian. At sea it calls the captain to the bridge to save the ship from destruction.

There can be few better measures of the force of international suspicion than the size of the armies which the principal nations of Europe thought it necessary to maintain during the years before the Great War. At the outbreak of the war the German Empire could probably reckon on some four million men fully or partially trained for war; but we now know that an army of a hundred thousand is quite adequate for the preservation of domestic order, so that thirty-nine fortieths of the total armament of Germany was due not to national needs but to the international situation. It was owing either to the apprehension that she would be attacked by her neighbours, or to strong international ambitions which could only be realized at her neighbours' expense.

But is it true that States have no obligations to one another? Is there no such thing as international morality? Is international honour a vain figment? Are we really to subscribe to the doctrine that every State is a law unto itself?

There is a school of political thought, represented in the age of Renaissance by Machiavelli and in modern times by Treitschke, which takes this view, which holds that the State is power, that the whole duty of the State is to increase its power, and no State is justified in taking any action which is likely to result in a diminution of its material force. From these premises it follows that treaties should only be observed so long as they suit the convenience of the signatory States, and should be repudiated without scruple as soon as they are found to present obstacles to aggrandizement; that small States, being deficient in power, are ridiculous and unworthy of preservation, and that since power is the be-all and end-all of States, and power is principally exhibited in war, every State should be organized for war; every State should regard war as not only an essential and valuable part of its national existence, but as the means by which it realizes its destiny and expresses its purpose in the world. In this view, war is not only part but the highest part of the law of political life. To attempt to banish war from the world would not only be futile, it would be wicked; for it is war that founds States, war that enlarges States, and war that gives to States dignity, courage, and meaning.

A few drops of corrosive acid are quite sufficient to dissolve this theory. If the State is power and nothing but power, it has no moral obligations. How then is it a moral obligation imposed on the State that it should increase its power? Or how is it a violation of any moral obligation that it should fail to attempt to increase its power? The notion of moral obligation does not apply. The professor of the doctrine of force is not entitled to lecture the small State upon its feebleness, or the large State upon the neglect of opportunities for further aggrandizement. The small State may reply : ' I have that measure of power which pleases me and I desire no other.' The large State, which has retired from the business of aggrandizement, may say, ' I am content with my present frontiers and am disposed to cultivate my garden ', and the apostle of force has no reply, unless he is prepared to contend that war is morally superior to peace and that States ought for that reason to desire it.

Now the apostles of the Gospel of Power never quite go to that length. They would not expose themselves by subscribing to the proposition that if all else failed moralists should get up a civil war in order to promote ethical development. However much they may secretly prefer a state of war to a state of peace and believe in the ethical value of preparedness for war, they do not go so far as to state openly that war is in itself and apart from its results and consequences desirable. It is only desirable as a means to an end, and that end the security, and as Treitschke would add, the enlargement of the State. Let us assume, however, that the State has been so enlarged that no further enlargement is possible ! Let us assume that a single State is enabled to achieve what all the great conquerors of the past have failed to achieve, the conquest of the world, that its power is unchallenged and unassailable in every continent, that its fleet dominates every sea, its armies every land, and that its writ runs in every court. What becomes of the desirability of war under such an hypothesis? Since there would be no external foe, war could only be civil war. It could only weaken, it could never strengthen the power of the State, and accordingly the apostle of the doctrine of force would be driven to the ultimate election between senseless violence and stable power. War he could have, but at the expense of the State; the State he could have, but at the expense of war. What would be impossible is that he should have both war and the State at the same time.

It is not difficult to appreciate the historical circumstances which led to the development of this materialistic doctrine during the Italian Renaissance and again in Prussia during the age of Bismarck. In the one case the spectacle of Italian impotence, in the other of the exciting experience of Prussian expansion and aggrandizement, pointed to the importance of physical force as the creator and sustainer of States. Machiavelli, the patriotic Florentine, saw that Italy would never be freed from the barbarian without statecraft of another order than that which too generally prevailed in his native land. He saw that instead of mercenaries the liberating prince must rely upon a native militia, and that his policy must be steadily and remorselessly directed towards the enlargement of the boundaries of his State and the increase of its material power. The deaf and fanatical Saxon professor who for so many years preached the doctrine of Prussianism from his Chair in Berlin was led to the same conclusion by the study of the rise and progress of the Hohenzollern monarchy. As Prussia had been made and enlarged by the use of force, as in his own lifetime Denmark, Austria, and France had successively yielded to the military power of Prussia, it was a temptation to suppose that Providence was on the side of big battalions, especially when they were Prussian, and that the more formidable the Prussian army might become, the greater the certainty that Prussian ideas and Prussian policy would be firmly imprinted upon the plastic surface of the world.   How ironical is Fate !   It was the strength of the German army, not its weakness, which proved to be the undoing of the Hohenzollern dynasty and the ruin of the German Empire.

Though the idea that the State is power is as old as Plato, who in the *Republic* puts the doctrine into the mouth of Thrasymachus, it has been greatly fortified in Europe by the political and intellectual development which succeeded the breakdown of the mediaeval system.   In the Middle Ages the coarsest and most savage rivalries coexisted with a political theory moulded by scholastic philosophers and religious mystics out of materials inherited from an order of things which had long since passed away.   The theory was that Latin Christendom was an unity, knit together by religious and moral ties under the rule of a single temporal and a single spiritual sovereign.   Pope and Emperor ruled the world, and if the world quarrelled, were at hand to arbitrate.   Might was subject to right, force to justice, the law temporal to the law spiritual.   The sword of the prince was at the service of the common creed professed from Cadiz to Konigsberg and from Syracuse to Edinburgh, and the political subdivision of Europe into small States, devoid of strong or stable military strength, contributed to preserve through many quarrelsome centuries an ideal unity which was in the strongest contradiction with material fact.

That unity was broken by the Protestant Reformation. And wherever Protestantism was welcomed by the reigning authority, its influence corroborated the authority of the State.   With a true political instinct Luther looked to the prince as the shield and buckler of the new faith in the days of trial, and on that point Thomas Cromwell and Henry VIII were much of the same mind as the Saxon reformer. The original Churches of the Reformation were, in Germany, in Scandinavia, and in England, dependent on the State, and contributed to fortify the rising spirit of nationality which was to be the great fashioning influence in European politics in the centuries to come. *Cujus regio ejus religio* : this maxim, recognized in the public law of Europe at the Peace of Westphalia after the wars of religion, was the assertion of the principle that the temporal prince was within his own territory supreme in ecclesiastical affairs.

The rise of the nation States was a second factor calculated to weaken the international idea and to corroborate the philosophy of power which insistently proceeds from the natural appetites and passions of man. The nation is an idea foreign to the politics of the ancient and equally alien to the philosophy of the mediaeval world. It is indeed the product of historic forces which have only fully worked themselves out in Western Europe in our own day. We need not here enter into a meticulous examination of the conditions which go to form a nationality. A common language is a factor, but not an essential factor, as the example of Great Britain and Switzerland may prove. Racial unity is clearly not essential, for where is the spirit of nationality stronger or where is there a greater mixture of races than in Great Britain? The example of Germany is sufficient to show that the fact and spirit of nationality are compatible with sharp divergences of religious creed. And legal unity is clearly immaterial, for we know that Scottish law is different from and, as some say, superior to English, and yet there is a common British nation to which both Scots and English belong. What is essential to the growth of the national spirit is a common history—common sufferings, common triumphs, common achievements, common memories, and, it may be added, common aspirations. Race, language, religion, law, geography, contribute to render this community of sentiment possible, but yet a nation is possible even if it be mingled in race and various in creed and language, provided that its inhabitants are bound together by that strong sentiment of community which the trials of historic circumstance can alone create. A nation then implies a common political sentiment, but it does not necessarily proceed from anything of the kind. It is an entire mistake to suppose that a nationality is a spontaneous exhalation of spiritual qualities of an exalted order. It is often the result of foreign conquest, and would have been impossible without the application of external pressure. Ireland is a small island, India a great continent, but they are alike in this respect, that such imperfect sentiment of nationality as they may now possess is alone made possible by the fact of foreign conquest. But we need not go so far afield as Ireland and India for illustrations of this historic truth. The unity of England was not owing to the political genius of its Anglo-Saxon rulers, but to the stern and equable pressure of Norman and Angevin administration. It was the conqueror from France who made out of a loose agglomeration of Saxons and Danes and Celts a single nation obedient to a single law, just as it was the conqueror from Prussia who beat down the Bavarians and Hanoverians in 1866 and so paved the way for German unity. The growth of British and German nationality are not, indeed, to be explained wholly or chiefly by the fact of conquest. There were intellectual, moral, and temperamental influences working for national nity in the soul of the people. But conquest was a contributing factor, and in an analysis of the causes which have diffused the idea of nationality throughout the world the pressure of external forces is of cardinal importance.

Nevertheless it would be idle to deny that the conception of nationality, whatever may be its origin, exercises a moral appeal which does not belong or does not in the same measure belong to other forms of political association. The argument that the State can do no wrong is for many minds rendered more plausible and less intolerable if the State is also a nationality. It is contended that where the government of a State expresses the national will, where the law is rooted in popular consent and authority is an organic part of a homogeneous social fabric, there is not only in all acts of State a peculiar force, but attaching to that force a peculiar moral sanctity. This sentiment is sometimes expressed in the proposition that a national government is alone legitimate and that all other forms are deviations from the norm of political justice. It does not necessarily follow that the nationalist government should be a democracy. The Tsarist Empire was certainly a nationalist government, supported by long national traditions, by deep national pieties, by living national aspirations, and reflecting both in its virtues and its vices the psychology of the Russian people. But right up to the end, despite the Duma, it was in all essentials an absolutist Government. The precise character of the political machinery is therefore not the decisive criterion of nationalism. What is essential is that the government of a national State, whether it be absolutist or democratic, should repose upon a common fund of nationalist sentiment, that it should not only guide the nation but spring from the soil of its being, that it should be the fruit of its character, the image of its temperament, the expression of its political thought and desire.

When such conditions prevail a Government is undoubtedly saved from many sources of trouble and perplexity. Nobody can doubt that nationalism is a source of strength to a Government, and the absence of nationalism a source of weakness. When law comes to a nation in a foreign garb, its authority is apt to be disparaged and contested. One of the chief sources of weakness in the political structure of Europe before the Great War was the inclusion within the confines of the great military empires of communities who felt themselves to be nations deserving independence but baulked of their destiny by external force. And accordingly the principle underlying the territorial provisions of the Treaty of Versailles was the rescue of the submerged nationalities of the continent and their establishment upon a level of secured and guaranteed autonomy. The treaties which concluded the Great War completed the task to which Napoleon, Bismarck, and Mazzini had contributed in their different ways. The old autocracies have vanished. The frontiers of States are roughly prescribed by the wishes of their inhabitants.

The general argument in favour of the national State is not only that it conduces to tranquillity and content, but that it is more likely to rouse its members to wholesome activities and to elicit whatever may be of latent value in the nature of the people. When during the Italian revolution in 1848 J. A. von Hübner was inquiring of a Milanese nobleman what the Austrians had done to deserve the fierce hostility of their Italian subjects, he was answered by the phrase, ' Ci a fatto cadavere' (you have made corpses of us), and he tells us that to this unexpected reply he had no answer, for he felt instantaneously that it was true.[1] However mild and benignant was the Austrian rule, it had in effect acted with all the effects of a creeping paralysis on the body of the Italian people. It had taken from them nerve, enterprise, self-confidence, political self-respect, and instead had given to those parts of Italy subjected to Austrian rule nothing better than material security and comfort. But does it necessarily follow that the invigorating influences which inspired the Italian *Risorgimento* and raised Italian political life to a higher plane must be

[1] J. A. von Hübner, *Ein Jahr meines Lebens*.

everywhere manifest in nationalist movements? Are we justified in concluding that because Italy, a country with a great historic past and clearly defined geographical frontiers and a well-marked and brilliant civilization of its own, can live more happily and effectively as a united nation than as a bundle of disconnected units, the same proposition will necessarily be true of every community which may lay claim to national status? Is the subdivision of the Austrian Empire into separate nationalities all gain and no loss? Is there not some advantage attaching to an organization which has the effect of forcing into combination a number of different races who might otherwise be at war, an organization which adapts itself to differences of creed, language, and race, and invites its citizens to treat them as of minor account? Was there no value to human society in the Pax Austriaca or the Pax Romana? And is there none in the Pax Brittanica? Should we in fact regard the establishment of a national State in Bengal and of another national State in Behar as an advance or as a retrogression? The French in Quebec differ in race, in language, in historical antecedents, and in sentiment from the British inhabitants of the Dominion of Canada. Would the world be enriched by the victory of a separatist movement in Quebec basing itself on the general principle that national States are alone legitimate, and that where they do not exist, they should be called into being? The question answers itself. It is clear that under the present Federal Constitution of the Dominion the French population of Quebec receive all the advantages attaching to the preservation of their own peculiar type of civilization, and are entitled at the same time to enjoy the privileges—and they are not slight—which flow from membership in the British Empire.

Another question suggests itself. We may admit that the principle of self-determination is a good rough rule for the guidance of statesmen who are called upon to redistribute territory after the convulsion of a war. It is, indeed, reasonable to suppose that if frontiers are drawn in accordance with the express wishes of the people most immediately concerned, they will prove to be more satisfactory than if the desires of the population are disregarded. But do these results necessarily follow? Clearly not. The success of the arrangement must obviously depend upon a number of circumstances over and above the wishes of the inhabitants as they might be expressed at the moment. It must be conditioned by the size and geographical configuration of the area, by the capacity of its inhabitants for self-government, and to some extent also by its economic resources. The question whether a State can live depends partly upon whether it is provided with a means of living. A *plébiscite* is one thing. A budget is another.

The triumph of nationalism at the Treaty of Versailles was won at the expense of the Teutonic and Magyar races. The long process of history, by which those vigorous peoples subjected to their rule the weaker Slavonic races of the Middle West, was violently reversed by a combination of forces never likely to be repeated in a European struggle. The Polish nationality, always restive under the eclipse of the partitions, was restored. The effects of the Catholic victory of the White Mountain, which had secured for the Germans three centuries of ascendancy in Bohemia, were suddenly undone, and the Magyars were stripped of territory on every side to enrich their Tchech, their Serb, and their Rouman neighbours.

Whatever the ultimate effect of these changes may prove to be, their immediate influence on the political temperature of Europe cannot be doubted. The little States which owe their existence or enlargement to the peace are passionately national. They rest their credentials on the ground that they have each of them a separate historic nationality affirmed in language and race and only adequately to be expressed and satisfied by complete political independence. Whatever separates them from their former associates is cherished ; whatever may tend to bind them with their alien neighbours is left out of sight. Nationalism may be wholesome, may, as some assert, be holy. But the apotheosis of the national principle in the recent settlement has certainly increased the political ' dissidence of dissent ' in Europe and multiplied the possible occasions of conflict.

If it be true that the State is ' above morality ', this is a serious consideration. *Entia non sunt multiplicanda præter necessitatem*, said William of Ockham wisely, and the multiplication of political entities, all unscrupulous, all anarchical, all guided in their policy by one motive and one only, the extension of their power at the expense of their neighbour, would clearly, in the absence of some compensating contrivance, leave the world more uncomfortable than ever.

But there is one simple and decisive refutation of the view taken by the school of Thrasymachus, Machiavelli, and Treitschke. If the State is power, ' above good or evil ', how is it that by the universal practice of mankind its activities are invested with an ethical colour and either praised as good or blamed as bad ? How is it that in judging of the State, whether it be our own or another, we cannot, do what we may, divest ourselves of the ethical bias ? Why do we in point of fact blame a State for breaking a treaty to which it has set its seal or for repudiating financial obligations which it has solemnly transacted ? What is the meaning of that continuous internal and intermittent external criticism of government if moral categories have no application to the case ? It is true that a State fighting for its life may feel itself impelled to courses of action which do not approve themselves to the moral conscience of mankind. So, too, may an individual. There is no valid reason why the single individual should be judged by one set of canons and the group of individuals by another. Every State is made up of individuals, is guided by a public opinion to which each individual contributes a quota, and justifies its existence by the measure of happiness which it provides for the individuals of which it is composed. How then can we justify the contention that while individuals are amenable to the high court of ethics, there is only one legitimate question which can be asked of the State, and that is whether it is efficiently organized for power? But, in truth, there is little need to labour an argument which finds so little weight in the ordinary converse of mankind.

The proposition that a State's first duty is to its own nationals, or again that 'La petite morale est l'ennemi de la grande', stands upon an entirely different footing. In accepting the first proposition we are in fact affirming the moral responsibility of the State. We are admitting that the State has duties, and are not denying the existence of duties to other States and to the nationals of other States. A famine occurs in Russia. Ought British citizens to be taxed to relieve it? It may be plausibly contended that the first duty of every State is to relieve the distress of its own nationals, and that so long as this task is unfulfilled, it is not entitled to compel contributions for the relief of the nationals of other countries, though it may very properly invite and even stimulate private succour as evidence of human solidarity. On the other hand, it may be contended that wherever great calamities occur which touch the human heart, it is right and proper that States should make a gesture of official sympathy, that government contributions voted by Parliament, however small they may be, make a greater impression upon the general mind than private charity, and that the disinterested assistance of one

State to the nationals of another in times of distress improves the relations between them and sweetens the atmosphere in which international business is conducted. But however the argument may be conducted, it is assumed on both sides that the State must justify its action both at home and abroad on ethical grounds.

So, too, the famous Napoleonic maxim as to the conflict of public and private morality is capable of interpretations consistent with an ethical and indeed exalted view of the mission and functions of the State. It may mean that a whole range of emotions and sentiments which are rightly regarded as valuable in private life have no place in great public emergencies, that there are times when the statesman must discard his most faithful followers, renounce his most cherished obligations of affection and gratitude, in the ruthless and single-minded pursuit of the public advantage. Or it may convey the thought that in the large foresight of public men measures may seem desirable in the ultimate interest of the State which are at the moment inclement and oppressive. Or again that the great original strokes of policy which change history can seldom be accomplished without private suffering and the disturbance of honest minds, or merely that in the rapid and sudden mutations and surprises of political life an excess of puritanical scruple may be an obstacle to large and fruitful decisions. But whatever the interpretation may be, the maxim assumes that statesmanship should be directed to an end which conscience can justify.

The drift of my argument so far has been to show that mankind does not subscribe in point of fact to the doctrine that the State is power ; that this theory, which has been used to buttress up an exclusive form of nationalism, is perverse and alien to our natural modes of thinking, and that some propositions which might, on a superficial view, be thought to lend countenance to the doctrine of mere force, do in effect assume a very different view of life.

At this point it is pertinent to add that there is no such thing as a self-contained and exclusive national State. The civilization of Europe, though rich in minor variations, is in essence a common civilization, influenced by a common religion, drawing upon a common fund of scientific ideas, confronted with common industrial and political problems, and using in all the arts of life ideas of liberty and of law derived from the ancestral genius of Greece and Rome. Nor is Europe itself self-contained. It has conquered the world. Indeed, the expansion of Europe has been the most important fact in modern history. European ideas, European knowledge, European fashions, European methods of government, go everywhere, a swift and all-pervasive electric fluid, creating uniformities of thought and experience, foreign to all anterior stages in our history. The civilization of the North American continent is almost absolutely homogeneous, and that of South America so feebly diversified that it would be reasonable to hope for a political federation of all the South American States. In India, English has to such an extent become the *lingua franca* of political life that no first-class agitator can do without it; in Japan a feudal society has been reorganized on the most modern European lines. The railway, the motor car, the aeroplane, the wireless message, the gramophone, the film, the cheap press, spread throughout the world a common fund of ideas and impressions, and break down dividing barriers. Indian villages, which ten years ago lived a secluded patriarchal life hardly different from that of Abraham, now listen to the vernacular newspaper and discuss the news of the world. Negroes in the recesses of Central Africa crowd round the chieftain's hut to enjoy the art of the London music hall. Chinamen trained in Western Universities build railways and bridges, and steadily work to Americanize their ancient country.   The mighty influence of scientific discovery, which owns no political passions and recognizes no political frontiers, is bringing everywhere ' that staring timid creature man ' face to face with his fellow.

Let it be considered also how the deepest influences which sway the mind of man take their root in a region of consciousness, into which the spirit of partisan nationalism does not enter.   The thirst for morality and truth, the two master passions of the noble nature, have nothing to do with distinctions of race, geography, or political constitution.   The great religions of the world have always owed their carrying power to a message directed to the heart of humanity itself. The first converts to Christianity were not the wealthy and the powerful, but the *déracinés* of the Mediterranean seaport towns.   There is nothing in the Hebrew prophets, nothing in Buddhism or Islam, which implies the thesis that religious truth is the perquisite of a State.   The world religions make an appeal which is universal, plastered over, as they may come to be, by national and political labels.

Science, too, has a universal appeal and is built up by international effort and co-operation.   The patent scientific secret, which is the perquisite of an industry or a War Office, is a comparatively insignificant exception to the generally acknowledged principle that in the sphere of scientific discovery knowledge should be freely communicated to all the world.   The idea that a single nation or a single industrial trust could ever be in a position to monopolize for its own advantage an important group of scientific principles is rendered happily impossible by the general diffusion of scientific education throughout the world, and by the zeal for truth and wide co-operation which animates scientific workers.   The spread of science then is one of the great forces tending to make the international mind.

That science should be, as it undoubtedly is, more international in character than religion, is easily explained when we consider that religion differs from science in three particulars, each of which is calculated to impair its universal influence. Religion is popular : science is technical. Religion is concerned with questions with respect to which there can be many equivalent opinions because there is no certain knowledge. Science, on the other hand, asks questions to which it expects and can often obtain precise, certain, and valid answers. Finally, religion influences the passions of man, science only his reason. Religion can therefore be employed as a political force, either to keep people submissive to government, or to rouse people against government, or to create prejudice between one nation and another. To such violent usage the cold impassive figure of physical science does not readily lend itself.

It follows then as one of the ironies of history that the development of scientific interests and habits is a greater power making for internationalism than the most enthusiastic religion of humility and love. Men do not kill one another for the law of gravitation. But how many feuds and murders and internecine hates and jealousies has not history witnessed in the name of Christ,

> Whose pale face from the cross sees only this
> After the passion of a thousand years.

Nor is it only the largest religious issues which inflame the passions of men. The struggles between Catholic and Protestant Christians have been just as bloody as the long controversy between Christianity and Islam, and even within the Protestant fold itself there have been bitter struggles, which, as Scotland knows, have not stopped short of bloodshed.

Nevertheless religion, like science, must be reckoned among the international influences. To these, too, must be added that sound philosophy of trade, which, starting from Adam Smith and the French physiocrats, has in various degrees captured the policy and coloured the thinking of civilized States. It is true that Free Trade is by no means universal : it is true that the original free traders overrated the influence upon international friendship of the removal of fiscal barriers. It is true that since the days of Adam Smith some objections not anticipated in the *Wealth of Nations* have been levelled against the extreme doctrine of *laissez-faire* in trade ; nevertheless there is not a Parliament in Europe to-day in which it would be seriously held by a leading statesman that a country could benefit economically by the ruin of its neighbours, or that foreign trade could be otherwise carried on than by an exchange of goods and services judged profitable at the time to either party to the exchange, or that a country was not advantaged economically by devoting its labour and capital to those branches of production which it could develop at the least comparative cost and by supplying itself from abroad with such commodities as it could only produce for itself at a great comparative sacrifice. In times of great political tension the solid advantage of a trade between two nations is often remembered. Self-interest supplies the place of sympathy, and eventually paves the way to understanding. Moreover, it is increasingly evident that the economic interests of the whole world are so closely intertwined that it is impossible that one country should prosper or fail without distributing some share of its prosperity or failure through the world. Recent history affords some striking illustrations of the extent to which this economic solidarity is now recognized by statesmen. The trade agreement between Great Britain and Bolshevik Russia was repugnant to many persons in this country, who regarded any connexion with a government stained by such crimes as those attributed to the Bolsheviks, and professing a philosophy so subversive of the established order of things, as dishonouring and savouring of impiety. Nevertheless the agreement was struck. It was contended that the convalescence of the continent of Europe was essential to the full employment of labour at home; that Russia had been and might again become a great market for British goods, and that the resumption of trade relations with a country so rich in foodstuffs and raw materials must in the end bring its own reward. Political antagonism gave way to economic good sense, hot sentiment to cold reason, well-grounded moral aversion to an appreciation of the complex bonds which unite nations far sundered in race, language, and psychology into a whole, every part of which is economically dependent on every other.

A second instance, even more striking, of the same perception of economic solidarity is afforded by the action recently taken by the League of Nations to retrieve the desperate economic fortunes of Austria. In this case a small State conquered in war, and owing a large debt to its conquerors, had partly by misfortune and partly by bad management drifted far down the road to irretrievable insolvency. Its currency was disorganized, its expenditure was far in excess of its revenue; its foreign trade was at a standstill; its government was too weak to face the unpopular measures through which alone salvation might be found. But the collapse of Austria could not be regarded with indifference by the business world of Europe. Even if there had been no place for sentiment, self-interest would have indicated the necessity of taking means to save from destruction the principal banking centre of South-eastern Europe. A country with an historic capital and with great potential assets could not be allowed to go down without involving all Europe in lasting discredit. So it was resolved to concert means for the relief of Austria. The foreign liens were released. An external loan was guaranteed by important Governments, and a scheme of economic and social reform was imposed upon the country. There are few more striking instances of international solidarity than this elaborate measure of economic assistance rendered to a vanquished people by the concerted action of their conquerors at the conclusion of a long and stubbornly fought war.

One other international influence of comparatively recent growth but of rapidly increasing importance may be noted. I allude to the doctrine of the solidarity of labour, which is the outcome of the industrial system combined with the spread of the newspaper press and of State-aided gratuitous education. That the interests of manual workers all over the world are identical is plainly contrary to the fact. They are often in the sharpest contradiction. But that the manual workers of the world may have a common interest in modifying the scheme of industrial society under which they live in some way more advantageous to themselves is an arguable proposition, and it is the belief that this proposition deserves to be argued which has given the world its international labour congresses and socialistic movements, and has spread the idea of the international co-operation of an oppressed class to effect, if not a violent revolution, at least an all-round improvement of social conditions. Socialism, Bolshevism, and their opposite, Fascism, are in effect not so much national as international phenomena.

It appears then that side by side with the growth of exclusive nationalism the world has been steadily developing an opposite set of tendencies, some religious and philanthropic, others strictly intellectual, others again social or economic, but all possessing this common characteristic, that they transcend national frontiers and contribute to strengthen an international view of affairs.

It is now pertinent to measure the strength of these international forces, to consider how far the world has actually progressed in subjecting the relations between States to the rule of law ; what still remains to be done and what chance there is of its being accomplished.

X

INTERNATIONAL LAW

' Find me an argument based on International Law and I will find you
a Professor to answer it.'—BISMARCK.

' Interest does not bind men together ; interest separates men. There
is only one thing that can bind people together and that is a common
devotion to right.'—PRESIDENT WILSON, 30 December 1918.

' TOUTES les bonnes maximes sont dans le monde, on ne
manque qu'à les appliquer.' There has probably been no time
in history since the emergence of organized States in which
there has not been some recognition of the elementary maxims
of international morality and some conception of the elementary principles of international law. To Aristotle the barbarian
was a natural slave and bereft of rights ; but within the wide
circle of Hellenic civilization there was ample room for the
development of an intermunicipal jurisprudence, which, though
it was never codified, came to be informed by similar, if not
identical, principles. No Greek State could lead a life of self-
sufficient isolation. Trade, religion, colonization, public games,
the need for contracting alliances for aggression or defence,
multiplied the relations between State and State, and created
the conception of a common Hellenic law and a common
standard of international justice. ' Have we not all ', asked
Demosthenes, ' the same laws and the same justice with regard
to commercial cases ? ' [1]   And apart from the laws to which
Demosthenes alludes, ' there were rules of public international law in case of peace concerning hospitality, asylums,

---

[1] Οὐχ ἅπασιν ἡμῖν οἱ αὐτοὶ νόμοι γεγραμμένοι εἰσὶ καὶ τὸ αὐτὸ δίκαιον περὶ τῶν
ἐμπορικῶν δικῶν ;—Dem. xxxv. c. 45.

extraditions, ambassadors, diplomatic negotiations, treaties, and alliances, balance of power and right of interventive arbitration; in times of war concerning sufficient causes of war, declaration of war, truce and armistice, ransom of prisoners, spies, hostages, reprisals, a certain neutralization, various mitigations of warfare, neutrality, maritime jurisdiction, embargo, blockade and piracy.'[1]   In particular the historian notes the frequency during the second and third centuries of international arbitration among the Greeks.   Now a dispute would be referred to an impartial city, now to an individual— how many were not referred to Alexander and his successors?— now to the Senate of Rome itself.   But it is hardly necessary to add that these refined and humane developments were consistent with a plentiful use of force in the settlement of disputes and a not infrequent disregard of the spirit of justice and legality by which they were inspired.[2]

The rise and spread of the Roman Empire opened a new era in the history of international jurisprudence.   The world of small city-states disappeared or rather was merged in a community coextensive with Western civilization and governed by a common political superior.   In such circumstances it was not possible to expect the development of a code of public international law, however numerous and intricate might be the relations of the Roman Empire with the barbarians on the frontier.   The course of development took another turn, and out of the relations between the Roman and the alien, since they could not be decided by the municipal law of either litigant, there grew up in contradistinction to the *Jus Quiritium* of Rome a law of nations administered by the Praetor Peregrinus, whose decisions were based upon principles assumed to

[1] F. E. Smith, *International Law*, ed. 5, p. 27.

[2] Vinogradoff, *Principles of Historical Jurisprudence*; M. N. Tod, *International Arbitration among the Greeks.*

be common to the legal systems of the world. It is easy to imagine how such a body of equitable principles, divested as it was of those special features which characterized the archaic law of Rome, and professing as it did to represent the common element in all legal systems, came to be invested with a peculiar authority. The Decretum of the Praetor Peregrinus—the decree, that is to say, in which the Roman judge whose office it was to adjust disputes between the Roman and the alien declared the lines upon which he proposed to administer justice—received the authority which must always belong to a statement of equitable principles believed to be universally respected. The commercial law of a commercial court, for such in origin was the *jus gentium*, was readily identified in the philosophic mind with that *jus naturae* or Law of Nature which Stoicism postulated now as the rule of a golden age, now as the ideal law which should govern a perfected society. So over against the particular laws prescribed for particular communities there grew up the conception of a law appointed by natural reason and common to all mankind. The contrast between these two systems, the one particular, the other universal, the one enacted to meet special needs, the other derived from the very nature of human reason itself, is clearly stated in the *Institutes* of Justinian, which summarizes the contents of Roman jurisprudence in the later half of the sixth century.

' All peoples who are ruled by laws and customs are governed partly by their own particular laws and partly by the laws which are common to all mankind. The law which a people enacts is called the civil law of that people, but that which natural reason appoints for all mankind is called the Law of Nations because all mankind uses it.'

This conception of a *Jus Naturae*, of an ideal system of jurisprudence, juster, more perfect, more congruous with the fundamental nature and needs of man and more self-evident than any of the existing bodies of municipal law, survived the chaotic struggles of the Middle Ages and was remembered in the closing stages of the wars of religion, when men began to turn their thoughts to a system of international relations reposing on some basis more satisfactory than force, fraud, or faithlessness. The great Dutchman, Hugo Grotius, whose famous treatise, *De Jure Pacis et Belli*, was published in 1625, in the middle of the horrors and atrocities of the Thirty Years' War, worked upon this ancient and fruitful conception of the Roman jurists. He assumed that States bore to one another the same relation as did the litigants of differing *gentes* who appeared before the Praetor Peregrinus of Rome. He assumed that they were in a state of nature, and that their mutual differences should be regulated by the law of nature. And as it was an integral part of the Roman conception of natural justice that all men were by nature equal, Grotius propounded the epoch-making doctrine of the equality of States.

It is no part of my present purpose to sketch the growth of international law since the days of Grotius. Partly through the work of publicists, partly through treaties and the decisions of prize courts and international congresses and arbitral tribunals, a great body of usage has now grown up which is described by the title of international law. What is, however, important to notice is that throughout all the changes and developments which have occurred in this region of public law and morality, the conception of the equality of States proclaimed by Grotius has been preserved as the foundation upon which the whole fabric has been erected.

Let us pause for a moment to consider this important doctrine. When two litigants appeared before the Praetor Peregrinus in Rome they were treated as equals before the law. One litigant might be powerful and rich, another powerless and poor. It was the duty of the court to regard them as equals and to see that the one litigant gained no advantage from his power and wealth and the other suffered no injury from his exiguous resources and lowly station. Whatever privileges might attach to the status of an individual by law and custom of his own city, these rights and privileges were of no account in a litigation with a foreigner. The Law of Nature recognized no adventitious distinction. It treated every man as equal to every other, as the subject of rights and obligations common to all humanity.

This principle was now transferred to the relation between State and State by Grotius and his successors, and is an essential part of modern international law. How far, however, is the analogy exact? How far is it right or possible to treat States as equals, when in point of size and importance and weight of intellectual and moral force they are clearly unequal? And how far is this doctrine of the assumed equality of States in effect observed?

It may be admitted at once that every State, no matter what its size may be, is entitled to equal and equitable consideration; that in any question of litigation between States the rule of equality should apply, and that no rule of international law could be regarded as fair or reasonable which differentiated against small States; that the United States, for instance, would not be justified in claiming greater privileges for its ships in foreign ports than Holland or Norway; and that any differentiation in domestic legislation against the nationals of a small State would violate the most elementary canons of international decency. But are we entitled to go a step farther and to maintain that States should not only be equal before the law, but that in any international organization they should be accorded an equivalent measure of authority? Surely not. Nobody would regard it as reasonable that the international relations of the world should be regulated by a majority vote in an assembly in which every State had an equal voice irrespective of size. Such an arrangement, irrespective of national prejudices, would involve too great a divorce of responsibility from power. How could it be reasonable that the voice of Luxemburg or Albania should determine the movements of the British Navy, that Costa Rica and Panama should dictate a policy only capable of being executed by the forces of Argentina and Brazil, or that in a matter gravely affecting her economic interest, such as the distribution of raw material, a combination of small European States should seek to impose its will upon the Federal Government in Washington?

In fact, though the making of international law has largely been the work of the small Protestant States (for the less powerful a State is, the greater its interest in the preservation of international order), the principle of national sovereignty has been far too jealously safeguarded to permit of any such usurpations either of small Powers over great or of great Powers over small being effected by a process of peaceful arrangement. Even the Federal Empire of Germany was not built up without the shedding of much German blood, so little did community of race and speech and economic interest avail to break down the obstinate body of pride and prejudice with which the life of a sovereign State, however small and insignificant, is invariably supported.

Nevertheless, within certain limits the small States accommodate themselves to habits of submission. Both in the New World and in the Old, material force carries with it a share of international superintendence, which is accepted as inevitable and convenient. The Government of the United States exercises such a superintendence over the States of the New World, and regards itself in virtue of the Monroe doctrine as specially charged with the duty of fending them from European aggression and of preserving the whole American continent (with the exception of Canada) from such serious internal convulsion as might degrade and dishonour the civilization of the New World. A similar office of superintendence over the affairs of the Balkans and the eastern Mediterranean was undertaken by the Great Powers in Europe after the War of Greek Independence; and the Concert of Europe, as it has been called, despite numerous evidences of discord and failure (for it could not prevent the Crimean War or the Russo-Turkish War of 1877), survived as a diplomatic force, sometimes relatively effective, as in its successful efforts to circumscribe the war between Greece and Turkey in 1897, sometimes openly flouted by one of its own members, as in the cynical annexation of Bosnia and Herzegovina by Austria in 1909, until the outbreak of the Great War.

Nor has the conception of a certain indefinite prerogative of police and regulation on the part of the greater Powers been extinguished by that great catastrophe. It survives in the organization of the Council of the League of Nations, which provides for the permanent representation of the five great allied and associated States which were actively prosecuting the war up to the day of the Armistice. Indeed, it is hard to see how any international system could achieve success which did not pay due regard to the sentiment and influence of the greater Powers.

The student who surveys the long series of wars and revolutions which have darkened the page of history may be tempted to disparage the credentials of international law. Despite Gentile and Suarez, despite Grotius and Vattel, despite the Concert of Europe and the Conference of The Hague, war remains, more costly, more destructive, more terrible with every advance in physical science and social organization.

What, he may exclaim, is the value of international law? It has not prevented war or the preparation for war. It has not availed against the competition in armaments. It has not averted the use of poisonous gas, or the sinking of merchantmen at sea, or the torpedoing of hospital ships. On the contrary, modern war is waged upon a huger plan, with greater ruthlessness, with more loss and injury to the civilian and noncombatant population, and carries with it a longer train of economic disorders than any war waged before the advent of physical science and conscription. The international lawyers may shut up their books. The fact of the Chinese Empire has done more to secure peace over a large tract of the globe than all the treatises which have been published by the jurists. It is rather to the formation of great States, like the British Empire and North America and China, than to the speculations of lawyers and moralists, that humanity must look for its relief from the scourge and the scandal of war.

The answer to such a mood of scepticism is supplied in an admirable phrase by Sir Henry Maine. 'What we have to notice', he wrote in 1888, 'is that the founders of International Law, though they did not create a sanction, created a law-abiding sentiment. They diffused among sovereigns and the literate classes in communities a strong repugnance to the neglect or breach of certain rules regulating the relations and actions of States. They did this not by threatening punishments but by the alternative and older method, long known in Europe and Asia, of creating a strong approval of a certain body of rules.' Thus there is a strong approval of the rule that a State is entitled to settle its own constitution, its own fiscal system, and to build such railways as it pleases, and however much apprehension may be caused on any one of these heads, it is now a fixed principle of international law that these are matters within the exclusive domestic competence of a sovereign State, and consequently that a remonstrance addressed upon any one of these questions by a foreign State would give legitimate ground for resentment. Thus while Great Britain waged war against revolutionary France in the eighteenth and against revolutionary Russia in the twentieth century, the ground of action was in neither case a denial that a country was entitled to upset its own constitution. William Pitt did not engage in war against France because a republic was substituted for a monarchy, but because the armies of the Republic invaded the Netherlands and proclaimed their intention of opening the Scheldt, which by international agreement had been closed to any but Dutch commerce. And much as the recent Coalition Government disliked the Communist Revolution in Russia, diplomatic negotiations would not have been broken off if the Bolshevik Government had not repudiated its obligations towards the Allies, refused to carry on the war with Germany, proclaimed a policy of world-wide revolutionary propaganda, and murdered a British emissary.

On the whole it cannot be doubted that the general acceptance of the rule against non-interference in the domestic affairs of another State makes for the general peace. A government may dislike the tariff policy of its neighbour or may suspect that its neighbour's railway developments have a strategic and not a commercial object; but if it were to expostulate, it would at once be told to mind its own business. There is nothing upon which nations are so sensitive as the attempt on the part of alien Powers to influence or deflect the course of their internal policy.

Such action could indeed only properly be taken in one of two circumstances. If, for instance, a country had come to the conclusion that the railway system of its neighbour was being deliberately planned with the view to an invasion, it might feel itself justified in risking a war by demanding explanations; or again, if a country allied with another country had reason to believe that the course of its ally's internal policy was such as to inflict injury upon their common interests by exciting the suspicions of a third party and provoking counter-preparations, it might take advantage of its friendly relations to tender advice. In general, however, the rule most conducive to the preservation of peace is that which assumes that every nation is friendly and animated by friendly intentions, until clear and unmistakable evidence is given to the contrary; and there can be little question that the rule of international law which prescribes non-interference with the domestic affairs of other States contributes greatly to diminish possible causes of international friction.

A further illustration of the value of international law is afforded by the history of the partition of Africa in the nineteenth century. This great operation, which in any earlier age would have been the cause of unending conflict between the partitioning powers, was effected by a series of agreements, in which France, Great Britain, Germany, and Belgium participated. Spheres of influence were marked out in advance, and all the unallotted land in a vast continent was divided among those few European nations who had already established settlements upon it and might be expected to extend their activities over the vacant spaces. It is true that this great series of operations was not effected by any process which could be described as judicial. The partition of Africa was the result not of legal judgements or of the application of legal rules, but of acts of policy; but the atmosphere which rendered such acts of policy possible was created by international law and by the sentiments from which international law draws its nourishment. For a violent scramble there was substituted an orderly and well-regulated process.

A third illustration of the value of international law is afforded by the steady growth of arbitration during the century preceding the Great War. The discovery and development of fresh modes of locomotion, occasioning and accompanying the expansion of commercial intercourse, have by increasing the volume of international business multiplied the occasions of difference between State and State. Every decade makes our Foreign Offices more sensitive to external events. And if there were no peaceful means of liquidating the diurnal variances which occupy their attention, the world would be a very grim and fearful place. Arbitration is a serviceable expedient to this end. Its development may in fact be regarded as a measure of the increasing interconnexion of States which results from modern travel, modern science, and modern trade. In the decade between 1820 and 1840 there were, according to Senator Lafontaine, eight cases of arbitration, in the succeeding decade there were twenty, in the decade succeeding that forty-four, and between 1880 and 1900 ninety. The first Peace Conference at The Hague, which met in 1899, drew up a Convention for the Pacific Settlement of International Disputes, and more than a hundred treaties of arbitration were subsequently signed between the Powers. It is then no exaggeration to say that before the outbreak of the Great War the progress made by the principle of arbitration had been one of the most remarkable and encouraging features in the international landscape. All the civilized States had signed treaties of arbitration with one Power or another. Many important matters, such as the Alabama dispute, had been referred to arbitration and successfully decided, nor had there been any case in which an unsuccessful party had refused to give effect to a valid award.

There were, however, very definite limits to the value of arbitration. The arbitration treaties in almost every case made an exception of disputes involving matters of vital interest or the independence and honour of the contracting parties. Treitschke ridiculed the idea that Germany could ever submit to arbitration the case of Alsace, and had some reason for his contention that arbitration was only employed in the settlement of disputes of tertiary importance. Yet even when full allowance has been made for the reluctance of States to submit matters affecting their honour and independence or some vital national interest to the decision of an arbitral court, it does not follow that arbitration is not to be counted among the effective agencies making for the preservation of peace. Wars often result from an accumulation of minor grievances and quarrels. If these are tended without delay, if little ailments are healed before they become poisonous and inflame the system, countries may continue to preserve good relations for an indefinite time, despite numerous collisions of interest. Great Britain has on more than one occasion in her history gone to war in a dispute far less serious than the variance with France over the conscription of British subjects in the French African colonies, which was recently settled by the International Court at The Hague.

Three other illustrations may be given of the importance attaching to the growth of a body of rules for the regulation of international intercourse. There was at one time a very prevalent idea that seas and even oceans could be treated as part of the exclusive dominion of sovereign States. The doctrine of the ' mare clausum ' found a champion in John Selden, who argued that the narrow seas belonged by right to the sovereign of Great Britain and could be lawfully closed to alien traffic. And in a form very much more extended and dangerous to the commercial development of the New World, the same philosophy was entertained by the two great navigating powers of the Iberian Peninsula. Now this doctrine was so inimical to the general interest of human society that it must in the end have given way to the pressure of circumstances; but that it was so speedily replaced by the existing understanding (i.e. that outside a three-mile limit the sea should be free to all nations) is due to Grotius and his successors. It was international law which gave the *coup de grâce* to the idea that the high seas could be converted into the private property of adjacent or pioneering States, and ruled that sovereign States were entitled to such rights only over the sea as were necessary to the preservation and protection of their territories. The rule was so congruous with common sense and the common interest that it has been generally accepted, and an ambiguity which might have been the cause of endless disputes has consequently been removed.

Again, the invention of the dirigible air-vessel has brought out very clearly the value attaching to the existence of a body of accepted legal principles capable of being extended to unforeseen cases. To whom does the air belong? Is air space free to all or is it the property of the subjacent sovereign State? The principle of international law which prescribes the three-mile limit at sea is clearly applicable to the decision of this novel and important question. A State is entitled to sovereignty over a belt of territorial waters, generally limited to three miles, because, if it were not accorded sovereignty to that extent, its territory would be insecure, and it would be unable to enforce certain laws and regulations (e. g. the collection of customs) essential to the government of its territory. It is not entitled to sovereignty over the seas beyond the three-mile limit, because the exercise of such wide rights would not add to its security and would be prejudicial to the general interest of the world. Let this principle be extended from the sea to the air, and it at once becomes apparent that the air should not be free to all, but that every State has a right to

regulate the user of the air above its territory in the interests
of its own self-government and security.

A third illustration is afforded by the special international
precautions which have been taken to regulate the status of
certain territories and waterways. Switzerland was neutralized
by the Convention of Vienna in 1815, and the neutrality of
Switzerland has been consistently observed despite strong
military temptations to violate it in the Franco-Prussian War
and in the Great War. The General Act of the Berlin Conference in 1885 neutralized the Congo and prescribed that
commerce and navigation in that vast region should be free
to all nations. The status of the Suez Canal was regularized
by the Treaty of Constantinople in 1888. The Panama Canal
was neutralized and opened to the navigation of the world
by the Treaty of Washington in 1901.

It may be argued by the cynic that such arrangements are
well enough so long as they happen to suit the convenience of
certain powerful nations, but that the world has no guarantee
that they will be permanently respected, and that the case
of Belgium, whose neutrality was guaranteed by treaty in 1837
and signally violated by one of the guaranteeing Powers in
1914, is a clear proof of the assertion. The case of Belgium,
however, affords a very interesting indication not of the weakness but of the strength of the sentiments supporting the fabric
of international law. The attack upon a small and innocent
country would in any case have aroused moral indignation
throughout the world, but that indignation was sensibly
deepened by the knowledge of the fact that in plain violation
of her pledged faith Germany was marching troops into
a country of whose neutrality she was a joint guarantor. To
the independent judgement of the world no apologies which
could be offered by the German Government as to the machina-
tions of her enemies availed against the patent fact that she

ad set her hand to a treaty and then broken it. And among
ιe causes which contributed to the defeat of the Central
owers in the late war none was more powerful than the
iscovery that they were prepared to defy the public law of
urope in subservience to national and military ends. The
pen cynicism which Bismarck infused into the conduct of
ιternational affairs brought at last the nemesis which always
vertakes those who persistently disparage the better impulses
f man and found their lifework upon a low estimate of human
ature. The violation of Belgian neutrality showed, what no
ιe has ever doubted, that under the overmastering temptation
ɔ secure an advantage in war, nations cannot be relied upon
ɔ respect the provisions of international law or morality;
ut it has also established the extreme danger which attaches
ɔ such lawless courses and the ease with which the sentiment
f that portion of the world whose partialities are not imme-
iately engaged in the conflict can be marshalled against the
ιwless aggressor.

The fact that international law is neither enacted by a
·gislature nor enforced by a police and that it is consequently
ιcking in two distinctive qualities of law, a sovereign originat-
ιg and enforcing authority and a definite and recognized set
f penal sanctions, imposes certain obvious limits upon its
sefulness and power. A system of law which is neither
ιacted by a single legislature nor interpreted by a single
ourt, which it is no one's business in particular to improve, to
xpand, or to adapt to the changing conditions of the world,
·hich may on occasions be disregarded or defied without
npleasant consequences for the contumacious State, which is
ɔ be gathered from text-books and legal decisions rather than
rom authoritative codes, offers a certain surface to criticism.
uch a system will present anomalies, incoherences; particular
rovisions will be subject to disputed interpretations. And

from time to time, when occasion serves, the authority of the whole system will be weakened by some act of defiance levelled against it by a powerful State.

Particularly is this likely to be the case in time of war. Indeed, the violations of the laws of war established by international usage which occurred during the last conflict were so numerous and flagrant that the world began to wonder whether this body of political morality, for such it is, will ever be invested with a sufficient measure of authority to restrain any Power who finds an urgent and immediate interest in violating one of its principles. The voice of the cynic will be heard declaring that the laws of war which compose a great part of what is known as international law are merely the rules which the belligerents in the last war have thought it convenient to adopt and will exercise no binding influence upon posterity. Experience, however, supplies a qualification to such wholesale scepticism. Terrible as were many of the circumstances of the Great War, the efforts of the international lawyers to humanize warfare were not entirely in vain. Prisoners were neither butchered nor enslaved, as in ancient times, but treated upon the whole with fair consideration. The Geneva Convention signed in 1864 and adopted by the United States of America in 1882 was in the main faithfully adhered to by all the belligerents, though some hospital ships were attacked and sunk by German submarines. Indeed, at no period of history have the arrangements for the tending of the sick and wounded during a war been carried to so high a point of humanity and scientific perfection.

A body of customs, rules, and precedents then exists which may be invoked for the settlement of international disputes or for the regulation of the conduct of neutrals and belligerents in war. Some of these rules are practically uncontested. Others, like the laws regulating blockade and contraband of var, may, as the letters of Ambassador Page remind us, furnish matter for vehement and even dangerous controversy between riendly nations. One of the real difficulties which impede he equal and ready acceptance of the laws of war by all the parties whom they may affect is that, war being a series of urprises, and each war presenting some special feature which ither could not be foreseen or had not in effect been foreseen, new rules are made by belligerents in the heat of the conflict, vhich have never been discussed in advance and to which violent objection is often taken. Thus in the late war it was found necessary by the Powers blockading Germany not only o give a great extension to the list of commodities which international lawyers describe as ' conditional contraband of var ', but also to widen the conception of an ' effective blockade '. Further, since it was necessary to prevent supplies passing into Germany through neutral territory, the blockading Powers were driven to an expedient unknown in previous wars, of placing a neutral country upon a strict ration of sea-borne goods estimated to be adequate for its internal consumption and of prohibiting the introduction into its harbours of goods in excess of the allotted share. It cannot be denied that so wide an extension of the law of blockade constitutes a serious infraction of the sovereign rights of a neutral Power, but since it does not entail any necessary diminution of the material comfort and well-being of the neutral community, and injures no interest save that of the war profiteer, it is not at variance with the essential spirit of that part of international law which deals with the rights of neutrals.

The value of international law is too often apt to be assessed by what is in fact, from the point of view of the interests of civilization, its least important function, that is to say, the success or failure which may attend its efforts to proscribe

certain methods of making war as barbarous or inhuman
That such efforts are more likely to fail than to succeed i
unhappily illustrated by long experience. Every new military
artifice—the crossbow, gunpowder, poison-gas, the Zeppelin—
is at first regarded with moral disapprobation as a violation
of the rules of fair play and chivalry which are supposed to
govern the conduct of military operations. By degrees opinion
hardens, and what was at first regarded as an atrocity i
tolerated as a necessary horror of war and an interesting field
for scientific investigation. Nevertheless, international law
expressing the general sentiment of mankind, deprecates the
use of weapons which, like the soft-nosed bullet, cause un
necessary suffering. No humane man will disparage the value
of such scruples. But it is difficult to see how, in view of th
great development of aerial warfare, high-explosive gas shells
and long-range artillery, it will be possible to avoid the inflic
tion of a great deal of unnecessary suffering upon combatant
and non-combatants alike in any future war.

The truth is that we have reached a point when we may
well ask ourselves the question whether it is possible to limi
the destructiveness of the weapons employed in warfare, and
whether any good purpose is served by the attempt to do so
What, it may be asked, can be more terrible than the effect
of a high-explosive shell? What outrage upon humanity can
be greater than the bombing from the air of the civilian
quarter of a town? Or than the dispersal of mines in th
high seas? If such occurrences are inevitable incidents i
modern warfare, why not accept the fact that war refuses to
be humanized, and that the true path of advance lies not i
the futile attempt to introduce temperaments and alleviation
into that which is in its essence an explosion of the savage
forces in man, but in a resolute effort to prevent war altogether

There is a school of opinion which takes the view that the

more terrible war becomes, the less likely are nations to engage in it. The efforts to humanize wars are, therefore, in any case misjudged. So far as they are successful, they tend to perpetuate wars; and so far as they are unsuccessful, they are a wasted and misdirected use of energies which might be more profitably employed.

The belief that Governments are deterred from going into a war by the formidable character of the weapons with which war is waged is not conformable to experience. On the contrary, most wars arise out of anxiety, out of a feeling that some other nation is plotting hostilities, or will become more formidable if left alone. The knowledge that aerial bombs had been increased a hundredfold in destructiveness would not deter any Government from entering into a war if a sufficient cause of quarrel seemed to present itself, for with the natural hopefulness of a belligerent it would calculate upon being able to repay with interest any damage which it might receive.

There is, indeed, an element of truth in the doctrine that wars become more infrequent in proportion as they become more destructive. The more destructive a war, the greater the injury inflicted upon trade and commerce and the longer the period necessary for convalescence. A war waged upon the modern scale and with modern appliances is a luxury so costly that it is only at comparatively long intervals that the well organized industrial nations of the world will be able to afford it. In this sense it is true that the increasing destructiveness of war may contribute to prolong the intervals of peace; but even this expectation may be falsified, for the discovery of some new lethal process of transcendent efficacy might tempt a nation not far advanced in economic convalescence to find an immediate pretext for its employment.

Too much weight, therefore, must not attach to the

argument that it is foolish to attempt to limit the barbarities of war, on the ground that barbarity in itself acts as a deterrent. Such attempts have often failed in the past, and will doubtless often fail in the future. But are they, therefore, not worth making? Let us consider for a moment the question of gas warfare. When this expedient was first employed by the Germans it was received with a chorus of indignant denunciation as an atrocity inconsistent with international law and the dictates of humanity. And the manufacture and importation of poisonous gases has been expressly forbidden to Germany under Art. 171 of the Treaty of Versailles. Nevertheless, in spite of this attitude, every great military Power, save Germany, is now engaged in perfecting its gas arm, and every year animals are submitted to painful experiments in order that a yet more lethal form of gas than any yet discovered may be placed at the service of the General Staff.

It is difficult to draw the line between gas and disease-bearing bacilli. The argument may indeed be, and has been, advanced that gas is in any case less painful than high explosive, and that science may in future discover various forms of gas which may effect the military purpose of an army with the minimum of suffering to its opponents. It may be possible to send an army to sleep by gas, or to drive it into an unconquerable fit of coughing and sneezing by gas, or to give it influenza by gas, or in some other gaseous method to incapacitate it during a period sufficiently long to enable victory to be secured. The advocates of gas claim in fact that we are on the threshold of a medical epoch in warfare, when victory at once moral and material will come to the nation which is most speedily able to incapacitate its enemy by the infliction of a mild, curable, but decisive disease. But how guarantee that the disease will be mild? A test-tube dropped into the water-supply of London or Berlin might put either of these capitals out of action. And if it be legitimate to undermine the lungs with gas, why is it indefensible to attack the intestines with typhoid germs?

It may be urged that these two forms of warfare can be differentiated by the fact that the effects of the one can and those of the other cannot be confined to the combatant forces. If this were true, it would be a valid distinction. But is it true? In modern war the distinction between the combatant and non-combatant forces of a nation is very fine, for the whole population is enlisted, in one form or another, in the common effort. And even if this were not the case, the gas bombs thrown from an aerial squadron sailing seven or eight thousand feet above the sleeping town are not very discriminating in the matter of the uniforms of their victims. The distinction, indeed, between poisoning by gas or poisoning by bacilli is so fine that its scrupulous observance in a future war would be a matter for surprise.

If this argument be correct, what is to be done? Should an effort be made to eliminate chemical warfare from legitimate military expedients? Or should an international congress be summoned at some convenient time with a view to the proscription of certain gases which inflict needless suffering? Or should the elimination or restriction of gas warfare be regarded as a hopeless endeavour, the clause in the Treaty of Versailles be annulled, and all effort be concentrated on an attempt to prevent the extension of medical warfare into other fields? Or should international law proclaim its impotence in this regard also, and allow science to do its worst without let or hindrance, in the hope that somehow or other the moral sense of man may, at the critical moment, apply correctives sufficient at least to save the fabric of civilization from destruction? These are grave issues, which when the fevers of the body politic are further abated, will deserve serious discussion.

When that time comes, two observations will certainly be offered : first, that it is vain to expect that the advance of physical science can be arrested by the fiat of the international lawyers ; and secondly, that the discoveries of science are of so impalpable and elusive a character that even if a League of Nations were voluntarily to place itself under restrictions as to the military use of scientific inventions, no member of the League could feel adequately secured that its fellows were observing the pact.

We have then to recognize the fact that mankind may fail to obtain any agreed restriction of these new and more terrible applications of knowledge to military purposes. It is, indeed, most probable that any endeavour further to limit or modify the instruments of war in the name of humanity will be foiled by the inexorable march of science. Just as the bow and arrow displaced the sling, and the bow was displaced by the musket, and this again by the rifle, so all our modern implements of war may in a short space of time yield to a machinery more formidable than any of which the world has yet experience.   There are only two methods of averting such a contingency, neither likely to commend itself. The first is a general and agreed determination on the part of the governments of the world to abstain from the use of new scientific expedients, and the second is the concerted refusal of the laboratories to supply them. Whether our men of science can ever be brought to such a point of pacificism may be doubted ; but if the laboratories are not converted, the American zealots for the ' outlawry of war ' will make little progress towards their end.

The real limiting force will, we suspect, be found in a very different sphere. International law will do something, but it will not do very much. What will abridge wars and divest them of some of their potential horrors will be the huge initial cost of undertaking them. If scientific warfare were as cheap as it is now fortunately expensive, there would be very little hope of saving humanity from evils which might shatter the fabric of civilization itself. But the cost of killing a single enemy under the conditions of modern warfare is equivalent to the value of an old master or a successful thoroughbred, and before expenditure upon such a scale even the most quarrelsome nation may be disposed to hesitate. The discovery of some really inexpensive means of wholesale destruction would change the face of the problem, and at once raise the question in its most acute form whether human society had the strength and wisdom to combine for its own survival.

In such a last emergency the sentiment which goes to the making of international law could alone save civilization.

XI

THE REDUCTION OF ARMAMENTS

'Ce qui compte pour la guerre ce n'est pas le nombre abstrait des hommes, c'est le total des hommes instruits.'—M. Paléologue.

'What counts in war is not the size of the population, but the number of trained men.'

'La guerre est une chose trop sérieuse pour qu'on la laisse aux militaires.' —A. Briand.

'War is too serious a matter to be left to the soldiers.'

The experience of the late war has imparted a new character of urgency to a question which has often been asked before, but without any sanguine or widespread expectation of an answer. Is war an inevitable outcome of human nature? Can it be averted either by a better organization of international relations or by a new direction of educational effort? Or must we to the end of time expect that wars will continue to be waged, each more destructive than the last, as science improves its lethal weapons, with every advance in patriotic self-discipline which the high organization of a modern State may secure?

This is no longer an academic question, the discussion of which is confined to a narrow circle of philosophical students. Plain men and women, who are neither philosophers nor students, are compelled to regard the problem of war and its prevention as one of the primary preoccupations of society. They see two things now very clearly: first, that the world may drift and blunder into a great disaster, without any clear-cut will to war moving the rulers of the contending States; and second, that modern scientific war takes on a character of mechanical destructiveness so alarming, so careless of the old immunity of the non-combatant population, so limitless in its possible extensions, that the problem of the prevention of war assumes a new form. It is no longer a question of an evil easily localized and by its nature so limited as to affect a very small section of the population in the combatant population, no longer a question of a malady which may easily have no injurious sequelae, but on the contrary effect an improvement in the health of the patient. Modern war differs so greatly from the wars of the pre-scientific age in its contagiousness, its range of destruction, and its cost, that it raises an entirely new problem. It compels us to ask whether if civilized society does not succeed in extirpating war, war will not succeed in extirpating civilized society.

One conclusion will be generally accepted. Though the incident which gives rise to a war may be trivial, the predisposing causes are for the most part weighty and complex. A diplomatist may commit an error, a Cabinet may be carried off its feet by a gust of passion or prejudice, and from either of these causes a war may result which with wiser or more prudent handling might have been averted. But nations are not brought to the point at which such accidents are possible save by a long train of exacerbating preliminaries. The fault of a diplomatist does not occasion a rupture between two countries unless there has been a considerable period of previous tension. A Cabinet in a democratic State does not lead a nation into war unless it is assumed in advance that it will receive support, grounded either upon adequate previous intellectual preparation or upon strong traditional antagonisms or else the clear and manifest sense of injury and indignity which the advertisement of the quarrel is likely to disclose. Great wars for the most part arise from great passions and involve great issues. In the first glow of controversial resentment a war may be attributed to this or that statesman; but history, gradually shaking itself free from the mists of contemporary prejudice, spreads the responsibility more widely, showing how all the various elements of national life which tend to inflame opinion or to make war an interesting or familiar thought to a people combine to create the atmosphere in which a single flying spark may spread a desolating conflagration through a whole countryside.

Among the larger predisposing causes of international suspicion, there is none more obvious than the growth of armaments. Every nation has the right to secure itself against attack, and if all nations were equally powerful and equally impregnable, any temptation to war which might arise from a reasonable expectation of success would be removed. It has therefore sometimes been argued that great armaments tend to the preservation of peace, and that the military weakness of a country is an invitation to its neighbours to invade it. We do not deny that weak countries have been attacked by powerful neighbours, or that under weak governments conditions of disorder may easily arise which are calculated to lead to forcible intervention from outside. A great disparity of military power between two high-spirited and ambitious States, whose political interests are divergent, may tempt the nation which is conscious of being possessed of the superior military force to presume upon its position and to adopt a dictatorial tone in its diplomacy which arouses resentment and produces reprisals.

But all this argument rests upon the supposition of a disparity of force, not of a balance either scale of which is lightly weighted by mutual agreement. And the case for such a lightly weighted balance rests upon the undoubted fact that heavy and expanding armaments lead to war, that a State fully organized for war is more likely to pick a quarrel than a State which realizes that it is unprepared, that vast preparations for war create vested interests, part material, part intellectual, in war; that an armed nation is compelled to write, read, and think about war, that it treats military service as one of its staple intellectual preoccupations, and that being saturated with the spirit and literature of conflict it is the more ready to believe in force as the normal arbiter of serious disputes.

The usual apology presented for expanding armaments is that they are required in self-defence. That was the case presented by Imperial Germany both for her army and her navy in the decades preceding the outbreak. That is the apology which France now offers for her large army and for her increasing expenditure in submarines and aircraft. That is the reply which Great Britain has always put forward when criticism has been passed upon the size of her navy. The misfortune is that these apologies, however sincerely they may be intended by those who make them, never obtain credence. Any armament strong enough to be used in offensive operations is held in suspicion by those against whom it may conceivably be employed, however pacific may be the present intentions of the country possessing it. The French argue, doubtless with entire sincerity, that their present military expenditure is required in order to maintain the treaties, and that they would be glad enough if Great Britain would relieve them of part of their military burden. Let Great Britain re-arm and France could partially disarm. But however much conviction this argument may carry to French minds, it does not impress public opinion on this side of the Channel. A disarmed country is always rendered uneasy by the spectacle of progressive armaments in other parts of the globe. Its apprehensions may be unreasonable. It may have nothing in reality to fear, but the nerves of nations are highly strung, and the intelligence of great activity in the docks or munition factories of another Power, however friendly, is always likely sooner or later to lead to political pressure being placed on the Government to adjust its own military preparations to the enlarged armaments of its neighbour.

There is then a clear case for an all-round limitation of armaments, or at least for a limitation of the armaments of the great military Powers, if it can be contrived. It is true that when a nation is once at war all limitations disappear, and that every ounce of national power, military, naval, financial, and economic, is thrown into the balance to achieve victory. But what influences the temperament of a people is the scale upon which its military and naval establishments are organized in time of peace. It is the peace effectives which it is necessary, if possible, to limit, and it is upon the problem of the limitation of the peace effectives that we should concentrate our attention.

The ease with which that problem can be solved differs with the character of the arm under consideration. It is easier to limit navies than armies, easier to limit armies than aircraft. A naval holiday can be contrived between certain great Powers, as the Conference of Washington shows, because a modern navy centres round the capital ship, and an agreement to abstain during a certain period from the construction of fresh capital ships or to reduce the construction programme is, especially if the countries concerned are anxious to economize and are tolerably satisfied with their relative naval position, comparatively easy of accomplishment. But even the limitation of naval armaments is not without difficulties. If a Power is ambitious of development, or if in the years previous to the Conference it has been economizing in naval armaments while a neighbour has been building, it will probably decline to come under a limiting agreement. Thus when at the third Assembly of the League of Nations a proposal was made for a conference to consider the extension to the minor naval powers of the principles governing the Washington Convention, Poland and Brazil raised a caveat, the first as a State ambitious of developing a navy, and the second on the ground that its existing naval establishment was inferior to its status and its needs. So long, however, as an agreement exists between the great naval Powers to limit their armaments, the absence of any agreed restriction of the minor navies is not likely greatly to disturb the peace of the world.

The limitation of land armaments is a matter of far greater complexity. Here there is no single very expensive unit corresponding to the capital ship, upon which all other parts of the organization depend and in relation to which they develop. Personnel and equipment, the weight of guns, and the strength of the aircraft establishment have all to be taken into account. A purely budgetary test, which seems so simple, is in truth delusive, so long as some nations have conscript and others voluntary armies, and while the level of wages and prices differ as between country and country.

And if we determine to concentrate upon the limitation of aircraft, the difficulties thicken. If air power depends on general industrial capacity, how is any nation to accept restrictions on that capacity? Then again, how discriminate between the needs of military and civil aviation, or secure that aircraft primarily constructed for civil needs will not be diverted to military ends in time of war? Certain countries may prefer to develop their air-arm in preference to their army and navy; others, on the contrary, may put their faith on sea and land. How, if there be such disparity in aim and practice, is the problem of compensation to be solved? It has been suggested that a limit might be placed on the number of air pilots, but even this proposal is not free from difficulty. One nation may have a conscript force. Another may recruit its air-arm by voluntary engagements. One nation may believe in long service; another may pass its pilots into a reserve after a short spell of active service. These considerations are sufficient to show that the problem of making a working and workable agreement for the limitation of the air-arm is not so simple as at first sight it might appear to be.

Still, it is probably sufficient for the broad purpose in view to take the numbers of men on active service in the land and air forces, and to assume that the equipment will adjust itself to the numbers. The assumption may, indeed, be very wide of the truth in many cases, and special allowances might have to be made for such deviations. There would, however, be few to contest the value of an international agreement under which all the great military Powers of the world would bind themselves down for a period of years to a peace establishment adequate to their domestic needs and to the fulfilment of their international obligations. But our difficulty consists in the measurement of those needs and those obligations. The view taken by country A of country B's needs and obligations does not necessarily coincide with, and is indeed likely to differ from, the views entertained upon the same subject by country B. But assuming that this difficulty is overcome in the only possible way, by each country being prepared to accept the estimate of its own peace needs put forward by every other party to the negotiation, there remains the further obstacle that some countries feel the need of some special measure of protection against the possible aggression of a neighbour. And so long as this sense of insecurity exists in any one country, it is difficult to reach any agreed scheme of limitation among its neighbours. Thus, if the small States neighbouring on Russia are doubtful as to the pacific intentions of their powerful neighbour, they may feel themselves compelled to maintain armaments upon a scale altogether beyond their requirements for the preservation of domestic order; and this high scale of armaments will inevitably, failing treaty stipulations to the contrary, exercise its influence over the preparations of their Western neighbours.

In one respect the difficulties of the problem have been theoretically diminished by the drastic measure of disarmament imposed upon the Central Powers and their Allies by the Peace Treaties. Germany, which is potentially the strongest military Power in Europe, has been forced to abandon conscription and to content herself with a regular military force only barely sufficient to maintain internal order. It would seem that the logical corollary to the disarmament of Germany would be the reduction of all the other land armies in Europe to a proportionate scale. Thus, if Germany with a population of 63 millions and a superficial area of 203,000 square miles was rationed with an army of 100,000 men, France with a population of 41 millions and a superficial area of 212,000 square miles might require an army of, let us say, 85,000, to which should be added such forces as were necessary to police her overseas possessions. The principle is clearly one which commends itself to human reason. Let the nations of the world combine to write off such forces as they maintain out of suspicion of their neighbours and agree to limit themselves to the effectives required for police purposes at home and in their overseas possessions. What could be more reasonable? What policy would be more welcome to the overburdened taxpayers? In what way could the growth and maintenance of international suspicion be more effectually checked? How could strained nerves be more speedily soothed and the world brought back to the paths of sanity?

Unfortunately there are obstacles, not insuperable, for no obstacle rooted in the political nature of man is insuperable, but serious. The first arises from the fact that some nations feel in need of a larger measure of security than is capable of being afforded by any scheme for the proportional reduction of peace effectives with reference to police standards. They see a neighbour and a possible enemy who by reason of a superiority in numbers, or technical equipment, or natural wealth, or by the possession of some geographical advantage, is potentially very formidable. They argue that in a war such a nation will possess advantages which must be expressly discounted in advance, and that it is only possible to consent to wholesale reductions in the peace establishment if there be adequate security that in the event of war breaking out, the disparity of force apprehended to result from these inequalities be effectually reduced. That, for instance, is part of the case of France in answer to those who urge that she may now safely reduce her peace effectives to the standard required by the needs of domestic police. She replies that Germany is a stronger and more populous country with a higher birthrate, a larger body of men trained to arms, a better railway system, and a superior capacity for mobilization, and that she dare not reduce her forces without guarantees. It is the provision of such special guarantees which creates the first difficulty.

The second obstacle consists in the circumstance that all nations are jealous of their sovereign power, and especially jealous of that part of their sovereign power which is concerned with the provision of means of defence. There is accordingly no type of international transaction upon which a State enters with more reserve and hesitation than one which even temporarily imposes a limit on the exercise of its freedom in the matter of armaments. Every proposal from the other side is jealously scrutinized by naval and military experts ; every concession is combated ; there is hardly a yard of the difficult road in which an ambush is not expected. A government must be very strong in popular support which comes out of uch a conference with a binding engagement to effect great reductions, so easily are such concessions misrepresented in the organs of the press or by an active opposition in Parliament as a blind surrender of supreme national interests.

Finally, there is the difficulty of securing the observance of the limitations consented to, or, what is perhaps more ineradicable, of preventing the growth of a suspicion that under the shelter of the pact a nation is secretly stealing a march upon its neighbours. This difficulty is no doubt greatly mitigated by the fact that in an age of popular institutions no government can conceal its budget and that the expenditure of a government, if carefully analysed, furnishes a rough test of its military preparations. On the other hand, the present state of the military art, and more particularly the development of dirigible aircraft, submarines, and chemical warfare, lends itself easily to forms of concealment which may evade detection in the public press of foreign countries. The march of science cannot be arrested, and the discovery of a solitary student in an obscure laboratory may give to his country a destructive process so powerful as in itself to upset the balance which had been so carefully arrived at by the diplomatist. Such contingencies are sufficient to nourish the plant of international suspicion in soil which is congenial to its growth.

A striking example of the difficulties which in the days before the Treaty of Versailles confronted the initiation and conduct of conversations upon this most delicate of international topics is afforded by the story of the abortive attempt of Emile Ollivier, the French Prime Minister, to secure simultaneous disarmament in France and Prussia a few months before the outbreak of the Franco-German War. Ollivier, who represented all that was best in French liberal thought, was anxious to lessen the financial burdens of France and to maintain European peace. To this end he conceived that there

could be no more effectual means than that Prussia should
express her willingness to enter into a scheme for a joint
reduction of armaments. But how was the suggestion to be
conveyed to Prussia without peril? If the French Government were directly to approach the Prussian Government
with a proposal for disarmament and the proposal were rejected,
what would be the effect on the public opinion of both countries? The Prussians would surely argue that the French
were suspicious of the friendliness of their intentions, and the
French that the Prussians had resolved on war. Nothing could
possibly have a more deplorable effect upon the public opinion
of both nations than the manifest miscarriage of an overture of
this kind. Even if the negotiations were kept a secret, it could
not fail to injure the relations between the two Governments,
either of which would suspect the other of unfriendly designs.
Accordingly, the French Prime Minister had resort to an
intermediary. He divulged his plan to Lord Lyons, the
British Ambassador in Paris, and requested the good offices of
the British Government. The Foreign Secretary at that time
was Lord Clarendon, than whom few British statesmen have
been more experienced in the handling of foreign affairs, and
so important did Lord Clarendon consider the preservation of
the strictest secrecy to be, that so far from communicating
the project to the Cabinet he only divulged it to two people,
the Queen and the Prime Minister. Nor did Lord Clarendon
think it advisable directly to approach Count Bismarck. He
wrote (2 February 1870) a dispatch to Lord Augustus Loftus
in Berlin to be shown to the Count, and in that dispatch
showed that he appreciated the reluctance which the King
of Prussia might feel in consenting to the reduction of an
army in which he had a paternal interest. Nevertheless, some
strong words were used by the British Foreign Secretary as
to the general desirability of disarmament. 'It is in the

general interest of Europe,' he wrote, 'of peace and of humanity, that I desire to invite the attention of Count Bismarck to the enormous standing armies that now afflict Europe by constituting a state of things that is neither peace nor war, but which is so destructive of confidence that men almost desire war with all its horrors in order to arrive at some certainty of peace—a state of things that withdraws millions of hands from productive industry and heavily taxes the people to their own injury and renders them discontented with their rulers. It is a state of things, in short, that no thoughtful man can contemplate without sorrow and alarm, for this system is cruel, it is out of harmony with the civilization of our age, and it is pregnant with danger.'

Bismarck, who had no intention of reducing the Prussian Army, readily found a reply. He urged, no doubt disingenuously, that he had not dared name the subject of the letter to his sovereign, who would have flown into a passion immediately at the thought that England was trying to weaken Prussia at the request of France. He said that Prussia was surrounded by enemies, that she was menaced with a war on two fronts, and that if she were to consent to reductions she must have guarantees from the neighbouring Powers to compensate her for the decrease of security which she had hitherto owed to her armies. And finally, he carried the war into the enemy's country. ' It is all very well for you,' he said, ' living in an island where no one can attack you, to preach disarmament, but put yourself in my skin. You would then think and act differently. What would you say if we were to say that your navy was too large, that you did not require so many ironclads, that you lavished too large a proportion of the taxation of the country in building ships, which in the peaceful disposition of Europe were not required ? ' Lord Clarendon, in fact, experienced a sharp rebuff ; but fortunately, neither the British nor the French public were made aware of an episode which, if known, might have exercised a disastrous influence on opinion.[1]

The whole problem of the reduction of armaments has now entered into a new phase with the foundation of the League of Nations. The fifty-four nations who have signed the covenant of the League have in effect bound themselves to co-operate in the task of reducing the burdens of armaments, and have accepted the principle of a full and frank interchange of military information. A machinery devised to promote disarmament and to maintain the world in a state in which armaments are reduced to the police level has been set up, and it will be to this machinery that the world will accordingly look for any comprehensive relief from the huge costs imposed upon it by international hatreds and suspicions.

It is, perhaps, too much to expect that the League, only now concluding the fourth year of its existence, and deprived of the co-operation of America, Russia, and Germany, should have made any great advance towards the solution of the problem. Armaments have indeed been reduced, but either by treaty compulsion or through economic necessity, each nation carrying out such reductions as have seemed convenient to itself. As yet no scheme of consentaneous limitation has been propounded by the League and accepted by its members. Not that the League has shown itself oblivious of the importance of the question. Indeed there is no issue of international politics to which the Assemblies of the League have successively devoted more attention or which has been more carefully explored by the committees appointed to deal with it. But circumstances have been difficult and progress correspondingly slow.

---

[1] Lord Newton's *Life of Lord Lyons* ; Ollivier's *L'Empire Libéral*, vol. xii, pp. 293–5, for a less exact account.

What principally retards advance is the search for some mode of effectually tranquillizing the apprehensions of France. A country twice invaded is twice shy; and France, which has suffered the humiliation and injury of two invasions during living memory, is, in spite of the overwhelming nature of her recent victory, full of angry and overmastering suspicion of Germany. The Rhine frontier, the goal of her political ambitions since the age of Philip le Bel, was denied her at the Peace Conference by the vehement opposition of America and Great Britain, anxious above all things to create no new Alsace-Lorraine in Europe. The Anglo-American pact of defence, which might serve as a compensation for so great a disappointment, was lost to her by the withdrawal of America, and the guarantee contained in Clause 10 of the Covenant of the League of Nations appears to the politicians of the Quai d'Orsay to be too generalized to furnish an adequate and effectual shield against the studied revenge of her powerful neighbour.

Principally to meet the special needs of France, the League has been considering the scheme of an open treaty of mutual guarantee to come into effect as soon as the nations concerned have carried out an agreed plan of disarmament. Such a treaty possesses many clear recommendations. Being open to all, it is not exposed to the reproach that it is calculated to favour the revival of those antagonistic groupings of powers which have been so fatal to peace in the past. Making the support of the guarantee dependent on the execution of an agreed plan of disarmament, it furnishes an important material motive to the reduction of war establishments. Finally, it is capable of being put into effect gradually, as State after State rallies to the idea.

To secure French assent to such a proposal two conditions are essential. A vague and indeterminate guarantee does not appeal to the military precisians who advise the Quai d'Orsay. If a guarantee is to furnish a basis for disarmament, it must be as precise as military conventions can make it. How, it is asked, can France be expected to put down two divisions, if Great Britain, assumed to be a guaranteeing power, can give her no information as to the number of divisions which she is prepared to furnish to France in case of invasion, and as to the number of days which must elapse before those divisions can take the field? It is, therefore, of the essence of the plan that the assistance to be given under the mutual treaty of guarantee should be according to a precise and detailed plan arranged in advance by the General Staffs of the countries concerned. A vague guarantee, such as was proposed by Mr. Lloyd George's Government to France, is not acceptable. It is not sufficient that the British Empire should be pledged to assist France in case of invasion. The French argue, with a logic which may be strictly military but is certainly not political, that a guarantee to be helpful to them must be based upon a military convention. The second condition, to which importance is not unnaturally attached, is the right of inspection and control. A nation which disarms itself by treaty has the right to be assured that her neighbour is conforming to the bond. She has the right to survey and scrutinize her neighbours' establishments, to take stock of her troops and her chemical works and her munition factories and her artillery. Only on such terms can a disarmament pact continue to bind a people.

The adoption of a general treaty of disarmament and guarantee, signed by all the nations of the world and maintained by the travelling circuits of commissions of the League of Nations, would connote so great an advance in the standard of public morality and international confidence that we should rightly regard it as opening a new chapter in the history of human relations. It is, perhaps, unprofitable to discuss at any length the various reasons which at the present moment might lead a British Government to hesitate before entering into such an arrangement, but one reason is so fundamental and the necessity of satisfying it is so important that it should be clearly stated in order to avoid misconceptions and disappointments. The British Empire for purposes of war and peace is a unity. A Dominion Government might, indeed, decline to enter into a war initiated by the Government of Great Britain on the ground that it was unjust, impolitic, or irrelevant to the interests of its people. But if it should take such action, if at a great crisis it should decide to dissever its course from that of Great Britain and other parts of the Empire, the end of the Empire itself would not be far distant. And as nothing would more certainly rupture the threads of sentiment and affection which bind the scattered units of the British Empire together than a severance of one member of the Empire from the struggles and sufferings and sacrifices of its fellow members in war, so there is no object which a British Government should keep more steadily in view than the alinement of its policy with the needs, aspirations, and sentiments of the Empire as a whole. If then the British Government signs a political cheque, it is well that it should be a cheque which the Dominions will consent to honour. If it promises to guarantee a foreign country, it must know that by that act it is involving the whole Empire. If it says to France, 'In certain contingencies we will land six divisions to defend your soil,' let it realize that by the mere fact of that decision it is determining that New Zealanders and Australians, that men from Canada and South Africa and India should be involved in that contingent conflict upon pain of the disruption of the Empire, for unless in the hour of peril the Empire moves into war as a unity, the process of dissolution will have set in.

This peculiar position of the commonwealth of British nations, scattered over every hemisphere of the globe, and yet, despite the great intervening distances, bound each to each by strong and supple ties of sentiment, imparts a difficulty into the arrangement of such a general treaty as that which we have been describing. France, let us assume, desires as a condition precedent to disarmament a guarantee not only for herself but for Poland, and this guarantee Great Britain, alone of European Powers, can most effectively give. But how can Great Britain give that guarantee to France unless she is assured that the Dominions will countersign it, and with what prospects of success could ministers in Ottawa, Cape Town, or Wellington enlist the interest of their respective parliaments and peoples in the defence of the eastern border of Poland against Russian aggression? A system of mutual guarantees limited to the States of a continent or a fraction of a continent seems a comparatively feasible project. A treaty coupling disarmament and guarantees might, one would imagine, be reached without an intolerable expense of statecraft by the States of South America, so near, one to the other, in speech, race, culture, and development, or by the small Balkan States, or again by the nations of the Scandinavian world; but unfortunately when we reach the most crucial and important problem of all, the full satisfaction of France, the guarantee can no longer be so limited. It must be a world-wide guarantee; a guarantee of the British Empire as a whole. Otherwise it is valueless to France and harmful to Great Britain.

The appeasement of the age-long feud between France and Germany is in fact the condition precedent to the effective disarmament of Europe. It is the poison of that dark and terrible quarrel infecting the mind and temper of the Continent which saps the vigour and hopefulness of movements having for their object a real as distinct from a mechanical pacification. But to the degree—and it is no slight degree—to which the ill-feeling of France is embittered by fear, the situation could undoubtedly be palliated by a system of sufficient but open guarantees; best of all, guarantees given by the American Republic in conjunction with the British Empire, but failing American assistance by the British Empire alone. If such guarantees are not forthcoming, France will continue to seek her security as she is now unhappily doing, in a course contrived for the partition of the German Reich.

The more the situation of the world is examined, the more clearly does it appear how great is the loss inflicted upon the cause of peace by the withdrawal of America from European affairs. If the Anglo-American pact had stood, the armaments of Europe would have been on a diminished scale, the French would not have been in the Ruhr, the Reparations question would have been settled, and Europe would have been well on its way towards convalescence. America has two special qualifications for playing an invaluable part in the affairs of Europe at this juncture of our history. She is very powerful and she is quite impartial. Her withdrawal from the Reparations Commission and the League of Nations and the Pact of Guarantee has been one of the great misfortunes of modern history, a misfortune comparable in scale and significance to the defeat of the German revolution in 1848, though happily not, like that great tragedy, beyond retrieval. Indeed, it can hardly be expected that so intelligent a people will long fail to recognize that if the problem of world armaments is to be effectually solved, their help is essential to the solution.

The truth of this proposition can be most easily tested by a consideration of that part of the problem which concerns the manufacture and traffic in armaments. In the decades preceding the outbreak of the Great War, peace-loving men and women were greatly concerned by the influence exerted by munition firms on public policy. There was no scandal in England, but there were scandals and rumours of scandals elsewhere. Newspapers advocating a provocative foreign policy were owned by continental armament firms. Small nations were tempted into extravagant military and naval developments by the skilful exploitation of their fears on the part of competing business men with ships or guns to sell. Barbarous or semi-civilized tribes who might have been well left to their bows and arrows were enticed into purchases of quick-firing rifles and even of machine guns. A fear grew up that the world was fast falling into the grip of an international armament group, without scruple or patriotism or concern for the sufferings of humanity, but solely animated by the economic motive of so playing upon the vanity or cowardice of governments as to obtain the largest market for their wares. So greatly impressed was President Wilson with this evil, that an article was inserted into the Covenant of the League of Nations drawing attention to the abuses connected with the private manufacture of munitions of war and with the un-regulated traffic in arms.

The evil is real. What greater offence could be directed against the common interests of humanity than the support of a Chauvin newspaper by an armament firm? How can a society professing itself to be civilized look on unmoved while semi-civilized and uncivilized tribes are supplied with its latest refinements in the art of destruction? But these evils can clearly only be dealt with by a general self-denying ordinance on the part of those nations which produce munitions of war, and of those nations the United States of America now plays the principal rôle. It is idle to suppose that the munition-makers of Great Britain or France will submit to restrictions upon trade and manufacture, if their competitors in America are free to trade and manufacture as they please. There must be an agreement all round or there will be no agreement at all.

Whether the pressure of powerful economic interests will prevail over clear public advantage remains to be seen. The League of Nations has asked for a conference to consider the private manufacture of munitions and the traffic in arms, and America has been invited to attend. If America complies with the invitation, something may be done in mitigation of a great public danger. If she elects to stand aloof, the world may go on arming itself without let or hindrance until a fresh catastrophe startles it into self-defence.

It is not necessary, nay, it is doubtfully expedient, that the private manufacture of arms should cease. What is necessary and expedient is that this branch of manufacture should be subjected to regulation, and that the traffic in arms should similarly be brought within the sphere of an agreed measure of control. A draft code of rules suitable for the governance of manufacture has already been accepted by a committee of the League of Nations, and now awaits the discussion of an international conference. Should such a conference come to an agreement as to the best method of regulating the manufacture of munitions and the traffic in arms, and should that agreement be subsequently ratified by the countries concerned, a sensible advance would be made in the direction of limiting a great and admitted evil. It is indeed humiliating to reflect upon the sufferings which have already been inflicted upon humanity by the non-ratification, after it had been signed by the principal nations of the world, of the Treaty of St. Germains of 1920, which was formed to regulate the export of arms and munitions of war to the less developed countries. The incident is one of the many instances which occur in the crowded life of modern communities in which a really valuable measure of reform fails to be secured, because in the crush and competition of claims upon the public notice it passes unperceived save by those who have an interest in defeating it. The more important then is it that peace-loving men and women all over the world should band themselves together to create a public opinion favourable to the great cause of pacification, and that when a measure likely to advance that cause comes up for the consideration of the legislature, it should be so vigorously defended and sustained on the platform and in the press that purely sinister interests have no chance of frustrating it.

The present situation of the world lends itself to the careful consideration of plans such as those which we have been describing. For many years to come a new world-war is made impossible by the hard logic of economic facts, and the nations of the world are accorded a breathing-space during which to arrive at an agreed and comprehensive limitation of their peace effectives. With goodwill much may be accomplished, either through the agency of the League of Nations or by separate and partial compacts, such as the recent Convention of Washington, or that famous arrangement concluded more than a hundred years ago between the Governments of Canada and the United States by a simple exchange of notes, in virtue of which each of the contracting parties bound itself to abstain from putting ships of war on the waters of the great lakes which intersect their common frontier. But it would be idle to ignore the serious nature of the obstacles which confront the would-be artificer of a universal peace, the fierce spirit of nationalism which has been excited in Europe by the war, the deep hatred which divides France from Germany, the uncertain attitude of Russia, the distracted condition of the Chinese Republic.

These obstacles it is the province of statesmanship to overcome. The general plan for the limitation of armaments may break down in detail ; but even so, the resources of statesmanship are not exhausted. What is important is that the habit of taking international action should grow ; that problems affecting the interests of the whole world should be increasingly regarded from the angle of that wide and universal interest, and that public opinion in the forward and enlightened nations should support the efforts of statesmen to explore in advance the deep underlying sources of international trouble and provide remedies while cure is still possible. In the formation of such an opinion there is not a citizen, however humble, who has not a responsibility to discharge. Even if he has no vote, from time to time he buys a newspaper which represents a certain frame of mind on international affairs. His choice may be guided by motives entirely unconnected with politics. He may like the sporting news, or the illustrations, or the society column, or the general make-up of the paper, or the serial story ; but if the paper, so far as it is political, lives upon the dissemination of international calumnies, he does wrongly to buy it. Papers do not continue to produce what they cannot sell, and if Chauvinism were known to involve a loss of circulation, the world would be relieved of much of that afflicting violence in the press which renders the task of statesmanship far more difficult than it would otherwise be.

It is to the encouragement of the international habit of mind and to the general growth of a preventive political medicine that we must principally look for the avoidance of future wars. So long as war remains a possibility, some training for war will continue to be regarded as a necessary and wholesome part of the national life. But in proportion as nations exact from their rulers higher standards in education and public health, a smaller proportion of the national revenue will be available for military and naval purposes. The development of the social services in all the progressive nations is therefore one part of that science of preventive medicine to which the world must look for effectual relief from the burden of armaments. Another and hardly less important part is constituted by diplomacy and conference and by the new chapter in the history of international relations which has been opened by the Treaty of Versailles.

XII

INTERNATIONAL RELATIONS

' Iti s on opinion that government is founded ; and this maxim extends to the more despotic and military governments as well as to the most free and popular.'—HUME.

IT is not surprising that one of the first intellectual reactions from the war should have been a deep and widespread dissatisfaction with the traditional modes of conducting international business. To millions of minds a system which had led to so vast a holocaust of human lives, to so senseless a destruction of human wealth, seemed to be condemned beyond reprieval. If that was what came of entrusting the governance of Europe to a trained political class, what was the good of training and experience? Let the amateur be summoned to the helm. He could not at least do worse : he might do better. If that was the fruit of secret diplomacy, let diplomacy forthwith be open. If that was the result of the labyrinthine correspondence of the Chanceries, let the leading men meet each other face to face. The peoples of the world whose lives were at stake had at least the right to know whither diplomacy was tending before their country was committed to a course bringing havoc and slaughter in its train.

The claim that diplomacy should be open and not secret is, with certain qualifications, founded upon clear grounds of justice and right reason. Every nation has a right to be informed in advance of the precise nature of the engagements which are being contracted in its behalf. That a great people should wake up one morning to find that it is involved in war by reason of some treaty or military convention with a foreign

Power of which it had no previous knowledge, is clearly intolerable. The self-respect of an intelligent nation is outraged by the mere suggestion. Apart from this, the knowledge that current international morality admits of secret treaties creates that very atmosphere of suspicion spiced with fear out of which wars most commonly arise. It is true that under modern conditions the fact of a secret treaty having been concluded does not long remain concealed, whatever precautions may be taken to hide it. This, however, does not diminish the evil which flows from such arrangements ; the treaty half known, hazily conceived, is even more dangerous as an element of international discord than it would be if the full text were given to the public. It is therefore a great advance towards the improvement of international relations that fifty-four States who have subscribed to the Covenant of the League of Nations should have accepted the principles of the publicity of treaties and have consented to register their treaties with the Secretariat of the League.

The principle of the publicity of treaties is so important as a factor in the establishment of international confidence, that deviations from it should only be permitted within narrow and preordained limits. In time of war, when surprise constitutes part of the value of the transaction, it may be necessary to make a secret treaty, such as the treaty under the terms of which Italy threw in her lot with the Allies in 1915. And in time of peace it is a matter for argument whether a nation should be required to disclose the military convention appended to a public treaty for defence. It may be held that if the terms of the published treaty reveal the governing political conditions which determine the *casus foederis*, the world cannot reasonably claim to be apprised of the military dispositions by which the contracting parties propose to implement it ; the more so as the only valid assumption in the case is that the parties to the treaty will employ all their available resources to win the war. In any case it is not to be expected that any nation will divulge plans which its General Staff has framed in the event of hostilities, and if such plans have been embodied in a convention, they will certainly be kept secret. Let us assume, for instance, that Great Britain should make alliance with France, and that as a corollary to that alliance a military convention were signed specifying in detail the number of divisions which Great Britain should supply in the event of an attack upon French territory, the number of days to be taken by the process of mobilization, the assistance in guns and tanks and aeroplanes to be rendered to the French armies, and all the other necessary details with respect to disembarkation and the like, it would be right and proper that the general political treaty should be given to the world, but absurd to publish for the benefit of a possible enemy the precise military arrangements by which the policy of the treaty was to be supported. Treaties made in the course of a war and as part of the belligerent operations are subject to similar conditions. It was not improper for the Allied statesmen to conclude the secret treaty with Italy to which allusion has been made, because being already at war with Germany and Austria they were bound to put military considerations in the forefront, and secrecy was an element of military success. But had such a treaty (involving as it did the transfer of important sections of Austrian territory to Italy at the conclusion of peace) been made in time of profound peace, while an Austrian Ambassador was accredited to the Court of St. James and a British Ambassador was enjoying an analogous position and analogous privileges in Vienna, the transaction would have been the climax of political turpitude.

It is also a matter of argument whether some conventions of a confidential or very technical character need be revealed.

It may happen, for instance, that one nation agrees to make a loan to another, and that the premature announcement of such an intention might be attended by unfortunate financial consequences. But the principle of publicity is so important that a certain amount of positive inconvenience may properly be risked, rather than that the moral obligation of every State to register all international arrangements (other than military conventions appended to treaties referring to the existence of such conventions) as public deeds with the Secretariat of the League of Nations should be diluted and attenuated by a multitude of exceptions and reserves.

Let us admit that a nation is entitled to know the terms of the treaties which have been signed on its behalf. Is it entitled to know more? Should the whole process of diplomacy proceed in public? Is a nation adequately secured against unpleasant surprises by the requirement that treaties should be published and registered? And may it not discover, when the treaty comes to be disclosed, that in effect its honour has been already pledged away in secret conversations?

The argument appears to assume that a debate conducted in public is more likely to end in a peaceful issue than are the conversations of trained diplomatists behind closed doors, that the great mass of the people is more likely to take a conciliatory and moderating view of a political situation than official personages schooled in negotiation, and that the fear of continuous public commentary will generally act as a restraint upon the adoption of hasty and vehement courses.

But every one of these assumptions is questionable. To reach an agreement in a complex international question one of the first requirements is a certain degree of flexibility on the part of the negotiators. On either side there must be a disposition to listen, to take up experimental positions from which withdrawal is possible without loss of prestige, to make concessions, to change ground as new facts and considerations come into view, to use strong pressure at certain points or to yield to strong pressure at other points, to disagree with violence if necessary, or to be lavish in compliance, and sometimes, though very rarely, to employ an argument which is intended as a warning.

To carry on a discourse so frank and flexible in the presence of the whole world is clearly difficult, if not impossible. In the House of Commons debate can be open and fearless, because every member has a tolerably good idea of the kind of attitude which different sections of his countrymen will assume on a given question and of the weight which they are likely to attach to a particular inquiry; but when the representative of one country is speaking to the representative of another, he has no such exact assurance. However skilled and experienced he may be, he is constantly liable to be surprised by some curious little aberration, as he is disposed to think it, in the mentality of the foreigner, or by the discovery of some highly sensitive spot which he had not expected. In the comfort of privacy a negotiator can afford to explore the temperament of the country with which he is dealing by the method of trial and error, and since he works upon the mind not of a people but of a single diplomatist, an error once made can easily be retrieved. Far otherwise is it if the negotiator is compelled to do all his work in public. An error in psychology reflected and enlarged in the million magnifying glasses of the press may then have very serious consequences. A false step is not so easily retraced. An experimental position is not so easily taken up. So long as there is a hope of reaching an adjustment of differences, it is best that the negotiations should proceed behind closed doors.

There is, however, a point beyond which privacy becomes injurious. Sometimes in private discussions a nation advances a wholly discreditable argument, which it would be very unwilling to publish to the world. In such a case it is very important to be in a position to insist on publication. Again, whenever a definite stage has been reached in a negotiation, the public has a right to demand papers and to know where it stands. If there is definite disagreement, the causes of the breakdown should be known; if there is agreement, the case for publicity is equally clear. The general rule should be that the Government should give to its Parliament at the earliest possible moment all the information which can be divulged without injury to the public interest. In this way only can a nation be assured that the conduct of foreign affairs is being carried on in general conformity with its desires and intentions.

It is not, however, to be hastily assumed that open diplomacy is more likely to avert international quarrels than the older method of negotiation. That the interest of the great mass of any population is always on the side of peace is incontestable, but interest and impulse do not always coincide. An emotional people, stampeded by the press into a mood of violent hostility against a foreign nation, may overthrow the plans of the shrewder heads of its government and compel a war when every dictate of sound policy counsels peace. History is full of examples of such perverse explosions of popular passion. Nations have their fevers as well as individual men. They become obsessed with the vision of some haunting danger, some obstinate obstruction to the shining course of destiny, some hateful encumbrance upon their present freedom, and in a mood of violent impatience determine to have done with it. All the million compensating arguments and possibilities are left out of sight. The dark incubus occupies the whole field of imagination to the exclusion of many helpful lights which the strong intellect of a cool and resourceful statesman might bring to converge upon the scene. In a kind of angry bewilderment, feeling itself to be so innocent and outraged, its adversary so perversely obdurate and injurious, and the problem of their mutual relations so insoluble by the patient processes of amiable interchange, a sensitive nation pricked and goaded by its hotspurs and alarmists stumbles blindly forward into war.

It may be argued that a better education will change all this, and that with universal suffrage and compulsory schooling we shall in the end reach cooler levels of rational civilization, in which society may be immune from such periodical distempers. But it is not any education which will effect this deliverance. A well-planned scheme of public education coupled with a system of universal suffrage had very little influence in checking the war spirit among the German and Austrian peoples in 1914. Indeed, the colleges and schools of Germany and Austria actively contributed towards its spread and sustentation, and the best educated country in Europe was in fact the most furiously unwise. What, however, is probably true is that the chances of a people reaching a sane and balanced view of international affairs would be greatly increased by the diffusion of that type of public education which is most calculated to give it. What that education should be in all its details is a problem beyond our present scope and deserving of separate treatment, but it is easy in the broadest outline to sketch its negative and positive characteristics. A system of school education controlled by the State in the interests of national policy is clearly a danger to be avoided, as inimical to that free development of criticism and initiative which are essential constituents in the formation of a sound national judgement. An education in knowledge only, such as is calculated by the severity and standard of the examinations which it prescribes to develop the memorizing as against the reasoning faculties of the young, is equally injurious. To be the slave of facts is as fatal as to be the slave of formulae. Again we do not want our schools to be seed-plots of national complacency or insular prejudice. A capacity to sift evidence, to weigh arguments, to distrust the written word, to bring a fresh individual mind to bear upon the questions which life successively presents, a disposition to pierce shibboleths with the needle of criticism and to react instinctively against the stress of unexamined emotions —these are the qualities which education should develop in the young. So far as the content of education goes, this too has an importance. Broadly speaking, a nation should be educated not for war but for peace. It should be taught something of the contributions of other nations and other races to the common heritage of civilized life. It should be encouraged to look at large maps and broad historical prospects. It should be taught how wars arise, and with what compelling motives on either side, and it should learn something of the character and consequences of war as it has now become. Of the past it should be invited to take a dispassionate view, in order that it may be trained to a temperate judgement on the events of the present. And these predispositions which are fostered in youth should be corroborated by institutions and public habits such as favour the lavish interchange and comparison of ideas, or contribute, like some features of the common law of England, to diffuse a respect for legality through the community.

Meanwhile we must not assume that the public temper of democracies, educated as they now are, is necessarily an influence making for the preservation of peace. In July of 1914 it was held in St. Petersburg, probably with justice, that a clear declaration from Great Britain that she would take sides with Russia and France in the Serbian question would avert a European war. But how could the British Government give such a declaration? The Serbian question as such created no interest in England. No Government could have come to the British people and said, ' There is great uneasiness in the relations between Serbia and the Austrian Empire. At any moment this uneasiness may produce a conflict between these two Powers, and in the event of such a conflict occurring, we have great reason to fear that Russia, France, and Germany will be drawn in. We are informed that a prompt declaration of our intention to draw the sword in favour of France and Russia in such an eventuality is the only effective and certain means of averting a conflict, and consequently we propose to make that declaration.' No Government could have said this, because the British people would never have consented, and quite properly, to fight in a Serbian quarrel in the solution of which they had no interest and the merits of which they did not understand. The reply would have been overwhelming. The nation would have said, ' A government has no right to gamble upon the success of a threat which may have exactly the contrary effect to that which is anticipated. Still less has it a right to commit the country to the contingency of a war on behalf of a cause in which it is not concerned. If the British nation is to be drawn into a conflict, it must be on an issue which appeals to its heart and conscience as just.'

That is a case in which a Government may have been deterred from taking the course best adapted in its opinion to make peace secure, by the knowledge that it could not in taking that course count upon the support of public opinion. Other cases may be cited in which governments are impelled into war or into provocative action leading to war by the inflamed state of the popular mind. The entry of Great Britain into the great war which became known as the War of the Austrian Succession, and gave rise to Walpole's famous remark,

' They ring their bells now, they will be wringing their hands soon,' is a famous example of popular intemperance. It is true that in these cases what is known as popular opinion is generally the opinion of a comparatively small section of the people ; but it is the opinion of that section of the people which makes and unmakes ministries, and cannot therefore be left out of account by the ministry of the day. Thus the fiery mood which prevailed among the political class in Paris in July 1870 undoubtedly encouraged the French Government to take action which Bismarck, who was anxious for war, was enabled to represent to the German people as a challenge and an insult. And even if Pitt had not been convinced that it was necessary to go to war with France in 1793, the popular indignation aroused among the British people by the execution of Louis XVI and by the proceedings of the Jacobins in the Netherlands would have compelled a conflict.

It is not unfair to urge that so long as the public are not taken into confidence as to the course of international policy, they cannot be expected to contribute to the rational solution of foreign problems. If the general mass of the nation are only called upon for an opinion on international affairs at a crisis, when relations are strained, a dangerous opportunity is given to the unscrupulous or headstrong politician to exploit the passions and prejudice of the mass. A public opinion generally characterized by ignorance and lethargy but occasionally stirred to a white heat of angry emotion is the worst of all possible auxiliaries to those concerned with the conduct of international business. The misfortune hitherto has been that public interest in international affairs has seldom been widely diffused in the past except in connexion with an acute suspicion of the intentions of some particular foreign power. Thus in the days when David Urquhart contrived to diffuse an interest in foreign politics among working folk, the *leit motif* of the movement was fear of Russia, whose sinister designs were found to be behind every occurrence which appeared to contravene the political interests of Great Britain. Other scares followed, and it is no exaggeration to say that each successive mood of apprehension has given rise to a fresh interlude of spasmodic interest in the problem of foreign affairs, which no force less closely associated with strong popular emotion would probably have availed to create.

There is now some hope that a sustained and rational interest in foreign affairs may, not in this country only but in all the civilized countries of the world, be nourished by something more respectable than international fear and suspicion. The League of Nations may not have realized as yet the dreams of its creators, but it represents an aspiration for a better and more civilized international order in which many enlightened men and women in every clime and country are deeply interested. A new stimulus to international studies, deriving its root from a desire to adjust quarrels and to anticipate difficulties before they become serious, is now making itself felt. And it may be hoped that under its influence public opinion may be more continuously instructed as to the true state of the contemporary world and more effectually armed against prejudicial and inflammatory appeals.

Among the contributions to political philosophy which have recently found some favour is the suggestion that the diplomatist should be superseded and that the main task of adjusting international differences should be performed in conference by the leading statesmen, who in most countries of the world are now responsible to popular assemblies. Diplomacy by conference has undoubtedly played a very conspicuous part in recent years, and clearly there is a great advantage in a political convention under which from time to time the leading statesmen of different countries may be brought face to face to thrash out their common differences. It would be difficult to exaggerate the value of the Imperial Conference which meets at regular intervals in Downing Street, and enables the leading representatives of India and the Dominions to exchange views over the Cabinet table with the leading members of the Home Government, and to be initiated into all the *arcana* of British policy. Indeed, without some such machinery for regular oral consultation, the widely scattered members of the Imperial Commonwealth might easily drift apart, each pursuing its own way, not out of hostile design but for lack of a common orientation. And so, too, during the war and in the years immediately succeeding it, the method of diplomacy by conference was essential to the preservation of some conformity of action and mutual intelligence of aim between the Allies. There are, however, certain clear limitations to the value of this particular instrument for the transaction of business. In the first place, it is only susceptible of occasional use. The burdens placed upon the shoulders of the head of a Government or a Foreign Secretary are of so exceptional a character, that these ministers can seldom be spared even for a few days, and then not without some risk that despite telegraph, telephone, and aeroplane, important political business at home will not receive the attention which it deserves.

In the second place, no Government cares to assume the responsibility of summoning an International Conference unless it is certain in advance that all its invitations will be accepted. And finally, a Government which summons such a conference cannot afford to fail. The publicity which attends an International Conference, the hopes which it arouses, the exaggerated expectations which are invariably formed of the range of its possible achievements, the impression made upon the public imagination by the spectacle of a congregation of distinguished men drawn from different lands, the rumours of intrigue and counter-intrigue, the suspicion of new combinations—all these circumstances attending a great international gathering make it an imperative counsel of prudence that the ground should be carefully explored before such a gathering is summoned.

And since nothing is more calculated to damage the prestige of a Government or to throw back the cause of international harmony than a conference which has failed, it is clear that diplomacy by conference specially convened must be regarded as an exceptional expedient, valuable on occasions, but always to be employed with circumspection, and in no sense as a substitute for the steady diurnal interchange of views which is carried on through the ordinary diplomatic channels.

Arbitration is another expedient, increasingly employed and recommended for the settlement of international differences. It is not, however, every question which a nation is willing to submit to arbitration. ' Subject to a few exceptions,' writes Sir Erle Richards, ' in all arbitration treaties hitherto the agreement to arbitrate has been directed to questions of a legal nature or to questions arising on the construction of treaties, and there has been added a clause excepting from arbitration disputes involving matters of vital interest or the maintenance and honour of the contracting parties.' [1] These are serious exceptions which are alone sufficient to show that arbitration in itself furnishes no adequate guarantee against the occurrence of war. Indeed, an examination of the wars which have broken out in Europe since the Treaties of Vienna in 1815 led Lord Bryce to conclude that ' comparatively few were susceptible of arbitration by a court on legal principles '. Out of sixteen wars, three only, the war between the Germanic Confederation and Denmark in 1864, the war between Prussia and Austria in 1866, and the war between

[1] *The Progress of International Law and Arbitration*, p. 19.

England and the two South African Republics in 1899, involved issues which, according to the same high authority, might have been settled by a judicial tribunal, but it is doubtful whether even in these three cases the legal issue was the dominant factor in dispute. In the two first instances Bismarck was playing for Prussian supremacy in Germany, and in the third the technical question of British suzerainty over the Transvaal was overshadowed by a fierce political and economic struggle, the rancour of which, spreading from Johannesburg to London and deepened by suspicions of German intrigue, made a judicial settlement unpalatable to the mass of the British people.[1]

Nevertheless it would be idle to disparage the value of arbitration as a factor making for peace. The settlement of the Alabama claims in 1872 and of the Behring Sea Fishing dispute in 1893 were both important questions which might have led to war between Great Britain and the United States if they had been injudiciously handled. As it is, the loyal acceptance by both parties of the award, which in the first case was favourable to America and in the second to Great Britain, has materially helped to improve the relations between the two great branches of the English-speaking race. And though it may be true that most of the issues submitted to arbitration have been of secondary importance—it is now, for instance, the custom to introduce into treaties of commerce a stipulation binding the contracting parties to arbitrate upon any disputes which may arise out of their provisions—nevertheless an accumulation of unsettled secondary disputes is apt to create a very dangerous state of tension between nations, and such dangers a free resort to arbitration upon minor questions is calculated to avert. Besides, wars sometimes directly arise out of minor questions. There can therefore

[1] Bryce, *International Relations*, pp. 229–30.

be no doubt that the growing habit of submitting ' justiceable' disputes to arbitration (and justiceable disputes have
been defined as ' Disputes as to the interpretation of a treaty,
as to any question of international law, as to the existence of
any fact which, if established, would constitute a breach
of an international obligation or as to the nature and extent of
the reparation to be made for any such breach ') has been an
important factor in spreading the idea of legality in the sphere
of international affairs. And the value of arbitration as an
influence making for peace is greatly increased where two
nations make a general agreement to submit such disputes to
a court.

Before the war international lawyers were wont to point
out that one of the principal defects of arbitration as a means
of settling international differences was that on each occasion
the arbitral Commission had to be constituted *ad hoc* by
agreement between parties who had already arrived at a high
pitch of mutual exasperation. That objection, however, no
longer stands so far as the fifty-four States who have signed
the Covenant of the League of Nations are concerned. They
have accepted the new International Court which has been
established at The Hague, and though it is only a minority
of the members (thirteen) who have so far pledged themselves
to refer their differences to that tribunal, it is to be anticipated
that by degrees an increasing mass of international business
will be referred to it. Already the Court has established itself
in the esteem of jurists and given some important decisions
upon questions which might otherwise have aroused an acute
and prolonged international controversy.

There is a body of opinion in America, prevailing rather in
religious and humanitarian than in strictly political circles, for
the ' outlawry of war '. The idea is that the world will never
be cured of this recurrent disease unless all nations submit

themselves to the rule of law and undertake to refer all their disputes, however vital, however much they may be deemed to affect national honour, national independence, or national existence itself, to the arbitrament of a law court. A nation declining to submit to due legal process should be treated like the criminal who defies the law of his own land. The peccant community should be punished not only by the public opinion of the civilized world but by a complete commercial and economic boycott, and if need be by other expedients in addition, until it has been reduced to a proper law-abiding frame of mind.

One of the difficulties overlooked by the advocates of this humanitarian ideal is that to which allusion has already been made, namely that the disputes between nations do not always admit of legal definition and are not always of a character suitable to the determination of a court of law; and this observation applies most forcibly to those disputes which are found most frequently to lead to war. They are political, not legal. They arise out of new aspirations and ambitions and new shiftings of material force : sometimes out of suspicions of hostile interest or sharp material antagonisms. A purely legal machinery, employing legal rules and legal methods, is inadequate to deal with them.

Legal arbitration then is not enough. It must be supplemented by expedients for the conciliation of differences in which the legal element, if present at all, is subordinate to the political and economic. The treaty between Great Britain and the United States in 1909, which set up a Commission for the settlement of any disputes which might arise between the United States and Canada, is an illustration of a very wise and effective method of settling international disputes between neighbour States, the value of which has already been proved in the working. The Covenant of the League of Nations embodies a larger and more ambitious plan. Under this instrument fifty-four States have already pledged themselves not to go to war with one another until the cause in dispute has been submitted to the consideration of the Council of the League or to arbitration, and a delay of three months has elapsed.

It is, indeed, in this double provision for delay and mediation that the chief value of the League of Nations as an instrument designed to make wars infrequent will be found to consist. The League will not change human nature or abate the combative instincts in man. It will be no wiser and no better than the men and women who form the population of the States of which it is composed ; but it has this great advantage over all previous expedients for the maintenance of peace, that if its members keep their bond, they are debarred from the tiger's spring. It will no longer be competent for a State which has become a party to this arrangement suddenly to snap the cords of diplomacy and to send hostile aircraft over the soil of its foe. At times of crisis diplomacy will not be flustered by the fiery pressure of the soldiers urging the claims of the mobilization time-table. There will be time for consideration. And time is all important. The new mechanical inventions connected with war and transport make of time the principal ally of peace.[1]

The Council of the League is not of itself a judicial or impartial body. It is in its present form an association of ten governments, each of which is represented by a statesman whom it nominates for the purpose, and who in many cases

[1] The sudden occupation of Corfu by Italy in August 1923 as a reprisal for the murder of Italian subjects on Greek soil was undoubtedly a violation of Article 12 of the Covenant. Greece, however, instead of going to war, appealed to the League, and the pressure of public opinion, exercised in the League and outside it, was such that the Italian troops were shortly withdrawn.

is a professional diplomatist. It is not, therefore, necessarily a body of eminent individuals or of the supreme controllers of national policy, or of men versed in judicial or semi-judicial inquiries. Its strength lies not in its individual competence but in the fact that behind each member there stands a government and a people. Its weakness consists in the fact that its resolutions, to secure validity, must be unanimous. How will such a tribunal acquit itself as a body for the conciliation of international differences? Can it be as effective as a council of jurists in securing for its decisions the name of impartiality? Will it not be a hotbed of intrigue? With what sort of interest or knowledge will the European member address himself to a South American question, or a delegate from Uruguay master the tangled issues of a Balkan feud? If the Germans are brought in, will it not be their object to block the French interest, and the French object to retaliate, and if the Germans are kept out, how can the Council be regarded as representative of the modern political world?

To such doubts and queries there are five answers. First, the Council is of such a size that no issue is likely to be raised at the Council Board with respect to which a considerable majority of the members will not be indifferent and disposed to give an impartial award. Second, it is always competent to the Council to refer a question to a committee of jurists, economists, or other experts who have no political end to serve. Third, the Council is assisted by a cosmopolitan secretariat, which has so far succeeded in maintaining a remarkable standard of political detachment and elevation. Fourth, acting upon the spur of public pressure, the Council holds most of its meetings in public and, even were no higher motive operative, would be deterred by the fact of publicity from any patent abuse of its trust. Moreover, the acts of the Council are annually passed under review by the Assembly upon which all the States of the League are represented, and though the members of the Council are not, strictly speaking, responsible to the Assembly, they do not altogether leave out of regard the probable attitude which the next Assembly will take ; and since the Assembly, being mainly composed of small States, somewhat over-represents the pacificist and idealist tendencies in current international policy, the course of the Council will be to some extent affected by these influences. Lastly, it is reasonable to expect that the ordinary desire of the average human being to secure the successful and honourable working of the institution with which he is associated will operate here. The main purpose for which the Council of the League exists is that it should smooth over international differences, and its *amour propre* is involved in the successful accomplishment of this task.

However little disposed the individuals who from time to time compose the Council may be to take what is called the pacificist view, however disparaging may be their estimate of human nature, and however low their view of the possibilities of political progress, they will be anxious that the particular adjustment which it is their duty to promote should turn out prosperously. They will endeavour to conciliate because they work in a council created for conciliation and because their personal credit as well as the collective credit of the body of which they are members is involved in their success. This is what is meant when people speak of ' the atmosphere of Geneva '. The Council no less than the Assembly is a gathering of people who for the time being are anxious to emphasize points of agreement rather than of difference, and desire to achieve conciliation, as one who follows the foxhounds may desire to come home with the brush.

The rule of unanimity is a concession to the deep-seated spirit of nationalism, which has been strengthened rather than weakened by the results of the war. A resolution of the Council must be unanimous. Otherwise a nation might find its will overborne by a collection of foreign States, some of whom might be acting under hostile inspiration. How impracticable and absurd! says the critic; the *liberum veto* of Poland was not more unreasonable. How can salvation come from a body whose purpose may be frustrated by the ill will and malice of a single member? Uruguay may defeat the combined endeavours of all the great European Powers. An irresponsible delegate from the headless and distracted Republic of China may for a period of four years reduce the League to a mockery by blocking every resolution taken by its executive body. Such sanctions as the League may possess for the enforcement of its decisions upon recalcitrant members may be rendered nugatory by the voice of a single opponent.

In effect, however, the rule of unanimity does not work out so disastrously. Many useful achievements of the League since its establishment are witness of the fact that there is a large field of action, political and humanitarian, in which, with a little goodwill, a number of very different nations may work together. And even if upon an occasion a single member of the League were to prevent the adoption of a resolution, it does not follow that the publicly advertised union of the other members of the Council would not exercise a great influence upon the moral opinion of the world. A proof of this may be found in the strong objection of France to any suggestion that the question of the occupation of the Ruhr should be raised in the Council of the League. The French are perfectly well aware that they could block a resolution in the Council. But they shrank from an open discussion, and intimated to the British Government that if the question were raised it would be regarded as an unfriendly act.

The incident reveals the presence of an obstacle which is

likely in the event to impede the effective working of the League far more seriously than the rule of unanimity, and that is the reluctance of members of the League to have their own policy discussed in a cosmopolitan gathering. If a nation is to be debarred from exercising the friendly right accorded to it by Article XI of the Covenant of ' bringing to the attention of the Assembly or the Council any circumstance whatever affecting international relations which threatens to disturb international peace or the good understanding between nations upon which peace depends ' by private representations from another member that discussion will be resented, then the League may easily sink into the position of a body of tertiary importance for the settlement of third-class issues. It is for this reason greatly to be regretted that the question of the Ruhr was not directly raised in the Council, as an exercise of the friendly right accorded by the Covenant to every member of the League, even though it was certain in advance that no resolution would be reached or action taken; for no real progress is made unless it be an established convention of diplomacy that in all grave international issues affecting peace the voice of the League is heard.

The question is often asked whether the fabric of a peaceful international order does not imply the establishment of an international army to keep the peace. Whatever may be the abstract logical argument for such a force, the present state of the world does not admit of it. The League is no superstate; its material power may be nothing or everything. If its members are but faintly interested in the enforcement of their common will, should they have a common will, the material force which they may put at the disposal of the League may be nothing or little more than nothing; but if the interest be fierce and passionate, then the efforts may be commensurate with the powers of the nations involved, and the sum of material force at the disposal of the League would be gigantic, exceeding even the huge effectives of the recent war. But the sanctions of the League are not necessarily military. There is the sanction of public opinion ; there is the sanction of economic pressure ; only in the last resort would the League have recourse to the sanction of physical force.

From the point of view from which these lectures are written, which is that of ethics rather than of politics, it is the first of these three sanctions which deserves special study. To what extent can the League mobilize the public opinion of the world against the transgressor? To what extent is the mere institution of the League a barrier against international ill-doing? How far may we hope that the League may embody the best moral opinion prevailing in the world with respect to the conduct of international affairs ?

The last question may be answered first. The Covenant of the League does embody not indeed a code of original morality, but a code of the best political morality current among civilized States at the conclusion of the Great War. All the great principles of international morality are embodied in the Covenant—that treaties should be published, that every opportunity should be given for conciliation before a shot is fired, that troubles likely to result in war should be treated in their incipient stages, that aggression should be resisted, that the government of the extra-European territories acquired from the vanquished parties in the war should be regarded as a trust to be exercised for the benefit of the inhabitants, that there should be a full and frank interchange of military information, that armaments should be reduced by agreement and the abuses incidental to the manufacture and traffic in armaments checked, and that international action should be taken to secure fair and humane conditions of labour for men, women, and children, and for the general supervision of agreements in regard to the traffic in women and children, in opium and other dangerous drugs. No one of these ideas is new, but their combination in a single document accepted as a binding political direction by fifty-four States is a fact which cannot fail to influence the practice of nations. How the spirit of the Covenant will work in detail we cannot predict, but the fact that an institution has been set up by the authority of most of the States of the world to give effect to its provisions must needs enlarge the sphere of international action and mitigate the flagrant insularity in which problems affecting the general interest of the world are too often considered. Steam, electricity, petrol, and the growing economic interdependence of nations will assist its operation.

Acting then as the focus of a growing mass of useful international work, the League will inevitably create a body of international knowledge and sentiment which will enter as an element of increasing influence into the political opinion of the age. A few strokes of disinterested and beneficent statesmanship, such as the rescue of Austria, will maintain or restore the wavering faith of mankind in the possibilities of fruitful international co-operation. Too much, indeed, must not be expected. Emotion is essentially inconstant, and mankind is emotional. Waves of war-feeling and peace-feeling, of fierce hatred and idealistic sentiment, sweep over the world. A statesman may often in a few brief years or even in the course of a single day give expression to views at once the most bellicose and the most pacific. Indeed, outside the narrow circle of the Quakers and their intellectual associates, who during the late war were known as absolutist conscientious objectors, how few human beings are thoroughgoing and consistent pacificists! The advocates of the class war are not pacificists, the friends of Armenia are not pacificists, the orators from the Labour benches who thunder against the French are not pacificists.

All these three classes of men desire to achieve a pacified world, but by the forcible removal of obstacles which intercept the realization of their ideal. And the more passionately and fanatically a humanitarian ideal is held, the greater will be the readiness to travel by the short rough heroic way of force to its accomplishment. Nevertheless, there are in experience and hard-thinking counterweights to the combative emotions which have their place in the scheme of things. And if the League of Nations cannot secure to these opposing agencies of reflection and sentiment a certain victory, it can at least provide for them a greater place and a fuller opportunity of effective influence than they would otherwise possess.

The League then may be trusted to exercise a certain moral influence in the direction of peace. It emphasizes the idea of human solidarity. What touches one, touches all. We may take it for granted that the government of a State which has undertaken obligations under the Covenant will henceforward reflect seriously upon those obligations before it will decide to break them. It may come to the decision to violate its bond, but not without grave misgivings as to the reactions which such a defiance of the common law of the civilized world would entail. Just as no Government willingly makes default when payment is demanded by a creditor State, so the breach of so important a system of obligations as the Covenant of the League would certainly involve a loss of international standing which wise men would not readily face. No nation is bound to accept the award, however reasonable, of the League, for the League is not authorized to impose its decisions; but the breach of the Covenant is a different matter, involving consequences which may extend from so light an indication of displeasure as the withdrawal of a consul to the extreme penalty of a general war. The prudent captain does not lightly steer for such perilous seas.

The lesson of the last war was that no country can affront the moral conscience of mankind without in the end paying the penalty. Germany lost the war because it was believed that when she might have had peace she preferred war, and that once embarked on hostilities she waged them without regard to the restraints of international law and humanity. The violation of Belgian neutrality, the introduction of gas warfare, the unrestricted submarine campaign mobilized opinion against her. With a tremendous initial advantage in material power, she fell because the world deliberately concluded that her cause was wrong. She was beaten by opinion. Human nature does not greatly change. What has happened once will happen again, and even in times of profoundest peace the fear of moral isolation will act with increasing power to shape the course of policies. A nation, it is true, does not readily admit to wrongdoing in face of foreign criticism. Rather it contends that the criticism is prejudiced, one-sided, ignorant, and that to know all would be to pardon all. None the less no Government and no Parliament can afford to flout the general opinion of the world. American opinion on the Irish question was, in the view of most British statesmen, largely misinformed and misdirected, but it had weight in every Cabinet notwithstanding, and was one of the factors which made a settlement of the Irish question upon liberal lines seem to be necessary even to men who on general grounds of temperament and political outlook were opposed to it. To that large body of opinion which will be reflected in the Councils and Assemblies of a League of Nations no prudent statesman will be for long indifferent.

We return then to the old maxim that opinion rules the world. But how is the ordinary man to form a true opinion on matters so far removed from his daily experience as international policy? Learned historians already dispute the origins of the late war. As documents are published we see more clearly the rôle played by the Serb, the Austrian, and the Russian. The responsibilities appear to be more widely spread, the nexus of events more intricate, the faults to have been committed in other places besides Berlin.[1] A doubt arises whether the case of a nation turning rogue and making an unprovoked attack upon society are really very common. Are there in effect criminal nations? as there are undoubtedly nations liable to fits of sheer lunacy. And if so, how is public opinion truly to assess the measure of the crime?

The principal moral issues of history are not, however, so complex but that they can be disengaged by the plain judgement of an honest democracy. The better opinion of Great Britain might legitimately decline to pronounce a moral judgement on the constitutional right of the Southern States of America to secede from the Union, but could hardly hesitate as to the ethics of slavery. The unprovoked invasion of neutral territory by an armed Power must always be wrong. The breach of a solemn international engagement must always be wrong. Though a policy which prohibits the sale of intoxicating liquors may invite criticism, who could doubt that a foreign government which attempted to discredit its success by giving encouragement to smuggling would be acting wrongfully? Finally, if a government which had taken upon itself the obligations prescribed by the Covenant of the League of Nations were to refuse to submit its quarrel to arbitration before beginning hostilities, that too would instantly be judged to be wrong by every thinking man and woman in the world whose conscience was not blinded by passion or prejudice.

The acceptance of such an engagement is in effect the best guarantee which statesmanship can contrive that nations will

[1] This must not be taken to imply that Germany was not the principal culprit. For conclusive evidence see Mr. Asquith's *Genesis of the War*.

regard themselves as part of a moral society to which certain duties are owing, and from which a due and reasonable consideration is expected in return. It is also the best means of furnishing to the plain citizen a moral criterion in the great crises of international affairs. The rights and wrongs of the secular quarrels of history are now so closely intertwined, justice and injustice are so subtly blended, that the historian can often do no more than state the facts. But if the nations of the world will submit to an undertaking to arbitrate and delay before plunging into war, one issue can be disengaged with startling clarity and presented to the conscience of the artisan and the peasant of every colour, of every speech, under every clime. Has the bond been kept? If not, if after such an engagement a State declines to submit to the dilatory process of the League, then it loses its cause forthwith in a court of morals, as wide as humanity itself.

To the student of history the unity of the world seems to be the unconscious goal of human effort. By the massive operation of forces, few of them avowedly pacific, most of them on the contrary springing from the acquisitive appetites of man, we appear to be approaching an era when civilization will be as uniform as the indestructible anthropological difference between the races and types of man will permit. Science, which annihilates distance, provides a common stock of cosmopolitan pleasure and experience. The great names and the great issues of contemporary history travel round the world. Literature and art and knowledge and business, all the higher products of the human intellect and imagination, now obey the impulsion of a time spirit which has very largely emancipated itself from the tyrannous accidents of space. At last after many hundreds of centuries man can find in every habitable portion of the globe fellow creatures to whom some portion of this dominating civilization is familiar. Europe exercises its influence on America, and America reciprocally influences Europe. In varying measures the races of Asia and Africa obey the common spell which has been woven by the ideas and efforts of the white men who on either side of the Atlantic have inherited the civilization of Greece and Rome. And this tendency to approximation, despite some reactions like the Slavophil movement in Russia, seems to be continuous and progressive. At no time in the history of the world were the real differences between man and man in respect of intellectual equipment and experience so small, or the social heritage common to all mankind so large, as upon the eve of the Great War. Industrialism was fast spreading its grim and levelling tentacles through the empty spaces. Parliamentary institutions were almost universal. Legislation, as a glance at such a periodical as the *Comparative Journal of Legislation* would suffice to show, was becoming rapidly more and more homogeneous, similar problems provoking in different parts of the world similar remedies. The spread of occidental influences in the Far East was so rapid and sensational as to give rise to a new branch of sociology concerning itself with the laws of imitation. Even in the subtler phases of the human spirit there was a growing appreciation of alien and distant manifestations. The mystical verse of a Bengali poet, rendered into delicate English, travelled round the globe and was read with pleasure under all the stars.

Will these tendencies towards a common human civilization be corroborated or weakened in the ages which are to come? We cannot certainly affirm that they will be corroborated. There was a common Mediterranean civilization held together by the strong clasp of the Roman Empire in the first century; it contained seemingly within its orbit all the intellectual and moral promise of the world, but it was swept away, dissolved into its parts, caught up in a hurricane of material forces which it had no strength to master. Are the signs and tokens of a world civilization to be realized in some future age destined to fail as did the sanguine vision of Virgil? No one can say.

It is easy enough to take a despondent view. Man is a combative animal, and the possible subjects of quarrel between man and man are infinite in number. Moreover, there is probably no nation in the world in whose eyes some cause, other than the defence of the homeland, does not appear worthy of the supreme sacrifice of war if challenged by a foreign power. It is true indeed that the prudential instincts of man have been fortified by the accumulation of knowledge. We attach more importance to preventive medicine both in the sphere of hygiene and in that of politics than did our ancestors. But how quickly does the national temperature rise under the flail of excitement! How easily are slight repugnances magnified by a sensational press into serious grounds of antagonism! If telephone or telegraph bind the world together, as is exemplified in the touching public monuments in Berne, how true is it also that they serve to increase international tension at critical periods! Nor can we take comfort in the thought that the world must necessarily be saved by the growth of the science of life. It is a depressing reflection that the fiercest war in the world's history and the most prejudicial in its effects upon the human stock was waged between those very races who stood first in the order of civilization, who were nearest to one another in culture, and whose impoverishment or destruction was calculated to inflict most injury upon the fortunes of man.

Skilfully as it may preach the dysgenic consequence of modern war, the new and promising science of eugenics cannot relieve humanity of these disquietudes. We are far from underestimating the influence which may be exerted by wise measures based on eugenic principles in arresting the process of race-impoverishment which proceeds in countries like Great Britain and America, where society dies at the top and breeds at the bottom. But we have yet to learn that there is any necessary correlation between anthropological improvement and the growth of political prudence and self-restraint; or rather if there be such a correlation it would seem to point in the direction opposite to that along which we desire to travel, and to indicate that the stronger the breed, the more energetic it is likely to be in asserting its pretensions by force and the more active in that form of political imagination out of which spring most of the troubles which have bathed the world in blood.

The true and only prophylactic against a fatal relapse and degeneracy will be found in the temper of the leaders of public opinion in the principal States of the world. If they are prudent; if they are prepared to recommend the sacrifices in national pride and susceptibility which will from time to time be demanded to save the general peace; if they are strong enough and wise enough to keep steadily before their eyes the great cause of human solidarity as a thing valuable in itself and only under the gravest and most exceptional provocation to be weakened and impaired,—then the forces making for a common civilization may work their way without impediment or rupture. But let us be under no illusion. The task of presenting to the mind of a proud, eager, and vigorous nation a constant and effective image of its wider responsibilities to the world is no easy one. The amount of prejudice to be vanquished is everywhere immense. The sacrifices demanded from time to time will be real: sacrifices of hate, sacrifices of revenge, sacrifices of impatience, sacrifices of jealousy, sacrifices of pride, in some cases even sacrifices of apprehension.

And the processes will not be assisted by the recent political education of the white races, which has for the most part been shaped by conceptions of nationalism steadily increasing in concentration and intensity. But hard as is the road, it is not so hard as the climbing pathway of religion. We are not asked for enthusiasm. We are not required ' to love those whom we do not like '. It is sufficient for the realization of a common human civilization that just so much enlightened self-interest, just so much sense of responsibility to humanity, should be imparted into the conduct of international affairs as to save us all, when quarrels spring up, from the imagined necessity of going with our opponents to the shambles.

INDEX

Printed in England at the Oxford University Press